Brian Lanker

WYOMIA TYUS was born and raised in Griffin, Georgia. She attended Tennessee State University in Nashville and ran under the tutelage of visionary coach Ed Temple as a member of the Tigerbelles until she graduated in 1968. A four-time Olympic medalist, and the holder of multiple world records, Tyus was also a supporter of the Olympic Project for Human Rights during the 1968 Olympics, doing her part to promote justice for oppressed people around the world. As a founding member of the Women's Sports Foundation, she continues to advocate for women's equality in sports to this day.

David Wakely

ELIZABETH TERZAKIS teaches English and creative writing at a community college in Northern California. Her fiction has appeared in *New England Review*, *Minerva Rising*, *Solstice*, and *Birdland Journal*, and her nonfiction publications include articles on the global AIDS crisis, education, free speech, human nature, and capital punishment. *Tigerbelle* is her first book.

TIGERBELLE
THE WYOMIA TYUS STORY

WYOMIA TYUS
AND ELIZABETH TERZAKIS
WITH A FOREWORD BY JOY REID

EDGE
of SPORTS

Tigerbelle is the latest title in Dave Zirin's **Edge of Sports** imprint. Addressing issues across many different sports at both the professional and nonprofessional/collegiate level, Edge of Sports aims to provide an even deeper articulation of the daily collision between sports and politics, giving cutting-edge writers the opportunity to fully explore their areas of expertise in book form.

Published by Akashic Books
©2018 Wyomia Tyus and Elizabeth Terzakis

The photograph of Wyomia Tyus on the first page of this book was taken by Brian Lanker and originally published in his work *I Dream a World: Portraits of Black Women Who Changed America.* It is reprinted here with the permission of Lynne Lamb.

Paperback ISBN: 978-1-61775-658-0
Hardcover ISBN: 978-1-61775-676-4
Library of Congress Control Number: 2018930200
All rights reserved

Edge of Sports
c/o Akashic Books
Brooklyn, New York, USA
Ballydehob, Co. Cork, Ireland
Twitter: @AkashicBooks
Facebook: AkashicBooks
E-mail: info@akashicbooks.com
Website: www.akashicbooks.com

*To my parents, Willie and Marie, for the great
foundation, wisdom, and encouragement you gave me.
You are loved and missed.*

*To Mr. Temple, my father figure, my educator,
and my friend. It is because of you that I am saying more
than four words now. I just wish that this story could
have been told sooner so that you could smell the flowers.*

*To my brothers: You always said you taught me
everything I know, and you did. And for that,
I am grateful. Thank you for making sure I got to play
and for making sure I always stayed in the fight.*

—W.T.

Table of Contents

Foreword by Joy Reid   11

Introduction   15

Chapter 1. Suster: Walking the Farm   25

Chapter 2. "You Just Ran Yourself into Some *Shoes* . . ."   49

Chapter 3. "Now Run Yourself into a Tigerbelle T-shirt!"   69

Chapter 4. First Gold, New Growth: The 1964 Olympics   93

Chapter 5. College As Usual   119

Chapter 6. Spiders and Fires and Bombs   142

Chapter 7. B2B100m   153

Chapter 8. After the Deluge   168

Chapter 9. Another Life to Live   185

Chapter 10. Making a Way   196

Chapter 11. Getting Out of the Blocks (Like Everybody Else)   210

Chapter 12. Mr. Temple's Legacy   230

Chapter 13. Black Women in Sports: Then and Now   248

Chapter 14. Blacks Lives Have Always Mattered   271

Appendix. The Tigerbelles   284

Acknowledgments   287

Foreword by Joy Reid

I was not yet born when Tommie Smith and John Carlos turned the 1968 Summer Olympic Games upside down with their fist-in-the-air protest (though I would come along not too long after). But growing up, that year's Games loomed large in the Black Pride origin story in our house, as dictated by my five-foot-three Guyanese spitfire of a mother. In our house, the Olympics was a time to gather around the family TV set, cheer on Black Excellence, and laugh in the face of supposed Black shame. We were achievers, not victims or merely "descendants of slaves." Every gold medal was a badge of honor we somehow pieced out among all of us. Say it loud: *I'm Black and I'm proud!*

For me—a skinny, bespectacled, nerdy kid who was nonetheless athletic, who could dribble a basketball like a boy, jump my Schwinn bike like a BMX, and sprint the 100, the 200, and the anchor leg of the 4x400 relay faster than the lithe, light-skinned, perfectly ponytailed girls in my mostly Black Denver suburb—seeing the Olympic runners, particularly the Black women who are so often not recognized as part of the sports world, was revelatory.

But even those of us who pride ourselves on knowing history often know almost nothing. We learn how much "nothing" we know with every new tale of triumph and overcoming that falls into our laps like a lucky coin.

The story of Wyomia Tyus is such a coin. For decades, it sat on a shelf, suspended above but never able to fill a blank space in my memory as I searched for more Black girl role models and found almost none to crowd out my male idols: Arthur Ashe and Muhammad Ali. Until there were the Williams sisters, Venus and Serena, "sporty" Black girls were an aberration, not the norm. Black women sports heroes were distilled down to a single name: Wilma Rudolph—a Black woman and a sprinter, but, as it turns out, not the only Black female sprinter to make an indelible (if for far too long invisible) mark on the world sporting stage.

Wyomia earned her place in the pantheon of American athletic greatness by doing something that no one—man or woman—had ever done before. Her story—growing up on a remote farm in rural Georgia and emerging onto the Olympic stage in 1964 and 1968 as one of the most decorated runners ever to don cleats—is one that every Black girl, every athlete, and every American should know. Hers is the legend we have never discussed. It was not until the second decade of the twenty-first century that America learned a small piece of the hidden history of Black women in the 1960s through the movie *Hidden Figures*. *Tigerbelle: The Wyomia Tyus Story* is the *Hidden Figures* of Olympic legend. Her athletic ability as well as her politics and her grace demand that we fight for her to be remembered so that we can not only revel in her accomplishments but also learn from them as a new generation of Black women leads the struggles of tomorrow both on and off the field of play.

Like most of the Black women who toiled in the trenches of the Civil Rights Movement in anonymity, Wyomia has yet to have her tale told on a scale equal to its magnitude. Now, we can hear it in her own voice. And in that voice we hear the distinct cadence of America's racial and gender history.

Joy Reid is the host of MSNBC's AM Joy. *She is also the author of the book* Fracture: Barack Obama, the Clintons, and the Racial Divide.

Introduction

If you want to get to know Wyomia[1] Tyus, there are two videos you should watch.[2] The first, in black-and-white, shows Tyus winning the 100-meter dash at the 1968 Olympics in Mexico City and becoming the first person—not the first woman, the first *person*—ever to win gold medals in the 100 at two consecutive Olympic Games. First in real time, then in slow motion, Tyus bursts from the blocks, establishes a lead, and leans over the finish line eleven seconds later. After the slow-motion runthrough of the race, the film cuts to Tyus on the medal stand, graciously shaking hands with bronze medalist Irena Szewińska and drawing the attention of teammate and silver medalist Barbara Ferrell to Szewińska's proffered hand. It is raining; all three women are dripping wet, but Tyus is laughing, shaking the rain from her fingers, maybe even dancing a little. She appears to be in a state of grace.

The second video also revolves around the women's 100-meter final at the 1968 Olympics. Although Tyus is not the primary subject of the film, she becomes the focus of attention as soon as the main contenders are introduced. A beatific grin

---

1 Pronounced Weye-OH-mee; the final *a* is silent.

2 "Wyomia Tyus Retains Olympic 100m Title—First Ever | Mexico 1968 Olympics," https://www.youtube.com/ watch?v=T2TOQU2T338. "Bittersweet Bronze: Mexico '68," https://www.youtube.com/watch?v=_76h0OCM558.

on her face, Tyus again seems to be dancing. A voice-over by Olympic medalist Dwight Stones describes Tyus as "a natural-born sprinter" and notes "the psychological strength that she would bring to a race." According to Stones, "She would just *intimidate* you out of any chance of beating her. And she really wasn't like that; she was actually kind of shy. But on the track, she was an assassin."

Tyus is shown in a preliminary heat, running, winning, smiling, waving to someone in the crowd. Then the footage jumps to the runners preparing to get into their blocks, and it becomes clear that Tyus actually *was* dancing: "She's standing there, and everybody else's faces are very nervous. At the beginning of a final, at the Olympics, of course you're nervous on some level—good nervous, maybe bad nervous—Tyus maybe even was nervous too," Stones admits. "But the way she chose to manifest it was that she got there by her starting block and she started doing the 'Tighten Up'—and what that did was it loosened her up and tightened everybody else up—and that's why she did it. It was just another technique, it was another thing that she thought of that she had never done, that they had never seen, that was going to take everyone else out of their game."

As Tyus dances the "Tighten Up," which she described to me as a "herky-jerky sort of dance" popularized by Archie Bell & the Drells, the camera pans the stands, where Black men—Jamaicans, according to Tyus—with rhythm sticks and hand drums of all sizes play an accompaniment. And then Tyus runs, and wins, and makes history. Twenty years would pass before Tyus's feat was equaled, and close to fifty before it was surpassed. Only four other runners have ever done what she did.

Wyomia Tyus—natural-born sprinter, shy assassin, and joyful dancer—is a sports legend and one of the Olympic giants of the twentieth century. Tyus won her first Olympic gold in the 100 at the 1964 Games in Tokyo, Japan, where she matched Wilma Rudolph's world record and helped her team to win silver in the 4x100 relay. In 1968, Tyus not only became the first person to win back-to-back gold medals in the 100 but also set a new world record for the event and racked up another gold in the 4x100 relay. In the years between the two Olympics, Tyus took the outdoor 100-meter Amateur Athletic Union (AAU) championship in 1965 and 1966, won the 220-yard dash in 1966, and, in indoor competition, won the 60-meter dash and set new world records in 1965, 1966, and 1967. Tyus is unfailingly modest about these accomplishments: "I don't focus on my records," she confesses. "Time never broke a tape."

Tyus's groundbreaking Olympic victory in 1968 occurred amid the political tumult of that era. The success of the Tet Offensive in January of 1968 increased domestic opposition to the American war in Vietnam while the assassination of Martin Luther King Jr. in April precipitated a radicalization in the fight for racial justice. Student protests were on the rise the world over, in Western and Eastern Europe, in South America and Asia, and in Mexico as well as the United States. Ten days before the Games began in Mexico City, students protesting police violence were massacred by government troops in Tlatelolco's Plaza de las Tres Culturas as part of the country's efforts to make the city "presentable" for Olympic visitors.[3]

As a Black woman from the Jim Crow South and a participant in the Olympic Project for Human Rights (OPHR), Tyus was acutely aware of the existence of injustice not just in the US but around the world. She also understood the significance of

---

3 See "Mexico's 1968 Massacre: What Really Happened?" December 1, 2008, *All Things Considered*, NPR, produced by Joe Richman and Anayansi Diaz-Cortes, http://www.npr.org/templates/story/ story.php?storyId=97546687.

Black athletes in the context of the Cold War and in light of the United States' self-proclaimed preeminence as an exemplar of democratic and individual rights: the Olympics made America vulnerable to exposure by providing Black athletes—including those who had grown up drinking from segregated water fountains and knew firsthand about urban blight—the opportunity to stand on a world stage. With this in mind, Tyus dedicated her gold medal in the 4x100 relay to Olympic protestors Tommie Smith and John Carlos, who shocked the upper echelons of the Olympic world and thrilled activists everywhere by raising their black-gloved fists on the medal stand to protest human rights violations at home and abroad. By throwing her support behind them, Tyus played a significant—if underrecognized—part in bringing the movement for human rights into the arena of international athletic competition.

For Tyus, the movement was all about inclusion: "We are all in this together. That's what the whole human rights project has always been about. And that's what I said to the reporters. But none of that got printed, of course."

It is also significant that Tyus demonstrated her solidarity despite the fact that the leaders of the OPHR—including Smith and Carlos—did not include her or other Black female athletes in their organizing. Talking about it, Tyus is neither bitter nor resentful: "Everyone wants to be wanted and needed and feel like they're a part. And that wasn't there for us. I'm not upset with them. It's just more that, 'How could you not think of us?'"

She holds true to the principles of inclusion and solidarity and has no regrets—even when it is suggested that her support for Smith and Carlos might explain the fact that her first-in-the-world accomplishment has gone largely unnoticed.

"It's either that," she says, "or the fact that I'm a Black woman." When asked if she considered the possible consequences of her action, she notes that she did, but, at the time, she didn't really care: "At that point, I knew that I was going to be me, and whatever else was going to happen was going to happen."

Tyus came to the Games as one of Tennessee State University's Tigerbelles, a women's track-and-field program that in its heyday produced forty Olympic athletes and twenty-three medalists. As a key protagonist in the triumphant tale of the Tigerbelles, Tyus provides a window into a remarkable—and remarkably overlooked—story. She accurately describes her coach, Ed Temple, who passed away in September of 2016, as a visionary: Temple led the program for forty-four years and was able to imagine a place for women in sports decades before the enactment of Title IX.

Like Mr. Temple, Tyus's parents had a vision: that their children should *be* children and not have to shoulder the responsibilities of adulthood until they were grown. In talking about her early life, Tyus describes the farm where her father worked and her family lived as a "safe haven" from the racism of the era—despite the fact that the Klan was a regular participant in local parades. She attributes some portion of her early athleticism to the fact that she played with, competed against, and often beat both her brothers and the male children of her neighbors, who were all white. Tyus had to—got to—play with the boys because the white girls "were never allowed to play with us—definitely not with Black boys, and not with me either. But that was okay with me. They didn't do too much playing anyway." The most athletic thing the white girls were allowed to do was ride horses, but even then, Tyus says, they had to be "prim and proper."

Tyus's parents would maintain their safe haven until Tyus turned fourteen and a family tragedy changed their lives forever. In the wake of her family's misfortune, Tyus began competing in track, primarily as a means to keep "busy" and "stay out of trouble." She was fifteen and running at her first state meet in Fort Valley, Georgia, when she was scouted by Ed Temple. Not long after, Tyus would take her first train ride to Temple's summer clinic at Tennessee State in Nashville. Following Temple's strict regimen of intense workouts, academic dedication, and mutual support, Tyus and her teammates, all young Black women, navigated the sea of racism and sexism that was the Jim Crow South and 1960s America to become world-class scholar-athletes and, in many cases, lifelong friends. Thrice-daily practices developed Tyus's speed and stamina while the generosity and guidance of "older" runners like the legendary Wilma Rudolph and Edith McGuire helped her to make her way both as an athlete and as a student. Mr. Temple insisted that the Tigerbelles earn their degrees and acquire skills to live on once their competitive careers were over, and this insistence—along with her own steely will and abundant raw talent—contributed greatly to Tyus's success both on and off the track. It also led to a 99 percent graduation rate for the Tigerbelles at a time when only a tiny fraction of American women—let alone American Black women—were able to earn four-year degrees.

The arc of Tyus's life—from her childhood as the daughter of a tenant dairy farmer in Griffin, Georgia, to her retirement as a naturalist in Los Angeles, California—would be worth following even if she had never medaled at the Olympics. Yet, as is the case with so many Black women of her day, her story has gone untold, her achievements unsung. One explanation for this is the fact that her ascent to Olympic glory occurred at a time when the editors at *Sports Illustrated* were less interested in covering the Black female athletes who would actually represent the United States in the Olympic Games than they were in promoting a white Texas coach nicknamed "Flamin' Mamie" and her all-white Bouffant Belles. The cover of *SI*'s April 20, 1964, issue features three heavily made-up and precipitously coiffed white women with the patronizing caption: "Texas Girls Aim for Tokyo."[4]

A breathtaking testament to the interlocking powers of racism and sexism, the article effortlessly erases the accomplishments of Black female athletes while simultaneously mocking the aspirations of white female athletes. Meanwhile, the story of Wyomia Tyus and her teammate Edith McGuire—who had been born in the same state, experienced similar family tragedies, and went to the same university—went unreported. McGuire was favored to take the gold in the 100 in 1964, making Tyus's eventual win a stunning upset and their uninterrupted friendship of considerable human interest—but where's the story in that?

It would be nice to think that the world has changed a lot since then, and progress has indeed been made—much of it thanks to the efforts of athletes like Tyus, who together with Billie Jean King and other female sports superstars formed the Women's Sports Foundation to promote the participation and publicity of women in sports. But there is still a long way to go, and the problem is not a lack of exceptional female athletes but a combination of structural barriers and widely broadcast individual bigotry. In March of 2016, tennis tournament director Raymond Moore made headlines by presenting his opinion that the Women's Tennis Association "rides on the coattails of men" and that, "lady player[s]" should go down on their "knees every night and thank God" for the male players who have "carried the sport." In making this statement, Moore demonstrated not only misogyny but ignorance: female stars like Venus and Serena

4 See *Sports Illustrated* Vault: http://www.si.com/vault/issue/43115/1/1.

Williams have been the face of tennis for the last twenty years, and the women's finals of the last two US Opens had higher television ratings than the men's. Despite this, female players still make less than male players overall, and their matches are all too often relegated to midafternoon while the men's matches occupy prime time.[5]

Women's sporting successes go unrecognized in other arenas as well. Sexism in the coverage of the 2016 Summer Olympic Games was a story in itself.[6] "Highlights" included Michael Phelps's tie for silver taking precedence over Katie Ledecky's world record–annihilating (by 11.83 seconds!) gold in a headline, and a marriage proposal being called "an even bigger prize" than Chinese diver He Li's silver medal.[7]

Racism, as usual, was also in play, for example, in the form of a photograph of gymnast Simone Biles misidentified in a column about gymnast Gabby Douglas.[8] When it comes to more permanent and in-depth coverage, the pattern repeats: of Amazon's first twenty "Hot New Releases" in sports biographies of

5 See "Women's Tennis Stars Paid Less Than Men, Despite Equal Popularity" by Martha C. White, http://www.nbcnews.com/business/business-news/women-s-tennis-stars-paid-less-men-despite-equal-popularity-n543496, and "Gender Equality? Women Are Already Tops in Tennis" by Stefanie Kratter, http://www.cnbc.com/2015/ 02/26/in-tennis-women-are-on-top-kratter-150226-ec.html.

6 See "Sure, These Women Are Winning Olympic Medals, but Are They Single?" by Katie Rogers, https://www.nytimes.com/2016/08/19/sports/olympics/sexism-olympics-women.html?_r=0.

7 See "Katie Ledecky's Record–Breaking Win Only Took Second Place in This Sexist Headline," https://mic.com/articles/151670/katie-ledecky-s-record-breaking-win-only-took-second-place-in-this-sexist-headline#.8lIfxvB4x. (As Twitter user Nancy Leong put it: "This headline is a metaphor for basically the entire world.") And "The Reaction to Olympic Diver He Li's Proposal Story Isn't All Praise," https://mic.com/articles/151534/the-reaction-to-olympic-diver-he-zi-s-viral-proposal-story-isn-t-all-praise#.mmlazXWNf.

8 Both Douglas and Biles are Black, which apparently means they look the same. See http://www.nbcphiladelphia.com/news/local/Philadelphia-Daily-News-Mistakes-Simone-Biles-for-Gabby-Douglas-390449411.html.

2017,[9] only two are by or about women—Caitlyn Jenner's *The Secrets of My Life* and *Women in Sports: 50 Fearless Athletes Who Played to Win,* which features one page of whimsical illustration and one page of biographical information apiece for fifty pioneering female athletes. And while stories of female athletes in general are difficult to find, the experience of Black women athletes in particular has been neglected by sportswriters and sports historians for as long as women have competed, much to the detriment of each successive generation of Black female athletes.

Wyomia Tyus's memoir represents an important interruption of this trend, not only filling a gap in the record but also providing inspiration for the athletes of today. Olympic medalist and International Olympic Committee member Anita DeFrantz has noted the vital role that just knowing about athletes like Tyus played in her development as a competitor: "The Tigerbelles helped me believe that African American women could be athletes; what they went through, the good, the bad, and the ugly, was amazing. It's a very important part of our history."[10]

Tyus's story, in her own words, also expands the historical record by providing the kind of nonstereotypical representation of Black women that, according to Black feminist Frances Beale, is most easily constructed through oral history.[11] Her account of her experiences includes her firsthand impressions of everything from Ed Temple's dress code, to the reason her team's plane wasn't allowed to land in Moscow at the height of

9 This list changes frequently, so there is some hope that more women's stories will appear.

10 Salisbury, Tracey M., PhD, "First to the Finish Line: The Tennessee State Tigerbelles 1944–1994," unpublished dissertation, 2009, p. 28.

11 Salisbury, p. 33.

the Cold War, to village life in eastern Africa during her stint as a Goodwill Ambassador. Her distinctive strength of mind and will—as noted above by Dwight Stones—is palpable in her thoughts about how to psych out a competitor, what it takes to get down the track, and the importance of losing. But the power of her thinking goes way beyond the boundaries of sport. Her explanation of her reasons for bringing her children "back South" is yet another testament to the inclusive way she sees the world; her method of coping with the loss of a loved one whose life was never celebrated as it should have been offers solace to anyone willing and able to take it in. Providing her perspective on American life from the Jim Crow South to sunny Southern California, Tyus tells a story not just about athletic greatness and political courage but about intellectual and emotional growth, gathering wisdom, and the evolving impact of race and gender in America.

Tyus's presentation of her past and her reflections on recent developments in organizing for gender and racial justice represent both significant additions to the history of the struggles for Black and women's liberation and important contributions to the movements of today. A new generation of politically conscious athletes is helping to shift the dialogue on race from false claims about "color blindness" to a horrifying but more honest account of the continuing discrimination, dehumanization, and terrorization faced by Black people in the United States, as well as highlighting the ongoing and systematic denial of the accomplishments of women in general and Black women in particular. Tyus's story, though long in coming—a full half-century after her groundbreaking achievement—strikes a chord that will reverberate for many years to come.

—*Elizabeth Terzakis*

Suster: Walking the Farm

My parents, Willie and Marie Tyus, early 1950s. (Photo by Gray's Photography, Griffin, GA.)

Up until my fourteenth birthday, my life was pretty much perfect. My parents were very different people—my father was a quiet man who believed in keeping to himself, while my mother would say anything to anyone at any time, no filter, none at all—but they both agreed on what they wanted for their children: a safe haven, a place where we could *be* children. They did everything they could to make it so, and they succeeded for quite some time.

My mother always told the story of how they met like this: Her family lived in a little town in Georgia called Pomona, near the railroad tracks, and along the tracks asparagus grew wild. "Mr. Will"—that's what my mom called my dad—would pick asparagus and bring it by the house to give to my mom. "One day," she told her mother, "I'm going to marry that man."

Not long after, she became Mrs. Marie Tyus, and she and my dad, Willie Tyus, moved from Pomona to Griffin, Georgia. I was born in Griffin on August 29, 1945, and lived there with my parents and three older brothers until I went away to school. My oldest brother's name was Jackie, the brother next to him was Jimmy Lee, and the youngest one was Willie, after my dad, but we all called him Junior. Junior is fifteen months older than me, Jimmy Lee was six years older, and Jackie was seven, which made me the baby girl—and the baby. "I'm the baby too!" Junior would say, but I would tell him, "Not so much. You're a baby boy. I'm a baby *girl. And* the baby of the family." Everyone called me Suster.

My mom worked in a dry cleaner's, and my father worked on a dairy farm, where we lived. The person who owned the farm was Ben Brown, and it was set up kind of like a movie, with the big house at the top of the hill and our house at the bottom. Our house was just as large as Ben Brown's, but it was not as nice. The lights would go out, off and on, because the wiring wasn't that great, and there was a well with running water in the backyard, but the plumbing didn't go into the house, so we didn't have indoor toilets. We did have three bedrooms, though, a long, long hallway, a living room, a kitchen, a big back porch, and a huge front porch.

Inside the farmhouse, there was a fireplace in every room:

my mom and dad's room and my room had adjoining fireplaces, my brothers' bedroom and the living room had back-to-back fireplaces, and in the kitchen we had a wood-burning stove. We would always eat all our meals in the kitchen. It was that big, big enough to hold the dining table and another table where we had our water buckets—what we had instead of a kitchen sink. We would go out to the well to get water, fill up the buckets, and scoop out the water when we needed it with something that looked like a ladle but was called a dipper. When I was very young, I remember using a hollowed-out gourd to scoop the water. At the end of the table was a pan where we would all wash our hands.

There was a big pantry in the kitchen, where my mom kept the food from the garden that she'd canned and preserved. We also had a china cabinet where we kept all of our dishes, and then we had the wood stove, with the wood stacked behind it, which took up a lot of room. In the winter months, we took baths by the fireplace in my brothers' room or in front of the stove in the kitchen, but in the summer we'd be out on the back porch, taking baths in a big No. 2 tin tub, and if someone came to visit, we'd have to jump out and run inside. We had such a long driveway that we could usually make it into the house before anybody saw us.

When we were very little, my brothers and I slept in dresser drawers, but after that I had a baby bed in my brothers' room and then a regular bed in my parents' room. Whenever I couldn't sleep in my parents' room, I'd crawl into the crib in my brothers' room, even at ten or twelve. I almost never slept in "my" bedroom because my mom's mom and her youngest daughter would stay there when they didn't have money for rent. My grandma, my aunt Nell, and my aunt's two kids would all stay in that one room until they could get back on their feet, and if someone else was having a hard time, they'd just come and stay with us too. We made it work because that's what family did—we took care of each other.

My mom's mom was named Pearl, and we called her Mama. She was a strong woman, a great woman, and we loved her dearly and always. She had rheumatoid arthritis, and in her later years she started to decline, but when she lived with us, she sewed all the time. We had an old Singer machine where you pushed the pedal to make it run, and when she couldn't do it because of her arthritis, we would do it for her. She would sit facing the machine, and we would be on the other side, pushing the pedal up and down with our hands.

She taught us how to sew, and when the machine eventually broke—we couldn't use it, couldn't fix it—we had to stitch everything by hand, so I learned to sew just like a machine, with straight little stitches; otherwise, I would have to yank them out and start all over. We made piecework quilts, and Mama made blouses for me and my girl cousins and shirts for my brothers and boy cousins out of the feed and flour sacks we got from the dairy. She was that type of person, always busy making something good out of what seemed like nothing much.

Outside the house, it was only seventy-five yards to the dairy, but the farm as a whole was huge. I can't say how much land the Browns had because when we were growing up we didn't think that way; for us kids, it was just open space, and we were always running through the fields and in the woods that made up the farm. Next to the dairy there was a big barn, and we used to jump in the hay or play hide-and-seek—nobody could ever find us; matter of fact, if there was enough hay, you could lose yourself. We would also play tag and try to get to base first, ride our bikes, climb all the trees, and play basketball and baseball. When we didn't have a baseball, we made our own. We would cut open a golf ball, take out the rubber from the middle, wrap it around a rock, cover it with a sock, add more rubber, and then cut up the cover of the golf ball and bind it up with whatever tough thing we could find: cowhide from the fields or another sock if that was all we had.

Playing those games and keeping up with my brothers kept me busy, kept me moving, kept me fast and strong. At least they did when it wasn't too hot; by late morning in the summers, we'd have to retreat to the house and play inside. We played so many games of checkers, *Monopoly*, *Sorry!*, and cards that you would think I wouldn't like them anymore, though I do. Cool or hot, outside or inside, we had to figure out how to amuse ourselves; there were no camps for us to go to, and no money to send us even if there had been. But it wasn't something we thought about; we could always find something we wanted to do.

All along his property, Ben Brown or someone who had the farm before him had planted pecan trees, like a fence—like in California, where they have the palm trees lining the streets. Once you came in from the highway, there was the road where his farm was and where we and the other people in the community lived, and on his side of the road, the east side, there were lines of pecan trees that went all the way to the end of the property.

As kids, we would shake the trees and pick up the pecans for my mom to put into cakes, or we would bag up the nuts and she would take them to the dry cleaner's to sell. That was how we got our Christmas money or extra money for whatever the family needed. In the evenings of the winter months, we would sit around the fireplace, put two nuts in the palms of our hands, and crack them open, and my mom would put them on a pan with a little butter and salt and bake them in the oven just until the smell came out—we called it parching—and then we would sit and eat them.

My brothers' room was right off the kitchen, and that was where we sat. We had a big wide radio with a phonograph in it, and we would listen to whatever came on—rhythm and blues, mostly, or the boxing matches if they were being broadcast. My dad was into boxing and baseball too, so we had to listen to a lot of that even though I hated baseball to death. Too slow! And when there was nothing on the radio that we wanted to hear, we had the phonograph, and we would play old records—45s— and do whatever dance was popular at the time.

There was always a fire in the fireplace, a big roaring fire, and if my mom wasn't roasting pecans in the oven we would put sweet potatoes in the ashes of the fire to bake, and that would be our dessert. We'd sit around with the music on, and play checkers and what we called checkers pool. Those times were just heaven to me—cozy kind of times when I was home with my parents and my brothers, listening to music and eating pecans or sweet potatoes.

All year round, we lived off the land. In the summer months, we'd pick blackberries and wild grapes—muscadines and scuppernongs—and we had a garden with fruit trees: pears and apples and figs. If we wanted fruit, all we had to do was go out and get it off the trees. Ben Brown had dug a pond on the property and stocked it with fish, and we raised worms and went fishing all the time. We ate a lot of catfish, bass, and brim, and when we weren't fishing, we would go hunting. My brother Junior got a rifle when he was about twelve or so, and we all knew how to use it to kill animals for food. We ate a lot of rabbit and squirrel, and sometimes, if there was nothing else to shoot, we had quail. We also raised our own meat: every year my dad's side of the family would get a pig together, and each family would take a turn at raising it.

We had other chores as well: we had to keep the house clean and the fires going. That meant we had to dust all the time; on Saturdays we had to scrub floors, and in the summer months we spent all day every Monday doing laundry. We did it in the winter too, but not as often. There was also sometimes work in the garden; we had to pull weeds and turn the soil, and when stuff was ripe, we would pick it. We didn't do any work for the dairy farm itself even though we wanted to—for one thing, we all wanted to milk the cows, but my dad wouldn't let us. He didn't want his children doing any kind of grown-up, paid work, and he especially didn't want us working a farm. Our job was to go to school so that, when we got older, we would not have to work as hard as he had to work. "This is not your job," he would say. "This is my job. You get your lessons and get out of school." So that was our work.

During the week when school was in session, we would come home, do our homework, chop wood, and stack it—both out in the yard and inside the house by the stove. I liked chopping wood because it meant being outdoors and being active; we would make it a contest: who could cut the most and stack the most and get it in the house the quickest. We had games for almost everything, and most of them were races, but that didn't necessarily mean that the work got done efficiently. At the end of the day, my dad would look at what we had done and shake his head. "You need to chop enough wood," he would say, "so you don't have to come home every day and chop wood."

My mom would get back from work at about five thirty, six o'clock in the evening, and we had to have the fire going in the stove so that when she got there it was hot enough for her to cook. She started supper as soon as she came home because my dad usually finished milking the cows right after she arrived. Ben Brown would help him, and they milked the cows by hand until I was about thirteen or so, and then they got electric milkers—just two for the twenty cows, but I guess that was enough. Fortunately, before that happened, my dad did break down and teach us how to milk. Pulling on the udders was an eerie feeling at first, but then it was kind of fun. We learned to squirt each other with the milk, of course, and there were a few other things he would let us do. When I was four or five, before I started school, my dad would go to work, and if my grandmother wasn't with us at the time, I would join him at the dairy when the school bus picked up my brothers. He would let me hose down the floors after they had finished milking—that was something fun to me then, hosing cow poo—and sometimes he would let me wash the troughs as well. I couldn't scrub them down; I was too small, and that would be too much like work, but I could put the water in, and he would do the rest.

My mom would already be at her job; her workday started at seven in the morning. My uncle John Henry, who had a car that was like a taxi but really wasn't a taxi, would pick up my mom and her sister Nell, who also worked at the laundry sometimes, and take them and about four or five other people to work and bring them home again in the evening. On some Saturdays we would go visit her at the cleaner's even though kids weren't allowed. It was just hot in there all the time, and my mom pressed clothes all the time. That's how I remember her: standing there pressing clothes. She worked in two dry cleaner's, one for fifty years and the other for twenty or twenty-five years after that.

My mom worked hard, but she was a real girly girl. She never liked the outdoors at all. We never ate outside, not even on a table in the yard in summer. She didn't like picnics, she didn't like animals, and she especially didn't like worms. I remember my older brother Jackie scaring her with a worm once. She ran, screamed, everything. But when he put that worm down, my goodness, did she beat on him. Even when she was a girl, she would always stay in the house; her sisters took care of the outside. She would do all of the cooking, but when you brought in greens from the fields, collard greens and things like that, you had to wash them for her because she couldn't do it herself, thinking there might be a worm in there. She would never husk corn either, or clean fish—none of that.

My mom was also a talker; she talked to everybody about everything. We used to call her "The Griffin Daily News" because she knew everything and everyone. She was nosey, only she didn't call it nosey. She called it "finding out things." And everything she would find out, she would say. In fact, there were not too many things that she would not say. Because I grew up with it, it just seemed normal to me. It kind of prepared me for Mr. Temple—but I wouldn't know that until later. You would come into her house—I would bring friends over, or my brothers' friends would come over—and she would say, "Where you been? Did you take a bath this morning? Do you know you smell? You know you don't be coming into people's houses smelling like that. And don't you sit on my couch. I don't want my couch stinking." To anybody. Their friends, my friends—anybody.

But even with all that, she was always smiling; my mom always had a smile for everyone. She was not a tall woman—five five, five six at the most—but she had big feet; even being that short, she wore size ten shoes. She would always point out that her big feet were flat feet too, and they were—completely flat from standing on the concrete at the dry cleaner's for all those years.

Different as they were, my parents were good at keeping up

what you might call a united front. If they ever did argue with each other, we were not in the room—although I would know when something had transpired between them if it happened on a Sunday because my mom would make me go to church. Usually, she didn't care if I went to church, but when she was mad at him, I had to go to church and sit up front with her. I would sit there and pout and think, *She's mad at my daddy and taking it out on me!* And my dad would sit in the back of the church or just wait outside.

My dad wore overalls all the time when he was on the farm, though he would put a suit on to go to church, and he would always have something in his pocket to rub on. Sometimes it was a worry stick—that's what he called it—and sometimes we would whittle him little things or he would carry his pocket watch, but he always had something. He seemed tall to me, but he was not big, more of a wiry type of man, and he had very thick eyebrows that grew together—a Tyus trait. Junior has thick eyebrows, just like our dad, and my son Tyus has those thick eyebrows too.

The Sundays when my mom wasn't mad at my dad, which was most Sundays, we did the thing that I loved best: my dad, my brother Junior, and I would go walking in the woods. Jimmy Lee was usually off hanging out with his white friends, and Jackie was already gone; he had lied about his age and joined the military when he was sixteen. But Junior and I would run and hide and climb trees, pick up rocks and see who could throw them the farthest—just be kids. At one point or another, we would stop walking and we would sit. We would always have our knives with us, and we would whittle while we were sitting; we didn't have to talk about anything although sometimes my dad would tell us about everything he saw, so we learned a lot about nature without really knowing that that was what we were doing. We would dig in the soil, and he would say what was rich soil, what was not, and I would ask questions: "How did they get all these trees here?"

"They planted some, for sure," he would say, "but then seeds just go places and grow."

"How could seeds just go places and grow?" I was always asking stuff like that. And he would explain it all to me. Not that he was giving out any great wisdom; more like he was telling us what there was to see, if you knew enough to see it. Sometimes it was just practical things like, "You shouldn't play in these bushes because that's where snakes hang out," or, "You need to watch out for this plant—it's poisonous." But other times, he wasn't so much explaining things to us as exposing us to the feeling of being free. I think that's how he looked at being in the woods, why he brought us there. "This is what nature is about; it's about freedom. This is all out there for you, this beauty, this freedom, this is how life is supposed to be— beautiful, calm, and serene." He didn't use those exact words, but that was the idea that I got from our walks. He had a sense of wonder about it all, especially in the springtime and the fall, when things were changing. He would say, "Look how pretty this is!" So it was never like he was teaching us a lesson. More like: "Look at this. Do you ever wonder how that got here? God put it here."

"How do you know God put it here?" I was always bucking up against the God thing. "You never seen God. How do you know the devil didn't do it? He has powers too!"

And my dad would say, "Now baby, you shouldn't be saying things like that." But I'm sure he got big joy out of the fact that I questioned every durned thing. My mom would say, "You are not to question God." But my dad was more like us. He had questions too. And he wanted us to be expressive. He didn't talk much, so he didn't really know how to teach us; his teaching was more through making us feel comfortable—through making us feel free. He wanted us to be able to express ourselves, to look at things with wonder *and* question them.

The farm was so big, but now, when I think back about it, we probably walked the same path all the time. The cows had to be milked twice a day, in the mornings and then at night, so at the end of our walks we would round them up and push them all the way back to the dairy. That was the best time of my life. I just totally enjoyed those walks. I think about it a lot of times now, and when I was working the last job I had, which was in outdoor education, sometimes in the mornings driving to work I would think, *This job is just like walking the farm.* It was all so pleasant. I just felt comfortable in my whole situation, and it was wonderful. My favorite remembrance still is of walking the farm with my dad.

We were not the only people living on that land, though. We were the only people working the farm, but Ben Brown had about three or four houses that he rented out when people would come looking for places to live. Some of the people who came didn't get along with us; they were white and didn't want to have anything to do with Black people. We kids would say, "Okay, we don't care, but then their kids won't have anybody to play with." Because if they were going to play with the other white kids in the neighborhood, they also had to play with us. The people who lived on the west side of the road, the other side of the road from us, were there before us, and we were all neighbors and acted like neighbors. For the adults, it was a white-and-Black thing: we didn't go over and sit with them and have dinner or anything like that, and they didn't come over and sit with us. But that was all it was. My brothers cut their grass and raked their leaves for money, and we all played together, us children—well, me and the boys, at least. None of the white girls were allowed to play with "the coloreds." But if any of the new boys came with the attitude, "I'm not going to play with *you people*," then they played alone.

"You people." I'm not going to use the words that they would use. That was a rule in our house. My dad would say to us, "You do not let them call you by any names but your name. They cannot call you the N-word."

So when new neighbors would come, we had to let them know that that was not something that was going to be tolerated. Sometimes it was a fight, and my brothers would make me do the fighting. One family that moved in had four boys, and they weren't the nicest boys in the world, but it didn't matter because we always felt we could beat anybody. So if they were calling us names, we just wouldn't play with them, or we would draw a line in the dirt and say, "This is our property, and that's your property. You cannot come over here. You can't play with us. Stay over there and you're fine. But you step across this line and call us names, then it's a different story."

Of course they didn't believe us. They had to cross the line and call us names. And my brothers would say, "We won't beat you up. We'll just let this girl beat you up." And I could do it. It was amazing. I don't think it happened but two times. No telling what they would call us after they left—but as long as they were with us, there was no name-calling.

In other places, it might have been dangerous for us to stand up like that. But where we were, like I said, it was kind of a safe haven. There were a lot of things happening in the fifties and sixties—bad things—but they just never really applied to us because we were kind of in a little cocoon. Not that everything was equal. We played with white kids, but we went to a

Black school. We could have walked to the white school, but we couldn't go there; we had to wait for a bus, and since we were the first to be picked up, it took us an hour or better to get to our school.

Going to elementary school, there weren't that many people in my classes, and then at a certain season of the year, during cotton-picking time, a lot of those kids would be gone for a month or two. That was just a part of going to school in the rural South at that time. The other part of school was that the teachers were always looking out for you, wanting you to do better. Because they were like my dad: they wanted you not to have to be on that farm, not to have to pick that cotton. That's what I felt then, and as I got older I could see it even more clearly.

When I wasn't at school, I played with the white kids—the white boys—and we really didn't think too much about it. Because it was just: white people live here, and we live here; what else are we going to do? Griffin was small, and it was rural, so people were pretty spread out. You could go a mile or two down the road, and there were other Black people that lived on other people's farms, but not near enough to be our neighbors. I never felt threatened by the white people or felt that someone was going to take our lives or harm us. Off and on, my mom would find people walking the roads, usually white people, and she would always feed them, and some folks would say, "Why do you feed those people? Why are you bringing those people onto the porch and all?" And she would say, "God probably had a reason for him to be here, and he needs to eat. No one should be hungry."

Both of my parents made sure the farm was a safe haven. They were helped along by the fact that we were not in town. I didn't live in town as a young child, and I didn't find out until after I was in high school, maybe college, that when they had a parade in Griffin, the Ku Klux Klan would walk through. According to my friends who lived in town, they would have on their hoods, but they were people that you knew—the people who owned the stores and ran the town. So I'm sure if you talked to Black people from Griffin who lived in town and not so much in our little refuge, they probably had a very different experience than we did.

Even in our safe haven, however, we were totally aware of the situation, of the separate-and-not-equal status of Blacks and whites. But we never really had any confrontations with grown people wanting to hurt us or make racial remarks or say much of anything to us. At that time, you just lived separately. "Look," my dad would say to us, "they don't want to be with you? You don't need to be with them. You're here now, but someday you're going to be out of this situation. You're going to grow, and you're going to do things in the world." And that was truth to me.

Being Black in Griffin was one thing. Being a girl was another. Along with the neighbors and some of the renters, we played with Ben Brown's boys. Ben Brown had five children—three boys and two girls—and like the neighbors' girls, his daughters were never allowed to play with us—definitely not with Black boys, and not with me either. That's what they would say. But that was okay with me. They didn't do too much playing anyway, because in those times girls did girl things, and boys did boy things. The white girls rode horses and played with dolls.

Playing with dolls was not my thing, although I would sometimes get a doll for Christmas. I would play with it for a while, but then the doll would become our football. Back then the dolls had devices in them that we called crybabies:

you turned the doll upside down and it would make a crying noise. One day when we were playing football with one of my Christmas dolls, it got ripped and the crybaby came out. We just looked at each other and thought, *Mom is going to be* so *upset.* We never told her. We went and buried that doll outside and had a funeral and said a few things over the grave. We kept the crybaby out because we would tip it to bother each other. That about sums up my thing with dolls.

During the Jim Crow era, Black women were less than second-class citizens, and they had to work—they had to work *hard.* But at the same time, they were supposed to be good in the kitchen; they were supposed to be nurturing and dainty and all that. Those things were not in my psyche; I grew up with three older brothers, and the only people I had to play with were boys. But when I went to school, it was a little different. The teachers would say, "Girls are not supposed to be playing with boys. Girls play over *here;* this is your place." It wasn't enforced so much as understood; I often left "my" area to watch the boys play ball, but when I started to play, they would call me back.

I also wore pants almost all the time because I couldn't wear a dress and play with the boys. One year for Christmas, my brother was going to get a cowboy suit, and my mother wanted to buy me the cowgirl version, which included a dress. "I won't wear it," I said. "I won't!"

In the end, they got me the whole Hopalong Cassidy outfit—the hat, the gloves, the gun—just like my brother, and you could not tell us apart. My mom took us to get our picture taken—that's the first picture I can remember us ever getting—and the guy who took it said, "What cute little boys!"

"I'm not a boy." I pulled my pigtails out from under my hat. "I'm a girl!"

My brother Junior (Willie) and me on Christmas day, ages six and seven. (Photo by Gray's Photography, Griffin, GA.)

And I guess that's why my mom was dead set against me getting the boy version of the outfit. But my dad knew I was never going to wear a dress, not even as part of a cowgirl outfit, and that it would just have been a waste of money. So I was off the hook that time.

At one point, though, it became a mission to make me wear dresses at school; the teachers *really* wanted me to wear them. "Okay," my dad told me, "now you're going to have to wear a dress to school. But you can put your pants on underneath." And that was how I would go to school: with a dress on and pants underneath. What could they say? I can remember a teacher asking my mom, "Does she *ever* wear a dress?" And my mom saying, "Yes—to church."

This was funny because I was never a regular churchgoer;

my dad didn't really go to church, and I wouldn't go if he didn't go. His feeling was that there were people in the community who needed us a lot more than the preacher. So when my mom would go to church, my dad and I and my brother Junior would go and visit the elderly people in the community and sit and talk. "You can learn more from these people," my dad would tell us, "than from that man up there preaching."

So we did a lot of that, going to visit the surrounding people. My father knew them well—we all knew them well—and that was another one of the finest things in my life: listening to my father talk to the elders. When grown people were talking, we were not supposed to be sitting around listening—most of the time, we weren't allowed to be in the same room. But when it was nice weather they would sit outside, and we could play in the dirt and listen to them tell stories.

They would talk about how each person was doing, or how the farm was, who had gotten sick, who had died, who had gotten put out the house, those kinds of things. Or they just sat. One of the people—Uncle Sam, we called him—taught us to whittle. We made popguns and slingshots and whistles and little cars and boats. Sometimes we whittled just to be whittling, for practice. We would sit and whittle, and they would talk, and sometimes Uncle Sam would turn to us and say, "You're not doing that right!" And then he'd show us the proper way of doing it.

We would also visit folks who were around the same age as my father; they talked a lot more, and they didn't go to church either. Not that they weren't churchgoing people; just that they were like me and my dad—not going to church *all the time*. I get my religion through a whole lot of things. I will go to church, but I like to go to different types of churches and listen to different messages and different ways of preaching.

Sometimes we would visit my dad's mom. Her name was Ada, and we called her Grandma. Grandma lived with her youngest son, and they had a farm in a town called Jackson, not that far from Griffin. It wasn't their farm, any more than the dairy farm was our farm. They were sharecroppers; they picked cotton and did whatever they needed to do to keep the farm going—fix the tractors, plant the seeds, turn the earth, all that. They raised hogs and chickens and kept a garden to feed themselves, and they had an outhouse and the kind of well where you had to drop the empty bucket down and roll up the full one with a crank—unless the well was dry.

Grandma was a very wiry, thin lady, and she chewed on a chewing stick all the time and sometimes dipped snuff—seems like everyone dipped snuff. They put it behind their lips or in their cheeks, and I just hated it. They would say, "Come give me a kiss!" And I would say, "Eww! No!" They had this little tin cup that they spit in—that drool, that snuff drool! But my dad's mom, Grandma—if she had snuff in her mouth in company, you never saw her spit.

Some Sundays we would go to church with them—not that we often went inside. They would sit outside the church and talk in the car, and I would sit in my dad's lap and listen to the conversation. I don't know why, but it was a little different there, somehow. There we were allowed to listen.

It was not that we never went inside the church; in fact, we were in church on my fourteenth birthday, the day my life would forever change. It was revival time. For Southern revivals, the pastor has a service every night, and a big church dinner on Sunday, and some people turn the revival into a way to honor their pastor. But on the evening of August 29, 1959, they were just having a service, and all of a sudden we heard a noise and turned around and saw four white men come into the church.

Everybody froze, and you could practically hear us all thinking, *Oh, wow, why are* they *here?* Because white people just did not go to Black churches at that time. And these were not just any white people. They were the white people from our neighborhood—our neighbors from the west side of the road.

As it turned out, no one had any cause to be alarmed except me and my family. Because those white men, our neighbors—I don't remember who it was exactly, but there were four of them—had come to tell us that our house was burning.

Looking back, I can see that being in church might have saved us; at least we were not at home asleep when the fire started. It's hard to remember that night. One memory is this: My dad is driving, and my mom is beside him. Jackie isn't there. So it's Jimmy Lee, Junior, my dad, my mom, and myself. And we're driving home from the church. Other than that, I don't remember the drive at all; I just know that it must have happened. The next thing I remember is smelling smoke, and once we got off from the main road, I could see the blaze. Church then seemed like it was eons away from the farm, but it wasn't; it was maybe ten minutes away. Still, by the time we got there, the house was totally engulfed in flames. We turned into our driveway and that was as far as we could go; it was too hot to get any closer. We parked the car right at the curb and got out.

It was a big house, a big wooden house, so the fire was huge. We were practically in the street, and we could still feel the heat. You couldn't really see the house anymore, nothing but the little sticks of the frame poking up against the flames, and the two chimneys, all black, so you could see those too. The house had been sitting up on bricks, and those were still standing and burned black like the chimneys, but other than that it was just flames, roaring.

For a while we simply stood there, staring at the fire. It was clear that my mom couldn't believe it. She was almost hysterical. She would grab one of us and hold on to us and cry and then let go and grab another. Finally my dad took her hand and my hand, and then I looked at him. And my dad—I will never forget the look on his face. He was crushed. The life just drained right out of him, right then, and he went limp, and to me, that's how he always was after that. Just didn't have it anymore. His whole life gone. The fire took everything he had worked for— everything we owned. We didn't have much, but whatever we had was in that house. And standing there, watching him look like that, listening to my mother cry, seemed to take forever. I had never seen devastation like that in my parents, not ever. They had always been the strong ones. And I think I was so overcome by seeing that in them that for a while I couldn't hear or see anything else that happened.

And then Ben Brown was there, and he was saying, "We got to get you someplace to stay. Everything is going to be okay." Those kinds of things. The fire department people had come, but there was nothing they could do. There were no fire hydrants or anything, so whatever water they had was on the truck, and it wasn't enough. All we could do was stand there and watch it burn.

The neighbors had managed to drag out a cedar wardrobe and the chair that my brother had had since he was two, which he still has. They saved about four things, and not the things that were important to me. Watching the flames, I kept thinking about our marble collection. But none of the trunks with our clothes or our marbles and other possessions were saved.

For my parents, the big question was: "What are we going to do now?" We had no insurance, none of that. Ben Brown owned the house; we were just renters—well, sharecroppers, basically. Tenant farmers. I really don't know how that worked. We didn't pay rent; my dad worked the farm and that was that. He must have got paid something, but what it was, I don't know. We had lost everything—we didn't even have any clothes except the clothes on our backs—and we didn't know what we were going to do or where we were going to stay.

Fortunately, friends and family came and helped. I stayed with a childhood friend of mine, Elaine, my mom stayed with her mother and her youngest sister, and my dad and two brothers stayed with other friends. By the end of the week, Elaine's family had found a place for us in the city. It had one bedroom, where my brothers slept while my dad, mom, and I slept in the living room; they had a bed and I had a rollaway, which was okay, because even though we had that big farmhouse, we were used to sharing. Lack of living space was not the problem. The problem was what losing the house had done to my dad.

We don't know if it was bad wiring that caused the fire because they didn't investigate things like that, and I don't know if they talked to my father about it, but we were never told anything about what happened or how it happened. We never thought that it was foul play; we had lived there for my whole life, and if someone wanted to chase us out, they could have done it many years before. It was more that the fire was just too much for my dad. Everything he had saved for us was gone. We had a desk—a secretary, an *old* secretary—and people used to see it and offer him money for it, and he would say, "No—this is for my kids! I'm leaving it to them." The secretary was not saved.

My father never recovered from losing the house. He was already ill, which we didn't find out until after the fire. He had a thyroid condition, which they call Graves' disease now, but then we called it goiters. At first he had a lump under his neck, and then his eyes started to bulge, but he wouldn't go to a doctor; he just would not. When finally he went, the doctors were surprised that he was still walking around living because he was that sick. But he always said he wasn't. "I'm going to be fine," he would tell us, "just fine."

He didn't work every day after that; he was too sick, and all his spirit, everything, just left him. You could see that he was less of a person, less of a man. Because his promise to us, to his children, was, "As long as I'm living, you're never going to have to work a day in your life because I'm going to take care of you." He always wanted to make sure we were taken care of, that we were safe, but after the fire, he could not take care of us anymore, and the next year he passed away. The fire killed him. You could see it.

My dad passing, for me, was just like the fire for him. I couldn't recover from it. I became a real recluse. That's when I went to one-word answers and not communicating very much.

It was hard for my mom because she and I never had a really strong mother-daughter relationship. My relationship was always with my father. If I got sick or frightened at night, he would get up and take care of me. He would lie next to me on the bed, and he would talk to me, or he would sit and rock me to sleep. It was not so much that my mom and I had a rocky relationship; we just weren't that close, which made it even more difficult for me when my dad passed. Even when he was still living, people used to say, "Anything ever happened to that man, that child is never going to make it."

When he died, it was kind of like that. I just couldn't think in my mind anything besides, *What am I going to do?* To have two devastating things happen right there, back to back, made me break. I just went totally inside myself. It lasted forever, ten years, I think—maybe right up until the time I ran in my second Olympics. And it would have lasted longer if it had not been for Mr. Temple.

"You Just Ran Yourself into Some Shoes . . ."

After my father passed away, I didn't want to go home once the school day ended because I knew he wouldn't be there, so I started playing basketball. Then I didn't have anything to do once basketball season ended, so I started running track.

There were not a lot of options for women in sports at that time, and the options we did have were especially restricted because they were for girls. When I started playing basketball, girls couldn't run up and down the court—you had to play half-court: three guards on one side, three forwards on the other, and you could only dribble three times before you had to pass or you'd be called for traveling. By the time I was a junior—maybe a senior—in high school, they allowed one person to roam from one side to the other. Of course I was designated to do that. I was not a shooter, but I could run up and down the court fast, and I could pass the ball. I had played like that already with my brothers; I always played that way when I wasn't playing with the girls' team.

Playing with the boys was what prepared me to be the athlete I became. And for me, playing with the boys was no big deal. Boys and girls are all about the same when they're close in age and haven't hit puberty. It's just a matter of who is best at doing whatever it is you're doing, not whether you're a boy or a girl. And I always had that competitive edge; I wanted to win, to be the best. "I can do it better!" I would say. "Let me try!"

My brothers knew I was good, I guess, but I don't think they thought about it that way. They just thought: *This is what you do.* If you played, you had to be better than the next person— you had to hold up your end. It didn't matter if you were a girl or a boy. Everybody had to be that way. Or you got your butt whooped and then you had to take it and keep going. There were a couple of kids that were crybabies, but we always felt: *That's on you.*

I didn't win all the time, competing against my brothers; there were things that I was really good at, and there were things that they were really good at. For example, I was not very good at playing baseball; I could play outfield because I could chase the balls, but I wasn't a good hitter. I didn't like baseball anyway. Basketball, I was okay at, but like I said, I couldn't shoot. We played football a lot, and I got knocked out a couple of times. My brothers would tell me, "Don't run here!" And I would run there anyway. I knew what I wanted to do, and I knew I was pretty good at playing football. But when it came to riding a bicycle or climbing trees, I was good at that. And when it came to running, I was *very* good at that.

My brothers and I fought a lot because they always thought they could beat me. Which in some things they could. But I would never be the person to stop. They could knock me down twenty times, and I'd be back up fighting. "Could you just stay down?" they would always say. But I never would. My attitude was: *You're going to know you've been in this war. I might get the worst of it, but you're going to know that you've been in a war.* They taught me all of that. And it's probably part of why I got my gold medals. My brothers always say they taught me everything about how to be tough.

All that ended, of course, when the house burned and we

moved into the city. I was in junior high, which at the time only lasted for one year—the seventh grade. After that, in eighth grade, I started high school. By that time, I'd had all those years running and playing on the farm, so I guess it would have made sense for me to go out for track even if my dad hadn't died and I hadn't needed somewhere to go besides home. But like I said: when I started running, it was just something to do after basketball season. Running kept me busy. It kept me out of trouble.

And I could run. I would go out on the track, and the coach would see me run, and she would say to me, "Can you run the sprints? Can you run the 100?"

In the beginning, I did not run the 100; I never ran any of the sprints. I high-jumped, long-jumped, and ran the hurdles. Those were the things I wanted to do, and I did them. I had no form, regardless of what I was doing; when I high-jumped, it was just sheer *I can get over that bar!* I'm a visual person, and I would watch someone jump and see what they did, and then go and almost duplicate it. Sometimes I would be good at it, and sometimes I would not, but basically I was high-jumping.

Same thing with the hurdles. No one taught me how to hurdle. I would run, almost stop, jump over, and then, because I had a lot of speed, I could make up for the stops. But hurdles are *hard,* and I finally came to the realization that there had to be a better way to get down that track—without banging up my knees! That's how I started running the sprints: because running hurdles was brutal. Absolutely brutal.

Even after I had figured that out, I still wasn't very consistent. I would only practice when I felt like it. Some days, I would just sit and look around and watch other people practice. Then when I did practice, my practice was pretty halfhearted. I knew enough to know that you had to jog around the field and run wind sprints, but I didn't put in much effort. I don't know why the coach let me get away with it, but she did. What could she say? Right from the start, I was winning. And I probably went to practice more than anybody else on the team. I and one other girl, Frances Dallas, lived walking distance from the track, but the other girls rode the bus. We were supposed to practice until five, though the bus would leave at four, so most girls weren't ever at the whole practice. Mainly, though, the difference between them and me was that even when I was there, I was not all there. I had to do something to occupy myself, yet my heart wasn't in it.

In high school, we had little track meets: Black schools would run against other Black schools in the surrounding towns and counties. At the end of the season, they had what they called the state meet at Fort Valley, Georgia, and that's where all the different schools came to compete. There was a lot more competition: girls who were much better than us as well as some who were not. Girls from my school usually didn't qualify for the Fort Valley meet, but my first year out I qualified for the sprints, and our relay team qualified as well, so my coach wanted us to go. I didn't think my mom would let me, and I knew that if my dad had been living, I would *definitely* have stayed home. He was never big on us leaving; I could not spend the night away from home, ever.

But he was gone, and my mom let me go, and because I won there, I got to go to the national championship, which was held at Tuskegee University. Tuskegee was well known for sports and especially track—not to mention George Washington Carver and the Tuskegee Airmen. Alice Marie Coachman, the first Black woman to win an Olympic gold medal,[12] was from Tuskegee, and Tuskegee and Tennessee State's women's programs were pretty much similar; you knew that if you wanted

12 In the high jump at the London Olympics in 1948.

to go to college and you wanted to be part of track, that's where you went.

To qualify for the meet at Fort Valley, you had to run a certain time; to go on to Tuskegee, you had to place first or second at Fort Valley. I was the only girl from our school who got to go to Tuskegee. Frances Dallas didn't qualify, and I think that was partly because she had gotten herself a boyfriend. There was a lot of backward thinking happening at that time. My school wasn't going to let me go either, because I was a girl, and girls never went, and no girls had ever qualified before, so how could I go? Where was I going to stay? Who was going to take me? If I'd been a boy, it would not have been a problem; boys from my school had gone and were going, but according to the school leaders, I could *not* be in the car with the boys.

I wasn't about to fight for it; I was not that engaged. But my coach fought, and she won, and that's how I ended up going to Tuskegee in a station wagon with the boys. It was one of those extra-large station wagons, the kind that takes a long time to drive by you, with lots of room in the back. But I got the prime seat up front because of course I couldn't sit back there with all those *boys*.

Fort Valley was where I first saw Edith McGuire competing, and right away I thought, *What a pretty runner! She can run so good!* At that point, I didn't know that she had been training with Mr. Temple for one summer. I also didn't know that Edith had lost her father at an early age, just like me, and that a fire had taken her family home; I wouldn't find that out until later, when we were at Tennessee State together. At Fort Valley, all I knew was that she was from Atlanta and could really run—that she was running so pretty, and I was running so ugly, just trying to get from one end of the track to the other.

Two other girls from Atlanta, Gloria and Cynthia, had that

pretty way of running too. My coach then was Coach Kimbrough, a very tall woman with really bowed legs—if she could have straightened her legs out, I bet she would have been six one. She was a classy type of woman, and when you looked at her you thought, *Hmm, how did she get to be a PE teacher?*

Coach Kimbrough and I watched the races together, and when she saw those Atlanta girls run she said, "You need to learn how to run like that."

"Okay," I said. "Somebody maybe should teach me."

"You need to look at them," she said, "and run like they run."

Coach Kimbrough left at the end of that year, right before I went to Tennessee State for the summer program, and another woman, Miss Susie Bonner, became the coach. Miss Bonner had a little more knowledge about running and tried to help me with my form, but I didn't really get better until I started to work with Mr. Temple.

Me and my second high school basketball and track coach, Miss Susie Bonner. (Photo courtesy of Fairmont High School, Class of 1963.)

* * *

I ran at Fort Valley in 1961, and that was when Mr. Temple first saw me. He came up to me after my race and started talking to me. I was fifteen, about to turn sixteen, and I was still not talking very much, so all I would say was, "Okay," and, "Yes sir." But I heard what he said to me: "I thought you looked really good. You look like you could get a lot *better*. I think that if you come onto my program, we could work on you. You need some work with your arms." He told me the program was at Tennessee State, in Nashville, and it would last for a month.

Right away I thought: *My mom is not going to let me go. And my dad would not have wanted me to go. I should not be leaving my house.* Because my mom would let me go to Fort Valley for a meet, sure, but to go away for a month? To Nashville? *That's not happening,* I thought. *And how am I going to get there, anyway?* All these thing were going through my mind, but I didn't say anything, not anything at all, and finally he just said, "Well, you'll be hearing from me."

He was at Tuskegee too, but I didn't know he was going to be there. He would do that; he would just go and scout and see who was there and sometimes not talk to anybody beforehand.

After my race at Tuskegee, he came up to me and said, "You looked a lot better today than at Fort Valley, so you're doing well. You need to continue to do well, and not just on the track. You need to continue to do well at school too. And you need to remember: always be a lady."

For some reason, that made me like him more; it made me appreciate him. Because it seemed like he was thinking about *me* and not just about how I could run. After that, he sent a letter to our house saying that he was coming to Griffin to see my mom and talk to her about the program.

My mom asked a friend of hers who had graduated from

college and had kids in college, Miss Jessie Lee, to be there, to make sure that we understood everything that was involved. We sat in the living room when Mr. Temple came, my mom and Jessie Lee on the couch, Mr. Temple in a chair, and me cross-legged on the floor, wearing my jeans, of course. Mr. Temple talked the most, explaining what it would be like for me to go to Tennessee State for the summer.

"It's not going to be an easy job," he told us. "It's a lot of hard work." He said there was a right way and a wrong way, and then there was *his* way, and if girls in the program couldn't do things his way, "they go home with a comic book and an apple." That's what he would say: a comic book and an apple—so that you would have something to read and something to eat.

All I could think was, *Oh. My. God!*

He stayed for what seemed like a long time, more than an hour, going over the different points of his program. "You always got to be a young lady, got to have good morals, no getting in trouble. This is what I expect of the girls in my program."

Oh wow, I thought.

Finally he said, "Well, what do you think?" And then he just looked at me.

What do I think?! "I think I would like to go," I said. "I think—yeah."

"Well, all right," said Mr. Temple, and then he looked at my mom.

She just said, "Yes."

They both—she and Miss Jessie Lee—thought that it was a good idea. That's the presence that Mr. Temple had. But also, I think that it was more that my mom knew I needed to be away. Because I was still having trouble with losing my dad. I was still struggling and still not talking much, and she would tell me, "You need to *talk* more. You need to be *yourself* more."

I knew she was right. But I would never say anything. Even though I disagreed with a lot of things going on around me—like them trying to not let me go to that track meet or not ride in a car with boys—the most I would say was, "Well, okay."

My mom wanted me to get out of my slump and start to see opportunity in the world. She wanted more for me—just like my dad had. I didn't know it then, but when I look back at it, I think the reason she let me go to Mr. Temple's program was that she recognized that I needed some help—to be around other girls, ones who were like me, who were my age and who enjoyed running and had some sense of themselves in the world. There was no way I was going to go and see a therapist or anything like that. That was never something that we talked about or would have thought of or could have paid for. But she knew I needed a change. So she agreed to let me go.

And then my biggest worry was, *How am I going to go? She said I could go, but I can't—we don't have the money. We can't buy a train ticket. I can't go.*

Fortunately, people at my school, Fairmount High, raised money for me to go. Coach Kimbrough might have been the one who organized it, but other people helped as well; everybody knew that we didn't have the money. When it was nearly time for me to leave, Coach Kimbrough handed me an envelope with some writing on it: *To Wyomia Tyus, to aid her in her trip to Tennessee.* And then there was a list of people and groups that had chipped in: three dollars came from Room 8-B, which was my homeroom, three from the Bogarzons, which was a social club for boys, as well as three from the Bogarzettes, which was the same club for girls. The student council pitched in five dollars, I got six from the school ice cream fund, and there was another three from Coach Kimbrough herself, for a total of twenty-three dollars. I'm sure people thought that it was for spending money so that I wouldn't just be up there and not have anything, but it was much more basic than that: they paid for my train ticket, which was about ten bucks, fifteen bucks—whatever it was, we didn't have it, and we were grateful for the help.

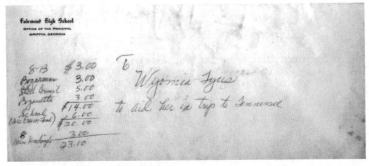

School support for my first trip to Mr. Temple's track camp.

When it was time to go, my uncle John Henry drove me to the train station in Atlanta, forty miles away, and Junior and Jimmy Lee and my mom came along to say goodbye. The trip seemed to take forever. I was anxious; it all seemed difficult and complicated: to get to Atlanta, find the right track, get on the right train. I had never traveled alone anywhere before. The train station was huge, but there was only so much for "coloreds"—only so many areas that you could go to and only so many cars you could ride in.

I was fifteen when I made that trip—all by myself with my little brown paper bag of food—fried chicken and an apple and whatever else my mom put in there so I wouldn't be hungry on the train. Because it was a long ride. We had to go through the Smoky Mountains, and with all the stops we made, it was probably about seven or eight hours.

The Fort Valley meet was the first time I had left Griffin without my parents, Tuskegee was the second, and this was the third. I don't have a good memory of the train ride. Miss Jessie Lee had said to me, "Now, you get on that train, and you don't talk to nobody, and you just sit there, and you sit there with confidence." Not talking to anyone was easy for me because, being me, I was not going to talk to anybody anyway. I didn't know the other people on the train, and if I had known them, I wouldn't have had much to say to them. So I sat there, like she said, with confidence.

It was summer and it was hot, and I'm not sure what I was wearing, but it was probably pedal pushers and tennis shoes—Keds—and a little blouse. I had long hair then, pressed and pulled back in a ponytail. My dad had never allowed me to have straight hair, and my mom was happy not to have to braid it.

When I got off the train, Mr. Temple was there. "Hi, Tyus!" He called everybody by their last name, except Edith; she was sometimes called Edith because her last name is McGuire, and Mr. Temple had a stutter—you would never know—and the *Mc* in McGuire sometimes tripped him up.

In any case, there he was, like he said he would be. Right there waiting for me. "Hi, Mr. Temple," I said.

Wilma Rudolph was with him, though I didn't know who she was. This was in '61, so she had already won her three gold medals, but I didn't know anything about *that* either. Her first Olympics was in '56, and she was there again in 1960, but the Olympics were not something that we paid attention to back home in Griffin.

Mr. Temple introduced me to Wilma. "This is Rudolph," he said.

"Oh, Tyus!" she said. "Come on!" And she just started talking and talking. Wilma Rudolph—if you ever met her, you'd know—was one of those people who never knew a stranger; no one was a stranger to her. She was that outgoing.

We got my luggage and went to the car, and Mr. Temple and Wilma talked the whole time. I just sat in the back listening, thinking, *God, they can* talk. I didn't know people could talk so much, not even my *mom* talked that much. But Wilma and Mr. Temple could just talk, and I cannot tell you what they were talking about. I was too busy looking around, trying to see where I was and what I had gotten myself into.

We came up on campus—the train station is about ten minutes from Tennessee State—and drove into the "horseshoe," a half-circular lane with the girls' dorms on one side and school buildings on the other. Mr. Temple was telling me what each building was, pointing out the track, explaining everything. We went around the horseshoe to the dorm where I'd be living. "You're going to have roommates," he said then.

I don't know how this is going to work, I thought.

"You'll be okay, Tyus," Wilma said, like she knew what I was thinking. "We'll take care of you. The older girls are on one wing of the dorm, and the younger girls are on the other, and you'll be okay. We're all going to have a great time." That was just how she was.

The other girls had been in Nashville for at least a day; I was one of the last ones to get there, or at least the last one that day. My roommates were Gloria, who I had seen run at Fort Valley, and Flossie, and of course I got top bunk because I was the last one to arrive. Flossie was from Mississippi, a really tall woman, five eleven at least, and I kept thinking, *I've never seen a girl my age so tall.* I'm five seven and a half, but there that was short because first you had Wilma, who's six feet, and then you had Flossie (who had *big* feet). Both she and Gloria were really nice and very friendly, and Gloria and I got to be close friends. Gloria could run.

We sat for a while and got introduced, but we didn't stay up late because Mr. Temple had told us, "You need to go up to your room and get a good night's sleep. You've got to be at practice at five in the morning."

Five in the morning?! But we got right into it because that's why we were there. "You don't have to worry about getting up," he had told us. "The older girls or the manager—they'll make sure you're up."

He had our "uniforms" ready for us: gray sweats and T-shirts and a pair of shorts. We didn't have Tigerbelle T-shirts because we weren't Tigerbelles yet. You couldn't just *have* that; you had to earn it. We just had plain old white T-shirts to work out in, and that was it.

You had to have your own shoes, and at that time running shoes were horrible. There were Adidas, Wilson, and Spalding—the Spalding spikes, they called them—and they were heavy, heavy shoes. They had spikes, but not the detachable ones; they were *old* school. Nothing like what they wear now. For years, Adidas used to make their shoes out of kangaroo leather, and then they had to ban that because they were killing too many kangaroos. Those shoes fit like a glove, but I wasn't about to get shoes like that at that point in time; those were the kind of shoes you might get if you qualified for an international meet.

Mr. Temple had a system, though. When Adidas was giving shoes to a Tigerbelle who, for example, made the 1960 Olympic team, that person wore five different sizes of shoe, according to Mr. Temple's order. That way everybody could get shoes when they were ready for them. He had stockpiles of shoes in all different sizes and levels of quality, so when girls just didn't have shoes, they could get some that were pretty good; or, when he felt that you'd done so well that you deserved some new shoes, you'd go in there and get a pair that was a step up from what you had. Which was good because most of us couldn't afford to buy shoes, and the school was not buying them for us—and definitely not for me.

What I had were some *old* Spalding shoes, and I couldn't wait to get a pair of new shoes—not top-of-the-line shoes, but an upgrade from what I had—and not just because I wanted nice shoes, either, but because when Mr. Temple said, "Well, you're running well, and we're going to give you a pair of shoes"—you couldn't beat that. You knew then that he saw something in you.

For me, that didn't happen right away. At the beginning, I didn't think it would ever happen. Practice was just *hard*. He loved to make you run hills because he felt it built a lot of strength and endurance, so at five o'clock in the morning we were on dirt paths running hills: up the hill and down the hill, up the hill and down the hill. We used to call it "Mr. Hill." It was not that it was very steep; it was that you had to run it so many times. Then it became very steep, and when you started to get tired, Mr. Temple would yell, "Get those knees up! Get those knees up!"

After we were done running hills, he would let us go to breakfast—whatever the cafeteria on campus had to eat—and lie down or maybe play some cards if you were feeling really energetic. That was about all you could do after five o'clock practice.

We would go back at nine. Nine o'clock practice was mainly working on technique—drill after drill after drill on how to run, how to use your arms, high knee drills, repetitive stuff. It was not about distance; we'd run fifty yards, maybe, lifting our knees, working on our arms. He taught us to think that you were pretty much shaking hands when you were running: reaching out, pulling back, reaching out, pulling back, keeping a bent elbow and not clenching your fists. Some people ran with straight hands and some with their hands cupped. "Think of holding an egg," he would say.

When nine o'clock practice was over, you would go to lunch and then come back at one. One o'clock practice was all about specialties: if you were a sprinter you'd work on starts, if you were a jumper you'd work on jumping. The length of each practice depended on Mr. Temple, but the five o'clock practice was usually the longest. He had a routine, and if the practices weren't always the same, the times were: five, nine, and one.

The older girls didn't usually come to the five o'clock practice, but if they came to the nine or one o'clock practices, they helped out. They were already in college, so they were either in summer school, or they had jobs, or both. Most Tigerbelles went to summer school because it was difficult to take a full load and compete at the same time. Even in summer school, you couldn't take a full load because that's when most of the competitions were held. Many people take four years to finish college, but for most runners it took five—and it would have taken me five even if I wasn't running.

So while we younger girls were just there to run, the older girls had other things to do, though they still had to come to at least one practice, and if they weren't doing that well, they had to come to two, usually the nine and the one. They had been in the summer program years before, so they had already been through what we were going through. Because of this, Mr. Temple arranged it so that there were always older girls there to support the younger girls and so that the younger girls got to be in contact with *all* the older girls instead of just a few. He knew that not everyone would connect in the same way, and he wanted each of us to be able to find someone we liked and could look up to who would help us.

There were about twenty girls in the summer program, three girls per room, and we had a whole wing of one dormitory. Living with those twenty girls, you got to know them pretty well because you didn't have anything else to do. You could go downtown with one of the older girls—usually two of them would take you, and if you had money, you could buy things, or you could go to a movie, but that was it. We were too tired to do much, anyway.

I was still the one who never talked, so I would just sit in the room and listen to the others. Their experiences were totally different than mine, and that gave me something to think about. I still didn't know where I was going or what I wanted to do or if this—running—was the thing for me. I just knew that it had gotten me out of Griffin. Listening to the other girls talk gave me ideas, and I think that was exactly the kind of exposure my mother had been hoping I would get.

Of course, one of the things that people would talk about was how hard the practices were. The older girls would say, "Now, it's not that bad. You're going to get through it. It gets easier." We would roll our eyes and think they were crazy. At one point, it got to be so hard that I just wanted to go home. It wasn't only me: one girl went home the first week, and more the week after. When girls started to go home, I thought, *I'm calling my mama!* Because everybody called their parents, everybody was talking about leaving, about how hard it was, about not wanting to take it. You're talking about girls who are fifteen, sixteen years old. They felt they could be doing something else. Not me—I knew I would have nothing to do if I went back to Griffin.

But still. And it wasn't only the practices; by the second week, we were in time trials, and Mr. Temple would shoot film of us, and at the end of the week he would hold meetings and put on the films. He'd stand there in front of the group and point and say, "Look at you! Look at your arms! That is *not* what you should be doing."

All the girls would be at those meetings, not just the younger ones. The older girls had to be there so they would know exactly what Mr. Temple wanted them to work on with us. One way they would help out at the track was by running beside you on the drills and showing you the correct form: *Stay relaxed, keep your knees high, don't clench*—all the things that Mr. Temple had said, but in a different voice. They could also tell when someone was getting frustrated and needed encouragement, and they were there to give us that as well. I don't know how Mr. Temple knew that we needed them, but he did.

Watching myself on film—I had never thought I looked like that, running. You'd look at it, and for the most part you couldn't really think anything because Mr. Temple was busy pointing out all the wrong and saying, "We can correct this." And then you would look again, and you would see yourself getting beat. That was deflating. More than anything, it was getting beat and *watching myself* get beat that wore me down.

My biggest problem was that I was never relaxed enough. Mr. Temple started calling me "The Mechanical Man." I wanted to say, *It's because you changed me! You* said *to run this way!* But I didn't say anything, and I couldn't relax. Between that and getting beat, all I could think was, *I gotta go home. I have had enough disappointments and enough bad things. This is not going to work for me.*

I called my mom after the second week. I had to go to the pay phone in the dorm and call collect. You had to put a dime in so that you could call the operator and tell her that you wanted to make a collect call, and then you would get your dime back, whether they accepted or not. I got my mom right away; I knew when to find her at home.

At first she was saying, "Oh, I'm so glad you called! We were worried about you." Because I couldn't call every week; you had to pick and choose your time. Mr. Temple had me call her when

I got there so she would know I was safe, and I used his phone in the post office where he worked for that call. But I hadn't talked to her since then.

As soon as she stopped talking, I said, "I'm ready to come home. This is not working for me. It's a whole lot of work, and I just don't think I'm getting any better. I think I'm getting worse. I'd prefer being at home."

She listened. Then she said, "Well. You can't come home. Because you decided you wanted to go, that it was something you wanted to do. You don't have to go back next year, but you've got to finish this out."

"But you just don't know!" I said.

And she didn't care. Her thing was that my coming home was just not going to happen.

I wasn't angry at her. It was more like, *Why don't she just let me come home? She knows I'm not a whiner, some crybaby type. She knows it must be hard.* But nothing had ever really been that hard for me before, so my mom probably thought, *She needs this test. She needs to be able to do this. She's never been a person who gives up.*

I'm assuming this. We never talked about it because my mom and I didn't have that kind of relationship. But I think she knew me a lot better than I thought she did at the time. Because for her to say what she did tells me that she saw something in me that I didn't see. She knew something about me and my courage, about what she and my dad had taught me, and she knew I could finish the program.

I'm glad she did what she did because I not only finished, I got better, and her saying I couldn't leave made a big difference. She made me stay, and since I knew I had to stay, I also had to tell myself, *I can get over this. I can do the next two weeks. Then I'll be done.* My attitude just turned.

I also knew that, if I had to stay, I did not want Mr. Temple talking about me, ever—or, if he talked about me, I wanted it to be good stuff. I didn't want it to be The Mechanical Man and, "Tyus, you need to relax."

I can remember Vivian, one of the older girls, saying to me, "Tyus, if you relax, you can do this. You got it. You *got* it. You're just too wanting it to be perfect. It's not perfect. *Run.* Just run."

And I started doing it. I started thinking, *Okay, if I can get this over with, I never have to come back here again.* And that's what got me through. After I got off the phone with my mother, I never talked about leaving again. I just kind of let go. I let go of feeling sorry for myself because I was getting beaten. I even started to let go of the fire and my depression over my dad's death. Because my grief over my father—that still had not left me. It was always there. At first, I didn't even want to remember the good times I'd had with him because all I could think was that I would never have them again. Of course I didn't talk to anybody about it. I wasn't ready for that. Matter of fact, I have just now gotten to the point where I can talk about it and feel okay. So no one else knew; it was just me and my battle.

At the end of the summer, in that first year with Mr. Temple, we went to the Amateur Athletic Union (AAU) championships in Gary, Indiana. They had the women's juniors and the seniors all competing at that meet, so the older girls came too. Mr. Temple would only take the younger girls who were doing well. "We only have three station wagons," he said, "so we're only going to take the best."

The station wagons were like the ones they had at my high school: big, long cars with the seat turned backward in the back. Mr. Temple drove one, the assistant coach drove another, and the athletic trainer drove the third. The older girls got to pick and choose where they wanted to sit, but the younger girls had to sit in the back. I was the youngest of all, and I sat with two other young girls in the *way* back.

I did well in that meet. I didn't win; I think I got thirds and fourths. But Mr. Temple told me I looked good and told me he thought I could do a lot better by next year. And then he gave me a pair of shoes. "You take these home," he said, "and you practice."

"Now Run Yourself into a Tigerbelle T-shirt!"

I took my shoes home, I went back to high school, and I practiced—every day. I didn't just sit around. I tried to do the things that Mr. Temple had told me to do. I didn't do them to the same extent I had in Tennessee, but then, I didn't have to: just by being there that one summer, I had gotten much better, and now that I was going to practice too, I was developing into an athlete. And I was happy—I didn't have to wear those old bulky shoes anymore. I had run myself into some *shoes!*

Not that everyone was happy. When I came back that first summer, my great aunt said, "Come here!" and started poking my legs. "What is that?"

"Those are muscles," I said. "All the girls have them."

"You're looking like a man! You need to stop all that running. No man likes to see muscles like that on a woman!"

"But this is what it takes to run!"

"That is not pretty *at all.* And it's not what women are supposed to look like."

Thank goodness I had thick skin. People would say these things to me, and when they couldn't get a rise, they started in on my mom: "You know, she's never going to get married—*or* have babies. Because that running just takes the womanhood from you—takes it *right* out of you."

Things like that and other things—I cannot tell you how

many things were said. And my mom was starting to say, "You know, maybe they're right."

"You should just call Mr. Temple," I told her.

And she did.

"Look," he said, "that's just not true. That's an old wives' tale. I've had girls who got pregnant while they were running and still in school."

Wilma had a baby out of high school, so she was proof. But my mom didn't know her, and when somebody's in your ear all the time, it can really affect your mind. Still, she didn't make me stop. She couldn't.

Because after being to Nashville, Griffin seemed all that much smaller. Everything seemed smaller. I had gone through some changes and was starting to see more of the world. Not that everywhere I went looked better than Griffin. When we had gone to Indiana, Mr. Temple said that we should try to see something of the place, but for me, there was nothing there to see. The next summer, though, in '62, we went to California. That was different. When we got to LA, I decided right then and there that that was where I wanted to live.

But that was down the road; I still had one more year of high school to finish before I could even go back to Tennessee State for the summer. And it was a busy year. The winter before I went back, I managed to run myself into another pair of shoes: Mrs. Marion Perkins was the coach at David T. Howard High School in Atlanta, and she also worked as an assistant coach for Mr. Temple in the summer and would help him scout at meets in the Atlanta area when he couldn't go. She had recommended me to a sporting goods store in North Hollywood, California, that sometimes gave her girls shoes, and the owner, Clifford Severn, sent me a pair of Adidas three-stripe competition track shoes for free. At the time, my mom was making about fifteen dollars a week and struggling to pay off the debts my father had left when he died, so every little bit helped. Fortunately, the second time I went to the summer program, I didn't need my school to take up a collection for me because my brother Jackie paid my way. He was still in the army, stationed in Germany, and he had some money to spare. Jimmy Lee was working too, and so was Junior, but the money they made was going into the household.

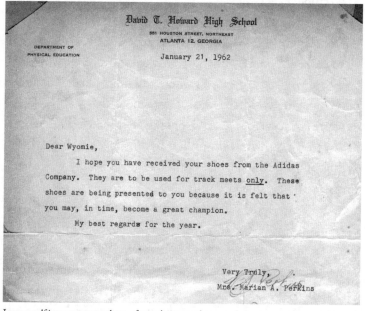

I ran myself into some more shoes—for track meets only.

* * *

When I got back to Nashville, Wilma was still there, and it became clear not long after I arrived that Mr. Temple wanted her to retire. One Friday afternoon he said, "I want to see McGuire, Tyus, and Rudolph at the track at nine."

We didn't usually practice on the weekends, so both Edith and I were thinking, *What did we do?* The next morning, we went to the track, and he told us he wanted to have a time trial. He wanted Edith, Wilma, and me to run against each other in the 100. And I tell you, I thought, *Run against* Edith? *And* Wilma?!!

So we warmed up, and it was just the three of us, him, and the team manager. Nobody else on the track. He didn't want anyone else to know. We ran a hundred yards, and from start to finish we matched stride for stride; it was the three of us, all steady, the whole way, and to this day I can't tell you who won. Mr. Temple never said.

He did that for Wilma, to show her what he had been trying to tell her: "These girls are going to beat you." He wanted us all to retire on top. "Once you've reached the top," he would say, "why are you staying on? Nowhere to go but down." It wasn't only about how old she was. It was more that he just knew: "They're gonna whoop you." Not long after that, Wilma retired. That was what that meant to her. But for me, keeping up with Wilma and Edith made me think that I was on my way to getting my first Tigerbelle T-shirt.

And I was right. When we went to Los Angeles for the AAU championships in the summer of '62, Flossie and myself were the only juniors, and the senior girls were Wilma, Vivian, Lorraine, who was from Panama, and Edith. The real thrill for me came when Mr. Temple gave me an opportunity to run the first leg of the senior relay. That was the time when Edith was really coming into her own and winning, and it was great for me to see that and to be a part of it by running with her.

Being in Los Angeles was exciting for all kind of reasons. For one thing, we got to run in the Coliseum where they had held the 1932 Olympics, the year that Babe Didrikson had set four world records at the qualifying AAU championships, and women threw the javelin and ran the hurdles for the first time in Olympic history. Running in that kind of environment just gave you a certain feeling, like you were doing something important. We also went on tours of Beverly Hills, Disneyland, Universal Studios, and the beach—all firsts in my life.

In addition to all that, I won. Mr. Temple had brought just Flossie and me, and he wanted us to try to win the Junior Championship all by ourselves. I won the 50, the 75, and the 100, and Flossie competed in the long jump and the 100. Flossie could really run; on most days she could beat me, but she just didn't have it in Los Angeles that year. If Flossie had gotten second in either the 100 or the long jump, we would have won the whole Junior Championship with just two girls. As it was, we got second—not quite what Mr. Temple wanted, but not bad.

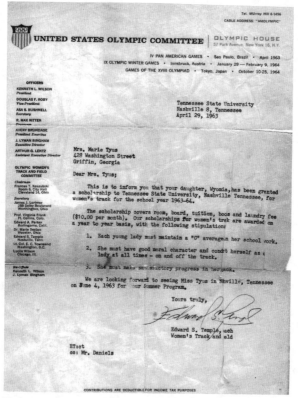

My dream come true: a scholarship for college!

* * *

That was '62. In '63, I graduated high school and went back to the summer program for the third time. I didn't turn eighteen until the end of August, so I could still run in the Junior Division in June and July. I was winning then too, and for me that was just gravy, because at that point I knew that I was getting a work-aid scholarship and going to Tennessee State in the fall. I was just so happy and proud. *Hey,* I thought, *I can do this! My mom doesn't have to worry about me—I'm going off to college on my own steam.* It wasn't all smooth sailing; we were still in the same boat money-wise, and I didn't know how some things were going to get done. Going off to college, you needed a trunk, which I didn't have, and I also didn't have the clothes to fill it; all my stuff fit into one piece of luggage.

Still, I was looking forward to it, and I was really coming out of my slump. I was talking a lot more—not yet to the point that I should have been, but more.

Then, that summer, I made the US team to go to the Soviet Union and left the country for the first time ever. When you went to the USSR, you got to go to Poland, Germany, and England as well—we left in the middle of July and stayed away until the middle of August—but it was always all about the United States versus the Soviets back then, so most of the fuss was about that leg of the trip.

It was the worst trip ever! First of all, it was the longest I had ever been on a plane. It was also the *second* time I had ever been on a plane—we had flown to California too, and that was it. We made it fun; we went as a team and played games and cards and talked a whole lot of junk. Of course, we had to wear uniforms on the plane—dresses, but not the full fashion outfits I would have to wear later when I traveled with the Tigerbelles. Still. Dress uniforms? On a ten-hour flight to Russia? Come on. But we did what we had to, and we had little bags with our jeans—our cutoff jeans—and T-shirts in them, and we went in the bathroom and changed for the flight, and then, just before we landed in Russia, we put our uniforms back on.

Except—they wouldn't let us land. We were supposed to go to Moscow, but when we got there, they had us circling and circling—they actually had to land the plane some place we weren't supposed to be to get fuel because we had been flying for so long. It was that whole Cold War thing. When we finally landed at something like four in the morning, we were dead tired. But that didn't change the fact that we were going to be running in the next day or two; they weren't going to postpone the meet so that we had time to recover.

It wasn't just the flight that went wrong. That was also the time when Mamie—Flamin' Mamie of the Bouffant Belles— was the coach of the team.[13] We weren't happy about it, but there was nothing we could do. It's not like it is now, when everybody has their individual coach and that coach goes too. Back then, you were stuck with the coach they chose. You still did your own workout, and the team coach would only put in her two cents here and there, but you were supposed to lis- ten to her like she knew something. Naturally, we knew not to do anything Mamie told us to do. We had seen her before at meets with her skintight outfits and her bouffant hair. She

13 Margaret Ellison, "nicknamed Flamin' Mamie for her strawberry-blond hair and flamboyant personality, had little track experience, but plenty of business savvy," ac- cording to *Runnersworld.com*. "Hoping to attract both spectators and media, Ellison brought her athletes to a beauty salon before every meet." In the words of one of her runners, "She just wanted us to be showy. Every year, she would design these fancy uniforms and she had this sewing lady in Abilene make red satin shorts and things like that." On April 20, 1964, Flaming Mamie's Bouffant Belles became the first female track athletes ever to be appear on the cover of *Sports Illustrated*. Gil Rogin, an *SI* editor at the time, "chose to write primarily about the athletes' beauty regimen rather than their running, and admits, 'It was all just a stunt. It wasn't a track story.'" See http://www. runnersworld.com/runners-stories/how-big-hair-got-these-runners-on-the-cover-of- sports-illustrated.

would come out to the track—heels *this* high—and you knew she couldn't coach. She couldn't tell us anything besides how to put on eye shadow, tease our hair, and wear skimpy clothing.

Between the plane and Mamie, we did poorly in the USSR—we got third and fourth, Edith and I. It was bad. And then they took us on a tour of the country, and *Sports Illustrated* shot a picture of us and printed it with the caption, "American girls having big fun, cannot compete against the Russians." No one said anything about how they made us fly around forever and ever. No one talked about that, but they talked about us, and Mamie was the main one talking, saying we stayed out all night and didn't come to practice on time. We didn't do any of that; we were never that type of people. And it wasn't just about what we would or wouldn't do; there were rules. If we had missed practice or even been late, there would have been consequences; we probably would have been sent home. So the things she was saying had no relationship to reality. But that didn't stop her from saying them.

For all those reasons, it wasn't a great experience, competition-wise. Still, it was exciting to be out of the country for the first time. Everything was so different. Even the smells were something else. That's something I notice in cities here in the US too, and in the USSR, the smells were both foreign to me and kind of like Gary—industrial smells, like diesel and tar and cement.

The reaction people had to us was totally different. We would leave the hotel to go out to practice, and people would come up to us and rub our skin and ask our interpreters if the color came off. And I would say, "No—this is us. It's not going to come off." We had been told they would do that, but nobody believed it before it happened, so it was strange.

Another special thing was being able to go to Lenin's tomb.

At first I thought, *What for? It's just a dead man,* but once we had seen it, I knew why it was important to people. I also noticed that, in Russia, the women did a lot of heavy labor. They worked on the streets, and you could see them doing the kinds of things that, at least here in the US, usually only men did. But even while doing that heavy work, they always wore dresses, peasant-looking dresses with lots of layers and colors.

Then there was the food they ate, and how they cooked it, and the whole thing about drinking a lot of vodka; they did do that. And caviar—it was the first time I had ever even seen it, not that I ate it. The food was difficult for me; I was a picky eater no matter where I was, so I didn't have very much to eat. We had been told by the older Tigerbelles that we needed to carry our own food—canned food, like peaches or Vienna sausages, and Oreo cookies and candy bars—because the food they served in those countries was not going to be anything you were used to. Those canned foods helped me out a lot because, other than that, I really didn't eat much at all, just bread and butter the whole time I was there—except when we were in Poland. They had this porridge there that was like oatmeal or something, but whatever it was, it was the best. I would get up early every morning just to have it because that would be my staple for the day.

The other thing that I noticed about Poland was that Warsaw, the city where we stayed, was still in ruins from all the bombing that had gone on in World War II. People were living with these bombed-out buildings everywhere. For someone like me, who had never seen anything like that, and being there and listening to how it had happened—I think my eyes must have stayed wide open the whole time. Going on those tours was eye-opening—whatever *Sports Illustrated* or Flamin' Mamie had to say about it.

* * *

After that trip, it was time to go to college, which changed my life a lot. For one thing, I started working: I had a work-aid scholarship, and I had to juggle that along with schoolwork and track practice. Mr. Temple tried to make sure we had jobs that didn't take up all our time and that we didn't work for people who would object when we had to go out of town for a meet. We had to work two hours a day, so it didn't take too much out of us. The football players didn't always show up for their work aid, but we Tigerbelles had to be at work, and we had to do the work, or we would lose our scholarships. Still, I got a full ride, and I didn't mind it. I worked in the off-campus student housing office, looking out for off-campus students, making sure they had their ID cards and helping them find housing.

Mr. Temple also made sure that we did well in school. You had to go to him every three weeks or so, and before that you had to go to your teachers and get a progress report. That's how he knew whether we were doing well—or not. The first year, the first quarter of my schooling, I didn't do well at all. My grades were so bad that Mr. Temple would say, "I just don't believe you!"

I tried, but I just couldn't get it—especially the classes that didn't interest me. I would always go to class, and I was okay in the classes that were more hands-on, like biology and kinesiology, or the ones that were about things I wanted to know, like history, but in some classes the teachers just talked on and on about nothing that seemed important to me. Like literature—I had that class at six o'clock at night, after practice—worst thing in the world. I went to class, but I was just not there. Why would I want to be talking about *The Canterbury Tales?* First of all, I hadn't even read half of it even though the older girls would say, "You know, they're going to talk about this book—

you need to start reading." I would look at that big book and think, *We got to read all of this in a quarter? No!*

So I did poorly. One day Mr. Temple called me into his office. "You're not going to stay with these grades, Tyus. You're going home with that comic book and that apple."

"Mr. Temple," I said, "I just don't know what's wrong. I go to class."

"Going to class will not keep you here. What will keep you here is raising your grades. Now you got to get all A's."

"But I'm not an A student, Mr. Temple! How am I going to get A's?" I knew I could be a good B student; I knew that. And his demand was only that all his girls have a C average—he demanded, really, that you have a C+. You could stay with a C, but basically you had to have a C+ so that, if you fell down, you had something to catch you. And here I was, needing all A's just to get back up to a C.

It was a rude awakening, another one of those moments when I had to start telling myself what to do: *I can go to school—I can do this. I got to really learn.* Mr. Temple wanted to help, of course, so he made a rule that I had to go to my teachers not just every three weeks but *every* week, and get them to write down what was I doing, what I was not doing, and what I needed to work on—and then I had to meet with him and talk about it. I did that for the next quarter. Oh God, I hated it. I felt just like a little kid. At one point, I had to go talk with him every day. I worked right next door to him, so it was easy for him to call me in.

"What'd you do in your class?" he would ask me.

"I'm doing fine."

"*What* are you doing in class?"

"I'm doing *fine.*"

"You sure? Did you talk with your teacher? I want you talking with your teachers every day."

"Okay."

"Do you hear what I'm saying to you, Tyus? That's the only way you're going to be able to stay here."

"I can do it," I told him. "I can." And I was thinking that if I could just get C's, that would be okay with me.

But he wanted us to want more. "The way you apply yourself on the track," he would say, "is how you got to apply yourself in your classes. We can't babysit you forever. You've got to do it. You *can* do it. That's why I put you in the room with Marcella!"

Marcella Daniel was my roommate that first year in college. She was a sophomore from Panama, and she made good grades. She was not like other girls on the team who did *really* well, but she had great study habits; she studied all the time, stayed up all night, reading and cramming. Her being my roommate, being who she was and doing what she did, was all part of Mr. Temple's plan. He paired me up with Marcella so that I could get the help he thought I needed. But I didn't believe Marcella could help me. We were too different. She followed all the rules while I just followed the ones that made sense to me. She was very good at studying, and I was not. She would go to the library *every day*, and she would take me with her, and I would wander around.

"Come sit with me," she would say, and I would try for a while. The problem was that it was too quiet in the library. If I studied in our room and there was noise going on outside, I did much better, because at least I could get up and go see what it was and then go back. It would break the monotony. Also, I did much better if someone else was in the same class with me, and we could talk about what we read. That whole just-sitting-there-reading thing did not work for me.

I finally kind of somewhat got it by the end of the year. I

kept on saying I could do it, and eventually I did. It was a big breakthrough for me. At that point, I realized that I had put my father's death and not having him aside—not all the way aside, but I could finally let myself remember the times I had spent with him. During my first year in the summer program, I had started to see that there was something else I could do besides sit around Griffin, missing my dad. I could do something more, which was what he had wanted. Sometimes I would fall back to thinking that nothing I did mattered because he wasn't there to see it. The next step was convincing myself that he did see it; I just didn't see him seeing it. And so on. And finally I was able to think: *If I can come to terms with my father's death then I can do well enough at school to not be sent home.*

And soon I was back to where I should have been. I had learned how to be a college student—though I had to learn it again every year. With school and track, you couldn't really have much of a social life, which was difficult. If someone said, "They're having a party—would you like to come?" I had to say, "I can't *go*. I got to study." No one could stay out late, of course—we had curfews. That was for all the freshmen, not just the Tigerbelles. All the girls, that is—the women. The men didn't have that. But we were in a dorm situation; you had to sign in and sign out. You could have male visitors, but you had to sit and talk with them in the lobby, or go outside, and that was it. Nobody could come upstairs or be in your room, not even with the doors open.

For Mr. Temple, this was a good thing; it was part of being "ladylike."

"First of all," he would say, "if you're running track, people look at you totally different. They look at it more as a male sport than a female sport. You're always going to get comments and things, so you need to be as ladylike as possible."

Whatever "ladylike" meant. We knew that it meant that you had to carry yourself a certain way, no cussing or fussing or fighting out in the street, always acting the way you were raised up to act. You had to dress up like you were going to church to go anywhere, that whole Southern thing. If you look at pictures of when the Tigerbelles traveled as a team, you can see that we were always decked out in our finest. That was a big part of the program. Tigerbelles *had* to dress up to get on a plane. That was *it*. We had to conform to the social idea of what it meant to be a lady—or at least Mr. Temple's idea of what it meant. Although it is true that most of the Tigerbelles enjoyed dressing up; I might have been the only one who would have preferred to wear jeans.

How to dress up was one of the things that the older girls taught you, from wearing stockings to having immaculate hair, which for Black women in those days meant pressing our hair all the time—straight and fried. There were always girls on the team that did hair; Evelyn, one of my roommates and a good friend, did hair. It was a big thing for us, for all the women at Tennessee State, but especially the Tigerbelles, because we ran every day, even in the rain. You're out there working out and sweating, and you have to care how your hair looked? I don't think so. But when you went on a trip, you had to have your hair looking great. When we went to Europe, we would take those little Sterno cans—can you imagine doing that today? You would light them up and use them to heat your straightening comb, and that's how you did your hair when you were in Europe. And you would hope that you didn't get on the wrong side of the girl that did hair because you wouldn't have a good hairdo if you did—or they wouldn't do your hair at all.

At the time, I thought that was part of growing up, part of being in the college life. But now I know that, mostly, wearing dresses and doing your hair was part of living in the South. That was when the Afro was popular, though with certain teachers at Tennessee State, you could not wear an Afro. If you had an Afro, you went into their classroom with a scarf or a hat on your head. That's what you had to do. And this was at an all-Black college—a Historically Black University (HBU). And then there were the teachers who didn't want women to wear pants to class. I had a Saturday-morning class at eight o'clock and I could *not* go in pants. I had to wear a dress—just like when I was a little girl in Griffin. But it was in the winter months, and the way I got around it was to wear my trench coat and have my shorts on underneath—cutoff jeans. Because I was not going to put on a dress if I didn't have to. I hadn't changed that much. I just sat there with my long coat on the whole time, and the teacher never knew.

Representing Tennessee, but not yet a Tigerbelle. (Photo courtesy of Tennessee State University Athletics.)

* * *

If you look at pictures of my early running, you'll see that I had on a T-shirt that said *Tennessee*. It doesn't say *Tigerbelles*. Mr. Temple had criteria for being a Tigerbelle, and you needed to meet his criteria if you wanted that T-shirt. You could be on the team, and you could say, "I'm with the Tigerbelles," but *we* knew that if you were not wearing that Tigerbelle T-shirt, you were not truly a Tigerbelle yet.

To be one of Mr. Temple's Tigerbelles, you definitely had to have good grades—that was number one. And you had to do well on the track. You didn't have to be a superstar, but you had to contribute something positive to the team at all times.

"My girls do everything," Mr. Temple would say. "There are girls on our team who have excellent grades, and there are girls running much faster than those girls, but they're all doing well at something. They're not just track athletes. They can be brain surgeons. They can be Miss Tennessee State University."

We had a diverse team, and everyone contributed. The girls who were A students kept the team's average up. My roommate Marcella, who studied all the time? She was also the one who was Miss Tennessee State. That helped us too; people thought it was good for our "image." The fact that everybody felt they could make a contribution was one of the things that made Mr. Temple's program successful.

Another reason Mr. Temple was so successful was because nobody else was doing what he was doing—hardly anyone else was even trying to have a women's program in track and field at all. Tuskegee had a program, and then Hawaii started a program, but it was not that big, and then, finally, Texas Southern started a program. But Mr. Temple was one of the few coaches who had the charisma and ability to convince parents to let their daughters run track. And once they did, he had the ability and fortitude to say to the girls, "You could be more than just a track star. This could propel you into your future. Track opened the doors for you, but education will keep them open."

He gave us a dream—something to look forward to. Most of us were coming from poor families, big families; I think Edith and I may have been the only girls on the team in the beginning who came from families of four children. Most of them came from families of nine, ten—even thirteen or fourteen. Girls wanted to get out of that and make a better life for themselves, and their parents wanted the same. Mr. Temple gave them that opportunity. He saw possibilities for women *way* before Title IX—in fact, Mr. Temple used to say that his program *was* Title IX before Title IX. He had a vision, and he let us see it too.

Even so, his becoming a coach was almost by accident. He went to Tennessee State for college, and he was on the track team and the football team. When he came out of school, he and his wife Charlie B. got married, and he needed a job, so they hired him to run the post office on campus. Then he needed another job because that one wasn't paying enough, and when the job coaching women's track opened, he took it. So it was kind of just by chance. But he was the kind of person who made it work—with all the odds against him. Not only was he coaching women, he was doing it at a school that was not behind him or behind women's sports in general.

Walter Davis was the president when Mr. Temple first started there, though he went through a number of them. That's what he always used to say: "I've been through a lot of presidents." Davis didn't support the program in the sense that he was not going to take away any of the scholarships from the football team or the basketball team to give to the Tigerbelles. Tennessee State had a great basketball team, a great football team, and a great baseball team. They had people who made the NBA, people who were on Super Bowl teams, and I don't know how many people who played baseball in the Major Leagues. Our band—the Aristocrats—was number one for years, and the Tennessee State and Florida A&M bands were always competing in the Battle of the Bands, which to us was the show of all shows—some people would come more for the halftime show than the games. All of these things were part of being at Tennessee State. In addition to being a great place to have your college experience and get a good education, it was a big sports school, so we were competing with all those other programs for funding and attention.

Fortunately, Mr. Temple was someone who could get a lot done with limited resources. One more thing that made him successful was the way he encouraged competition and the kind of competition he encouraged: competition with support—and loyalty. We all felt that if we were going to get beat by anybody, it might as well be a Tigerbelle. There was never any shame in that. There were a lot of girls who didn't get to wear the Tigerbelle T-shirt, but nobody talked about it. It was competitive, but competition and camaraderie were intertwined. I don't know exactly how Mr. Temple managed to make it so. But no matter how competitive it got, it was never that you hated each other, and I feel that he was responsible for that.

Part of it was his whole method of having the older girls helping the younger ones. The older girls knew, firsthand, what we younger girls were going through, and they knew Mr. Temple. It made us feel that we were all in it together. It also helped that in general he didn't play favorites—although we all felt that Wilma *was* his favorite. You could see the connection between the two of them. But that was nothing to us. He never stated that she was his favorite, and he never did anything special for her that he wouldn't do for us. In those early years, after my father died, he was a father figure to me, and he was definitely that for her too, though our relationship was different; she was always hugging him, and I would *never* do that. If I did well at something, Mr. Temple would say to me, "Tyus, you did a good job," and give me a slap on my back, and I would say, "Thank you." That was our relationship. He had a different relationship with each of us because we were all different people.

No matter how different we were, however, we all wanted to be Tigerbelles. For me, the Tigerbelles were the essence of being a woman who was going places and getting things done. It wasn't just about being able to run—you had to have goals in life and you had to be able to talk to people. "And not," Mr. Temple would always tell me, "just sit up there and *not* talk—like you, Tyus."

He used to get on me all the time about my not talking. He would make me sit by him on trips so that he could talk to me, thinking that would get me to start talking more. *You're the one who does all the talking,* I would say to myself. *I'm just listening.* Still, I understood that Mr. Temple wanted me to be able to express myself, and that he wanted it for *me*—because he knew that it would help me later in life. Everything he wanted was for his girls. He wanted us to do well, and we could feel it.

Not that we always did do well. If you did something that he was not pleased with, he would call you into his office, and you did *not* want to go to his office. Yet as much as he criticized, he also gave you your accolades. He would talk about how promising you were, and how well you were doing, and if you weren't doing all that great on the track, he would say, "Well, you're not doing so good now, but you'll come around. You'll have to work hard, but you know that you can contribute to the team in other ways."

One way the older girls could contribute had nothing to do

with the track or getting good grades. It was to help out the ones who had less by taking them shopping—not by buying things for them, but by showing them what things to buy and how to look for bargains. Mr. Temple would help us with those kinds of things too; if we broke a record, sometimes he would take us to buy dress shoes and things like that. My mom couldn't give me all the things I needed to fit in at college, and I was not the only one. Every year I went to school, I would come a couple days before the quarter started in September, and Mr. Temple's wife Charlie B. would take me to town and buy me two or three outfits and a big coat, so that I would have something to wear.

Mrs. Temple had a lot to do with those kinds of things. Mr. Temple was used to having a lot of women around him, but when it came to talking about clothes and female problems, he would say, "You need to talk to Charlie B." He had female assistant coaches in the summer—Mrs. Perkins, who I've mentioned, was also a teacher at one of the high schools in Atlanta—and they would help out with those kinds of things too, but that was just in the summer. The rest of the time, it was Mrs. Temple. After meets, Mr. Temple would bring home our uniforms, and she would clean them. She would also make German chocolate cake for us on our birthdays. She was not a person I would open up to—I barely talked to her husband. But she was always on me, just like he was. "Tyus, you need to talk more," she would say, and when I came up early to buy my clothes, she would ask, "Do you like this?"

"Yes, that's fine."

"But what is it that you *really* like?"

"What you bought me is what I really like."

She wasn't any better than he was at getting me to talk. Still, she was a big influence. She was not liked by everyone, but we all knew she was there for us, and she was always there for Mr. Temple. When she passed away in March 2008, Mr. Temple had three different generations of Tigerbelles speak at the service, and I was one of them. It was very difficult for me because I had just lost my mom too, but I got up and I said to the people in the church, "One thing that I have to say to Mrs. Temple is, thank you for letting your husband hang out with fast women."

We could be like that, because it was like a family, and it was a family that I pretty much needed at that time. My dad was gone, and Mr. Temple was there for me. I didn't so much see Mrs. Temple as a mom, but I did see Mr. Temple as a dad—looking out for me. Not everybody appreciated him like I still do or like Edith does. There were girls on the team who really didn't care for him. I don't understand some of it. You went to school and you got an education, free, because of this man, but you're angry because of something he said in the whole course of the four or five years that you were there, and you let it come between you? And when they say, "Well, he could have done more," I think, *Yeah, well, he could have done a lot of things.* But he did what he could do. Of course, he didn't pull punches. He never did. He said what he said, and sometimes it was not the best thing. Sometimes Mr. Temple would say things, and you would think, *Oh God, he didn't just say that, did he?*

Not that he was ever trying to put anyone down; it was just him. He was so *real.* I can remember one of the girls having trouble with her weight. He rarely put me on the scale—I was always too skinny—but some of the girls had to weigh in, and if he saw you gaining weight, he would say something. One girl was having trouble with shin splints, and he told her, "Well, what do you expect if you put a car on a tricycle?"

And when he showed those training films, he would say the first thing that came into his head, and it wasn't always the kindest thing. But he would talk about the good things too. He would show films of the older girls running in meets where there were eight people on the track and six of them were Tigerbelles, and he would say, "That could be you. You could be one of those Tigerbelles."

And I knew that's what I wanted to be. And I knew how I wanted to get there: sprinting. The distances were 100, 200, and 400, and at that time, 400 seemed like a mile to me. But it didn't matter because I was not going to run the 400 nor the 200 either. All I wanted was to run the 100 and be on the 4x100 relay team.

Mr. Temple had a different idea; he wanted all his sprinters to run the 100, the 200, and the relay. He tried to convert me to that race from the start, but I wouldn't. Or I would, but it was like pulling teeth. And I didn't care if I won. He would say, "You're a good 200 runner. You need to do that race."

Don't think so, I would say to myself. *Why do I need to run that far?*

Still, he tried to get us to do it all. In the fall, we ran a lot of cross-country—a lot of hills—because when the snow came we would be stuck running around the gym. Mr. Temple had certain times he wanted us to be able to run before the indoor season started: if we had to run a mile, he had a time for us to do it; if we had to run the 400, he had a time.

For me, the 400 was too far. I wasn't going to do it. So let's say he told us we had to run the 400 in under sixty seconds. I would run 59.9. Edith and I would run that race together, and he would yell at us: "You're not going to make it! Pick it up, pick it up!" But we could pretty much pace it and know that we would make it fine. "You can run better than that!" he would say. But we knew: if we ran any faster, that was going to be a part of our race. So we paced ourselves and ran our 59.9. All those five years I was at Tennessee State, I never ran the 400. Every year I would run 59.9. I would never do fifty-eight; I would not do fifty-seven. Same thing with the 200. I would say, "You tell me what you want, and I'm going to give that to you, and then I'm done with it." And that was it.

A lot of times at practice he would say, "We're going to have time trials, and if you run eleven flat for 100 yards, you don't have to practice anymore." I'd run the eleven flat and go home. I didn't want to do anything extra, ever. I just wanted to be done with that track because while I loved to run, practice was just work.

All the years that I was there, though, I never missed a practice. That was also a big part of the program. If you were sick, you still had to show up; Mr. Temple would determine whether you ran and what kind of practice you did. The only way you could not be at practice was if you were at the hospital. And you could not be late. If you were late, you had to meet with him afterward and do an extra workout. I was never late. I think one person was late once; she did not want to be late again.

It certainly wasn't true that all of us always did what he said. Some people claim that Mr. Temple controlled us, but I don't think so. I think he tried to create a safe place where we could learn our own minds. Just like my parents. And I think that what helped to propel me into running was the fact that I was going to be under Mr. Temple. He was so much like my father—a man of wisdom, in my eyes. Nobody was ever going to take my father's place, but at least I could listen to some of the things that Mr. Temple had to say and know that he cared about my future. He was clear about what he thought, and it helped me to be clear about what I thought. I didn't fully accept a lot of the things he said. Not so much that I didn't believe in them; I just thought that he was a little bit harsh. Yet his harshness was for a reason: he had all these girls on his team, and he had to be that way. As time went on, I learned to really appreciate him. He gave me the opportunity to break out of my reclusive state and see what I could do. He gave me the chance to become a Tigerbelle.

Funny thing is, I don't know what year I got my Tigerbelle T-shirt. I probably got it that summer when I was fifteen, after I won in the meet in LA. I think I got one to *practice* in, then. But I didn't race in one until after Tokyo—or maybe just before Tokyo. Maybe just before I went to the Olympics.

Putting up a win for Tennessee State. (Photo courtesy of Tennessee State University Athletics.)

First Gold, New Growth: The 1964 Olympics

Going into the '64 Olympics, I had no idea that I would win a medal or break the record for the 100-meter sprint that Wilma Rudolph had set at the previous Olympics in Rome. I wasn't even thinking about it. In fact, Mr. Temple had told me, "Tyus, we really don't expect much from you. Your year is '68."

Which was fine with me. People would ask me, "How can you even let him *say* that to you?" But I knew it wasn't a derogatory thing. Mr. Temple liked to bring us along deliberately. He felt that if you got exposed to top competition too quickly, you would get a "big head"—as well as a lot of pressure to do interviews before you were mentally ready. He wanted us to be exposed to the track aspect of competition, but he also wanted us to know how to handle the press: to be able to talk to people, to be able to make an impression, to be able to do all the things that an athlete needs to do to be successful. You have to be able to manage all sides.

It wasn't just me; he groomed all his girls that way. You took baby steps: first you would maybe run a relay and trail an older girl who was being courted by the press. Then you would try out for events and maybe not make the cut but still get to see who was there. Only after all that, when it was time, would you start to have your own races and do your own interviews.

I can remember him saying, "Well, Tyus, we're going to take you to the Olympic Trials. I'm not expecting you to make the team, but this way you'll get a feel for how people get themselves ready—so you know what I'll expect from you over time."

That's all Mr. Temple expected, so that was the attitude I carried into the Olympic Trials, both the semifinal in New York on Randall's Island and then the Trials themselves in Los Angeles. Going to Randall's Island, I just thought, *Edie's going to do this; she's definitely going to make the team, but I'm just here to have fun and do my best.* When I made it to the finals, Mr. Temple kept to the same line: "Tyus, you made it to the finals. That's really good. Still not expecting much from you. Just go out there and do the best you can do."

Then, in the finals, I placed third in the 100. They only take three: Edith was first, and then Marilyn White, who ran for the Los Angeles Mercurettes, and then myself. There's always been a rivalry between Tennessee State and the Mercurettes. Marilyn is short, about five feet—I'll give her five two—and Edith and I used to say, "Look at those little-bitty legs—we can't let somebody that short beat us!" But when Marilyn came to those trials, she was *on*. She always had a great start, and at the trials she was coming out of the blocks and just *eating* everybody else. All we could say then was, "She is really ready for the Games."

When the gun went off for our race, Marilyn White came out like a rocket. She was so far ahead of us that I thought, *I can't catch her, but Edie can.* And Edie did. I was coming on, but it was late, so I got third.

Mr. Temple was really happy. "Look at that, Tyus," he said, "you made the team—first time out! That's okay, though. I don't want you to start thinking that you *need* to do this. I want you to be very comfortable and learn as much as you possibly can about being in major meets and have the experience of going to the Olympic Games and being in a different country for a long period of time."

At that point, Edith and I thought we were going to be having that experience without Mr. Temple because they had not yet agreed to let him be the coach. Mr. Temple coaching the Olympic Team in '64 was unprecedented. Because he had coached the 1960 Olympics team, he was supposed to sit out '64. After the Trials were over, Edith said to him, "Mr. Temple, I would like for *you* to be the coach of the team."

"Somebody else needs to do it," he told her. "I've already been there."

"But you have all the girls on the team!"

"That's all right. We have to give somebody else a chance."

In the end, they made an exception because, as Edith had said, Mr. Temple had all his girls on the team.[14] The Tigerbelles *were* the US team, basically. But even after Mr. Temple found out that he would coach the team, he never changed his tune with me: I would be there for the experience. His whole thing,

---

14 It was neither the first nor the last time an Olympic team was dominated by Tigerbelles: all four runners in the 4x100 relay teams in both the 1956 and the 1960 Olympics were Tigerbelles, just as Tigerbelles were three of the four 4x100 relay team members in 1964. Nor was it the first time Mr. Temple was chosen as coach in an unprecedented manner: When the US was putting together its national team to go to the Soviet Union in 1958, they had never had a Black coach, and were not thinking to ask Mr. Temple. In an interview with Kenneth Thompson of Fisk University, Mr. Temple tells the story of how he came to be coach: "I called [the chairwoman] aside before they went into the meeting because I wasn't involved in the meeting, and I said, 'Frances—' her name was Frances, Frances Kosinski—I said, 'Frances, we come up here on a charter bus. I got eight girls on this United States national team. Now, when you go on in there and have your meeting, you tell them that if they don't come out with me as coach, those eight girls are going to be back on that bus going back to Nashville the next morning.' She looked at me and turned red, and she went in there and told them, and when she came out, she said, 'Ed, you the coach.' And I said, 'Thank you.' And from that time on, I didn't have no problems." See the complete interview at https://www.youtube.com/watch?v=q_q3NnejsJQ.

the whole time, was, "Tyus, we're just happy you're on the team. Now we're going to go home and train like we always train."

So we went back to Tennessee, and then Edith and I got on the train to Georgia together to go back home and prepare ourselves to travel. You had to make sure you had your passport in order, let everybody know that you had made the Olympic team, and say goodbye to family. It wasn't like it is today when the whole community comes out and gives you a big send-off—that didn't happen. The sendoff was just your family, and for me that was my mom and my brothers. They had a sense of what the Olympics was, sure, but mostly they felt: *This is what you wanted to do, and now you're going to do it.* They didn't make a big hoopla. I was not the one to do something like that for anyway because I was too quiet and barely spoke. So if they asked me, "How do you feel?" all I would say was, "Okay. Fine."

"But it's the *O-lym-pics!*"

"Okay. Fine. I'm going to the Olympics."

That was just me, and my family knew me, and they knew: not getting anything out of that girl. They wanted to know a lot more than I would tell them. But for me that was just my life. Nothing to talk about. I went out there and did what I did, and if that meant going to the Olympics, so be it. I trained to do it, I was asked to do it, so that's what I did. I was still just a girl of few words.

Everyone was really happy for me, even if there was no sitting down at meals and talking about what I was going to do and how great it would be. It was more like, "You're going to the Olympics, you'll need some spending money." At first, we didn't know where that was going to come from. But then people started stopping by to wish me luck—because my mom had told everybody in the world—and before they left, they would say, "Here's a piece of money, bring me something back!" It could be a dollar, it could be five dollars, but it added up, and in the end I went to Tokyo with thirty dollars in my pocket.

After we had said goodbye to our families, Edith and I got back on the train and headed to Nashville to meet up with Mr. Temple, and from there we went to Los Angeles to get fitted for our uniforms. The track-and-field team and the women's swimming team were all about the same size, which was a problem because the swim team got their things first, and we got what was remaining. They had enough for most of us, but they didn't have anything that fit Earlene Brown, who was a shot putter—a *big* shot putter—and they refused to give her a men's sweat suit because that's how they were about all of that. What Mr. Temple had to go through just to get Earlene a uniform was ridiculous. Still, the rest of us got fitted with a workout uniform and a uniform to compete in, not to mention luggage and a little bag with everything you needed to travel, including toothpaste, which was welcome to me—I'd never gotten that much stuff at once before. We were also given a traveling outfit with a blue straight skirt, a white shirt with a tie, a blue sweater with red piping, a red blazer, and a big cowboy hat: Lyndon Johnson was president at the time, so they had a Western theme. For the opening ceremony, we each got a white dress, a little red bag, gloves, and a pair of high-heeled shoes. And raincoats—capes, actually, checkered red and white. Nothing I would ever wear again although I probably still have it, somewhere.

After we were fitted out, we stayed at the training camp for a couple of weeks before heading off to Tokyo. That was another long ride, but I remember enjoying it because we got to travel with other athletes. Not all the athletes came over at once; they would fly us in so that we had time to adjust to the time zone before we competed, and different athletes competed in different weeks. Track and field went all together, something like a month ahead of time, and I think we had all of the men's track team and all of the women's track team on the same plane.

In '64, everybody participated in the opening ceremony—everybody who was there and wasn't competing the next day—even though for us that meant standing in heels for hours and then having to go out and run. At that time, there were close to one hundred countries competing, and all those people had to march in, and other people had to speak. So it was a lot of standing and waiting. Mr. Temple had told us that marching in the opening ceremony was the best part of being in the Olympics, but I didn't see how it could be until I participated in it, and then I understood. To walk into the stadium—and that stadium was *so full*—I can't find the words for how it made me feel. I was just totally in awe. And to be out there with so many people, representing so many countries, some in uniforms like ours, and some in uniforms based on their traditional clothing—like traditional African garb, for example—just to be able to see that was mind-blowing for me as a nineteen-year-old, something that I never in my life thought I was going to see. And then to be a part of it, and a big part at that, was just amazing.[15]

It was also the first time I had really seen all the people that were on the American team, and it gave me a different outlook on the whole event. I was only used to being with the track team, but in Tokyo, athletes I had only heard about and read about were suddenly right there in front of me; it had never

---

15 "I was very happy," Wyomia said in a later interview, "to see that so many American athletes took part in the opening ceremonies in Rio in 2016. When I competed in '64 and '68, it was an unwritten rule that everybody would participate in the opening ceremonies, and most of the athletes and their coaches felt that it was an important part of being at the Olympics. But after '68, it seemed like a lot of people kind of let that go. So it was nice to see the young athletes getting that kind of experience—an experience that meant a lot to me when I had it."

crossed my mind that I was of their caliber, that I belonged on a team with so many great athletes—it was just like meeting your favorite author and finding out that he or she is just a regular person, a person like you.

That wasn't the only time on that trip that I was blown away; I was also amazed by the sheer number of people in Tokyo. We came in at dusk, and just seeing all the lights was almost overwhelming for me. I had never thought about what it would look like to have so many people all in one place. And then getting on the bus to travel to the Olympic Village through all the tall buildings and cars—so many cars! The honking horns reminded me of New York City, and after I had been to a few different places in Tokyo, I started thinking: *It's not too much different from New York.* The only difference was that it was bigger—that, and the friendliness of the people. Even though they didn't speak our language, they were still very friendly, which reminded me of being down in the South. People would always look at you and say hello as you approached them instead of glancing down like they do in New York. I appreciated that about the Japanese. Still, it was a lot of people, very close together. And it was a long way from Griffin, Georgia.

The Olympic Village was an old army barracks, and at that time athletes had to stay in the Village, not like some subsequent Olympics when a number of the athletes have stayed in fancy hotels.[16] Personally, I don't see why you would do that, because

---

16 "I also was pleased," Wyomia said in the same interview, "to see that, in 2016, a lot of US athletes stayed in the Olympic Village. The basketball teams—both the men's and the women's—were the exception of course; they stayed on a cruise ship. But when the press did little pop-up interviews with other athletes, many of them talked about how much they enjoyed staying in the Village and what a nice feeling it was to be with other athletes from around the world, meeting the people they were competing against and eating the different foods in the different food halls—experiences that were unique and life-changing for me. And for some of them I was thinking, *You stayed in the Village? Times have changed.*"

staying in hotels, you don't get to meet anyone, you don't get to eat in the Village dining halls or go to the Village parties. In the Village, you could eat in your own country's dining hall or you could be adventurous and sample foods from other countries— taste what they eat in Japan or Mexico or Jamaica.

In the American dining hall, we had a lot of potatoes— potatoes and rice and bread. I gained weight there, and Mr. Temple was highly upset about it. Before that, he had been highly upset because I was too thin, and he told me that I needed to eat more—I was such a picky eater. His dietary recommendations for me up to that point had been, "You need to eat more! You have to be stronger!" Then, in Japan, I gained weight, and it was: "Now you're too big!"

I was at around 125 pounds when we arrived, and I think I went up to 130. "I gained five pounds at the most, Mr. Temple. I mean—"

"That's just too big! You've never been this big, and here it is, the most important race of your life. We're going to have to do something about that. You need to push away from the table. You need to push away from those potatoes, you need to push away from the rice, and you need to push away from that bread."

That was pretty much everything I was eating. And it wasn't as if I was eating all the time. I was a breakfast person, so I would eat in the morning, but at lunchtime I just showed up to see who was there. That was the main reason I went to any of the meals besides breakfast: you never knew who would be there to sit next to or talk to or connect with. In the barracks where we stayed, most of the US women's track team was on the second floor, the volleyball players were on the third floor, and the swimmers were on the first floor. You would pass people from other teams on the stairs and in the hallways and going to the showers—it was just like being in a dorm at college. But at meals, you got to actually sit with people from different teams who you never would have met otherwise.

Walking to practice was another great way to meet people. Each country had its own dorm building, but they were right next to each other, and when you went to practice, you walked through a whole international community. And even though the dorms were not coed—they had the men on one side and the women on the other—whenever you walked through the Village, you would run across all kinds of people. I met Flo Hyman, the volleyball player who died so young, and Joe Frazier—I still have pictures of how he looked in '64. He was a lot smaller and much younger, of course, and he was always talking. We got to be friends with a lot of the boxers because Martha Watson, who was on the team with us, was a very outgoing person; she was great at telling jokes and making everybody laugh. So it was not so much that *I* got to know the boxers, but because of Martha, the women's track team always had a relationship with the boxing team, both in '64 and in '68. We went to a lot of their matches, and they came out to the track-and-field events.

For me, it was wonderful just to be in the Village. I was like a little sponge, seeing all those people every day. Before that, we only saw the US men's track team, and we already knew most of them: Bob Hayes I had known years before the Olympics—he went to Florida A&M, and they and Tennessee State were rivals, both in football and with their marching bands—but at the Olympics I got to know him a lot better. He was a carefree guy, a really nice person. Henry Carr and Ulis Williams, who went to Arizona State together, were also there. Bob and Henry are no longer living, though I still talk to Ulis based on that connection. And of course there were Ralph Boston and Richard

Stebbins—people on the men's team that we had known before the Olympics.

We would go to the track, and one group, say the Polish group, would be practicing here, and another group, say the Japanese, would be practicing there. We all had specific times to practice because they only had a certain number of tracks, and if you wanted to practice at other times you had to go off into the city to find another track. But Mr. Temple always had us train at the track in the Village, so we got to see a lot of different people from a lot of different countries and cultures. It made me appreciate them and want to learn more about them. It's not that I made friends with them—there was often a language barrier. But people would come up and ask me questions as best they could in English, and I would try to put my answer back to them as best I could, and just having that interaction, that contact, was new.

Most people just wanted to make sure they knew your name so they could say hello when they passed you in the Village, which I thought was cool. A lot of times, especially out on the track, the athletes would be with their coaches, who usually spoke English. That year, Irena Kirszenstein and Ewa Kłobukowska were like the Edith McGuire and Wyomia Tyus of Poland. Their coach kept talking to Mr. Temple about our strides and how he wanted to measure them. "The stride, the stride!" he would say. Edith and I would look at each other and say to ourselves, *It's not that serious, you just run.* But the Polish runners knew how long their strides were, and that mattered to them. Coaching was totally different between the two countries in those days.

In the evenings after dinner, we would go to the area where everybody socialized, and some of the athletes could speak multiple languages, and they would talk and translate and play music in the meeting room where everybody congregated. Some groups had their own little tape recorders and would play their music—whatever was popular in the sixties—and other people would come over and sit and listen or get up and bob around. Once the music was on, everybody could converse because everybody could dance—maybe not all in the same way, but they could dance, and there was a lot of that kind of conversing.

Being in the Village and having access to all that diversity was just incredible, and I grew a lot from that experience. Coming from Georgia and Tennessee, not knowing anything but "You're Black" and "You're white," and then seeing all these different hues and colors, all these different ethnicities, there was nothing I could do but grow. It made me have a better understanding of people in general—and of myself. Everybody always talks about the differences between Blacks and whites, but the truth is, certain aspects of the Black and white cultures in the South were pretty much the same: people who came from the farms ate mostly the same, talked mostly the same, dressed mostly the same, depending on their class. But in the Olympic Village, there were all these people who ate different foods and spoke different languages and wore different clothes—they lived differently, and they had a different understanding of how we lived. I had always known these other types of people existed, but before that I had never been around many of them or even tried to have conversations with them. In the Village, that type of thing happened every minute of every day. And it changed me, all that learning about different cultures.

I also got to learn a lot about Japanese culture in particular. The reporters would take us out to dinner, and that was the first time I was exposed to sushi. Mr. Temple would say to me, "Tyus, you know you got to eat here. You can't just not eat. Don't be embarrassing us and making these people feel bad because you're not eating their food." And I like fish. But, you know, at home we'd catch a fish, we'd clean it, we'd fry it, and *then* we'd eat it. Still, I told myself, *I can do this. I can eat their rice*—which I did. Although I still cannot use chopsticks.

I remember one time we went out to dinner with some photographers and reporters who were interested in writing stories about Edith—they were courting her—and the first course that came out was this big fish on a platter with its head still on and its eyes still there and a cherry or something in its mouth. And I thought, *We're supposed to eat that? I don't think so.*

They started taking it off the platter and putting it on our plates, and Mr. Temple said, "Only give her a little."

Thank goodness I needed to lose weight. But that was the first time I was exposed to anything like that. All the different tastes. Mainly I grew up on fried food, but there had soy sauce, sushi, and spices that I had never heard of or seen before. It was a good experience. Although I didn't eat most of the food, it was still eye-opening, and it broadened my horizons, made me more understanding, made me want to try more things.

I also went with other people—I didn't go on my own—to the dining halls of other countries, just to observe, to walk past, to see what was being served, and that was how I learned about Latin American food. Not that I was eating it—I was *exposed* to it. I saw it, and that's a bigger part of the experience than you might imagine. It makes you think about the different countries, which Mr. Temple encouraged us to do. He thought that when you were in a country, you needed to experience it, to try to understand it, because you never knew when you were going to go back there. "If nothing else," he would say, "go and *see* it. Lay eyes on it. Then you can say, "I've seen this." Whether you've tried it or not. You have a memory." And that was very important to him, to give us another type of education—not only a college education but also an education of the world.

Of course, this didn't mean we could just do anything and everything; Mr. Temple was very strict about things that we could do and things we couldn't; we could not, for example, climb Mount Fuji or do anything else that might put our legs or feet in jeopardy. But there were lots of things we could do. Since the press was courting Edie, they would take us shopping down in the Ginza district, and whenever reporters asked Edith to go somewhere, Mr. Temple would say, "If Edith goes, Tyus goes. She can't go without Tyus." He was always that way, whether it was me and Edith or others: he felt that if you were going to be exposed to something, you had to bring people along with you. It's kind of like the whole shoe thing—when companies offered someone shoes, the athlete did not just get shoes for themselves, but for everyone.

Just getting to the Ginza market was an experience, with all the cars and people and everybody looking at us kind of strange—and we were looking at them kind of strange too. For them, I guess it was because we were the only ones who looked the way we did. And I think I was reacting to the fact that it was so very tight there, in Tokyo, everything so close together; it was kind of shocking, especially for me, coming from a dairy farm where there was space galore.

Once we got downtown, we went into the department stores, and they asked us what we wanted to look for and offered us things like shoes. There were no shoes to fit these big feet of ours. We have pictures of them bringing out shoes for us to try on, and we could only get our toes in. It was funny to be trying on shoes for the public—for the cameras. And the Japanese store workers were extremely accommodating. They really wanted to find us some shoes that we could buy, but it was just not happening.

After we made it past the shoes, we got to discover what the Japanese are known for, like their silk. It was wonderful to be able to touch the silk and see how they made things to order. They kept saying, "We could make you something before you go back to the States!" So different from shopping in America. Of course, we didn't buy much because, as usual, we didn't have a lot of money. I had the thirty dollars that had been given to me, and I bought my mom a piece of silk because that, to me, represented part of the Japanese culture. I also bought little things for all the people who had been so good to my family, knickknacks and coasters and ashtrays that said *Tokyo* or *Japan* on them—things that didn't really cost much. This was 1964, so the little things weren't very expensive; thirty dollars was actually a lot of money when it came to buying trinkets. And when you were being taken around by photographers and journalists, you got a better deal too, for bringing publicity.

Although the press arranged for us to go shopping, it wasn't as if they were buying us anything. Mr. Temple would never hear of it, and not only that, it would have taken away our amateur status. At that time, you couldn't accept a gift worth more than fifty dollars. So there wasn't much actual shopping happening on our shopping trips. We had to stop a lot so that they could stage the pictures, and we always had a lot of people with us, but still, everywhere we went, there was something new for our eyes to see.

Even though they asked us where we wanted to go, they only took us to what they actually wanted us to see. We were sheltered. They didn't take us to the poorer neighborhoods or tell us what was going on politically and economically in Japan or even in Tokyo. If there was unrest anywhere, we didn't see it; they showed us the best side of everything. But it was still a mind-altering experience. The Japanese looked at us strange, but they treated us with respect. Imagine what that felt like to us, coming from Tennessee and Georgia, where we were so used to society not being integrated. As Mr. Temple said, "They treat you better in another country than they do in your own. Someday that will change, but right now that's the way it is."

During the Olympics, though, it wasn't just the Japanese who treated us differently. At that time, the Civil Rights Movement was just getting started, so I had a very particular experience coming from the South. Tennessee State was a totally Black school, and I was from Griffin, Georgia, where Blacks had gone to one school and whites had gone to another. I never went to school with any white kids at all, and I have never had a white teacher in my life—not in elementary, junior high, high school, or college. It was simple: they had their lives, and we had ours. But when we went to the Olympics, we were all on the same plane, and they didn't make the Black athletes sit in the back— there was no assigned seating, none of that. And once we were on the plane and at altitude, we went into the bathroom and changed into our T-shirts and jeans as usual, and then we would sit and play cards and walk the plane and talk to anybody we wanted. We were like a big family.

In Japan, it was the same kind of thing. We were all in the same barracks; they were not segregated by race, just country and sex. In our dorm at the Village, I roomed with Edith, Estelle Baskerville, Eleanor Montgomery, Martha Watson, and Debbie Thompson—a huge room with all Black women. But that was because Estelle, Eleanor, and Martha were not Tigerbelles at the time; they were coming into Tennessee State for the fall. Mr. Temple had put us all together because he was recruiting Martha and the others, and he wanted them to know: *These are going to be your teammates, the Tigerbelles you're going to work with, and we want you to get a good start.* He was all about that. His thinking was to have us all together so that when they came to school, they would know us, and we would be a team already. They could either like us or not, but that would already be broken in by the time they came.

There were other Black women on the team—in addition to being mostly Tigerbelles, the women's team was predominantly Black—and I don't know who their roommates were, but some of them had to be white. The field eventers—except Earlene Brown—were white, so there were probably about four or five white women on the team. I knew those white women because we ran together at different meets, though I wasn't friends with any of them. But even for us, in our all-Black room, it was different from what I was used to because of where the other girls were from: Estelle was from Columbus, Ohio, Eleanor was from Cleveland, and Martha was from Long Beach, California, so all their schools had been integrated. There were lots of people on the team who didn't come from the South and whose situations were different from mine and the other Tigerbelles.

For me, we were a team, and we were all there together. That's how I looked at it. I can't say how the white athletes looked at it because we didn't talk about race relations—we were playing cards and joking around and trying to make the trip feel as short as possible. I'm thinking about the white athletes who were on the track team. I don't know if they were racist or if they weren't. I do know that when we got back to America, they went their way and we went ours, and that was it. But we still had that experience, and it made a difference. It was also different to see the white managers—the managers of the women's track team were almost never Black—working under Mr. Temple.

For all that was different, however, there were some things

that were still the same, like when we had an issue with the men's coach and the starting blocks. At the Olympics, each team brings its own starting blocks. In 1964, the American runners used Arnett blocks, the men and the women both, no matter where we went. Starting blocks had been shipped to Japan for "the team," but when we got to Tokyo, the coach of the men's team refused to let Mr. Temple use them.

"What are you talking about?" Mr. Temple said to him. "I thought we were the American team—that we were *all* the American team."

But no. According to the men's coach, we could not use those blocks, and for a while it looked like we were going to have to use the blocks that were there, the ones the Japanese runners used. We didn't know anything about their blocks, didn't know how to set them, weren't accustomed to starting from them, but somehow the men's team's coach thought it would be okay for us to use them—in the Olympics.

Mr. Temple just could not believe it, so he was talking about it, and we were talking about it, and when Bob Hayes heard, he said, "What kind of craziness is this? You can use my blocks any time you want."

That's how we ended up using the Arnett blocks: because the male athletes themselves made a point of sharing. Was it a racist thing? I say yes, definitely, but also a sexist thing; the coach was not trying to make the Black male runners use the Japanese blocks. Mr. Temple wrote about this in his biography, *Only the Pure in Heart Survive,* and he used to speak about it all the time. As far as I know, the men's coach has never explained himself; he never had to, because nobody would talk to him about it. Mr. Temple definitely didn't have anything else to say to him.

* * *

All that was going on before we even got to race—all that and more. For example, '64 was the first time South Africa was banned from the Games. At the time, I wasn't totally aware of all the political implications that went along with that, but it was not something that you could go to the Olympics and not know. I didn't have discussions with people on the team about it, but I think that was partly because the only thing that could have been said was that they should have done that years before.

Of course, we didn't spend all our time shopping at the Ginza or eating foreign food or thinking about how integrated we were or weren't. A lot of the time we were simply busy preparing for our races. And for me that meant eating lots of rice and bread and potatoes. Because I actually believe that gaining the weight helped me get stronger—although Mr. Temple didn't think so. He just thought I was too big. But I was *growing*—I was growing in more ways than one. That's what I felt, although I never conveyed it to Mr. Temple. And when he said, "I'm going to have to run you some more, we're going to need some extra practices," I just said what I always said: "Okay, Mr. Temple."

Regardless of who was right, it worked out. Between his hard practices—which everyone had to do—and preparing for the relay, I got those extra workouts. For the relay, Mr. Temple couldn't decide how to configure our team. We had two new people, Willye White and Marilyn White, to add in. He always wanted me to pass to Edie, and that's how I thought it should have been. But he didn't want Marilyn White running the second leg because that could be the "longest" leg, nothing but straightaway, depending on how far you move your mark back. He was thinking that, because Marilyn was small in stature, if he had her run that leg, whomever the other teams had could really eat up a lead or, if we didn't have a lead, get far ahead. So in practice, he kept changing it up.

And it wasn't just the second leg he couldn't figure out; he also didn't know which girl he wanted to put on the first leg, Willye White or Rosie Bonds. He tried several people, and they were always passing to me, so I was always running. I guess that was his way of getting me to run off the weight. Instead, it just made me really strong—good and strong.

When it came down to qualifying for the final in the 100, I was running well in every heat; in fact, I was *winning* each heat, and easily—easily meaning that I wasn't struggling or really trying hard to win. Even Mr. Temple had to say, "Tyus, you look *so* good."

When I had made it to the finals, he came to talk to me. "Tyus," he said, "I am very proud of you. A lot of people train all their lives and they don't ever make an Olympic team. But you've made the Olympic team your first time out, and here it is, you're going to be in the finals."

"Yes sir."

"Well—how're you feeling about it?"

"Okay."

"Is that all you have to say, Tyus?"

"Yes sir."

"Well. Okay. I don't expect you to set the world on fire. I'm just happy you're in it. Just go out there and be relaxed and do the best you can do."

I felt that he really wanted me to be me—to be nineteen and not worry. "Okay. Thank you, Mr. Temple."

He started to walk away, but then he came back and said, "You know, you keep running like you're running, you could win a medal."

"Okay. Thank you, Mr. Temple," I said, but in my head I

was thinking, *I could win more than just a medal. I could win a gold—maybe.* And then I thought: *Oh God, I can't go there.* It was like that—a flash—and then back: *No way.*

In '64, the track was *perfect.* Even with all the rain we'd had, there were never any puddles; the Japanese workers kept it immaculate. Every day, they would fill all the holes, skirt off the water, and make sure it was a perfectly dry, perfectly flat surface. When we lined up for the 100, Marilyn White was in lane eight, Edie was in lane seven, and I was in lane six. The two Polish women, Halina Górecka and Ewa Kłobukowska, were in lanes one and two, and then there were Marilyn Black from Australia, Miguelina Cobián from Cuba, and Dorothy Hyman from Great Britain.

When the gun went off, I just remember running, not thinking, until I was at the 80-meter mark, and then asking myself: *Where's Edith?* Because Edith was always catching me at 80 meters. *Where is she?* I wondered. *I can't hear her. I can't see her. But it don't mean anything because she'll be here.*

Mr. Temple had taught us never to look from side to side because if you looked one way, somebody might pass you on the other. *Stay relaxed,* I thought, *stay relaxed!* At first it was just: *Where's Edith?* Because Edie could beat me! Then I thought: *I must be out front!* And right after: *No, I can't be out front.* And then: *That's the 80 mark; Edie will be here at 90.* And then I could hear her coming. I could *hear* her. We were on a cinder track—it was red clay, actually, and it was packed firm, hard like a table, and I could hear her footsteps. You can hear a lot of things, going around that track. I've thought about this a lot because people always ask you, "What were you thinking about during the race?" And you wouldn't believe all the things that can go through your mind in eleven seconds. That's what we're talking about—11.3, 11.4 seconds. I didn't know at the time, but when I analyze it now, I could tell it was her because I knew she was on my right. I never even thought about those Polish girls.

Another big thing that Mr. Temple always taught us was to lean at the tape; I mean *lean,* not just dip your head, lean with the whole upper part of your body. Of course I did that—all the Tigerbelles did that. I knew Edith was coming up on me—I felt like she was *right there*—and then all of a sudden it was over. I couldn't even tell who won.

Edith and me in the 100 in Tokyo—leaning at the tape! (Photo courtesy of Tennessee State University Athletics.)

I turned around, and Edith ran up to me. "Who won?" I asked her.

"You won!" she said. "You did it!" And she was hugging me and hugging me.

Then one of the high jumpers, one of the pentathlon girls—Pat Winslow, who used to coach Evelyn Ashford—ran out. "Tyus, Tyus! You beat Edie!"

And then all three of us were hugging, and I was wondering: *Who got third?* We thought maybe it was Marilyn, but as it turned out, one of the Polish runners—Kłobukowska—got third, and Marilyn got fourth.

I was excited. And for me to say I was excited means I was *excited*. I had to wait a minute before I could go and get my medal, and once I was on that victory stand, I started thinking, *I've got to do this four years from now.* Instead of standing there feeling everything and enjoying my win, I was thinking: *I've got to try to be here in four years—I've got to come back here and do this again.* That's what went through my mind. Not, *Yay! I won! I did it! I won a gold medal!* That was not even going through my head. It was: *Four years? Oh my.*

But after the ceremony I started thinking, *Who knows where I'll be in four years. Who knows whether I'll even be running.* It was time to celebrate. Mr. Temple was so proud. "Who would'a thought," he said. "A little girl from Griffin, Georgia, gone and won herself a gold medal."

"Yes, Mr. Temple. I'm sure my family is very happy." I think that's probably all I said.

Everyone was thrilled that Edith and I had come in first and second. We went back to the barracks, and just being in our room with Edith, Martha, Estelle, Eleanor, and Debbie—all of us about to go back to Tennessee State—was perfect. We sat there and took turns holding our medals and looking at them, and people came around to see the medals and congratulate us. Just to take that in was wonderful. I was excited, even if my excitement never really shows in a bubbly type of way. I can't get behind that jumping-up-and-down thing. That's not in me. But I appreciated all the people who came up and said, "Gosh, Tyus, we knew you could do it. You were always good." Because they used to say all the time that I wouldn't beat Edie since she was my best friend. They kept saying, "You and Edith are so tight."

Which was true; we had been friends since I started at Tennessee State, just best of buddies who'd been through everything together, though we never talked about our races. We'd go and compete, and she'd beat me, and I'd take it and keep going. And then in the Olympics, I beat her, and she took it and kept going, and we continued to be friends; the friendship was never in jeopardy. And it wasn't friendship that kept me from beating Edith; I just wasn't ready before then. Like Mr. Temple said, "You have to groom. It takes time for you to grow into yourself and feel good about yourself."

I think I became ready because of all of the experiences that I had in the Olympic Village and out in Tokyo, as well as all the training: having to run so many different times on the relay, trying to get a pass right, someone passing to me, then me passing to someone else, and next time to yet another person—not to mention all those potatoes and all that rice. All of those things made me a stronger person.

Not that Edie wasn't strong, and plus, she had other things to think about: she had a 200-meter race to run and win. She told Mr. Temple that, and he said, "Well, McGuire, you shouldn't be saying that."

"That's all right," she said. "I'm going to win that 200." And she did.

Edie had a lot of pressure on her because the press had put her up as the one who would get three gold medals like Wilma Rudolph, and I stepped in there—I ran in there—and took one. But she never let that get her down. And if she had gone into that 100 like she went into that 200, I might not have won. I don't know. Either way, it would have been a good battle.

The Gold Dust Twins and Mr. Temple. (Photo courtesy of Tennessee State University Athletics.)

* * *

The 4x100-meter relay was the only other race I ran in the '64 Olympics. When Mr. Temple finally felt that he had found the group to run it, it was Willye White passing to me, me passing to Marilyn White, and Marilyn White passing to Edith. He thought that combination gave us our best chance to win.

Marilyn was very good off the blocks, but it was her first time at the Olympics; Mr. Temple didn't want an inexperienced person on the first leg because there's so much riding on that first-leg person: they have to be able to get out of the blocks and not jump the gun, and Mr. Temple didn't want Marilyn to get nervous and jump. Willye White, on the other hand, had been to the Olympics before, and I think he felt that with her experience, she would be a good person to run the first leg, and that while she might not really gain anything, she wasn't going to lose anything, either. "And Tyus," he said, "you have that long straightaway, and you should be able to put us in the lead."

When you're running in the relay, you have a certain zone where you have to make sure that you've got the baton, and you can move that zone way back so that you get the baton much earlier. That means that the second-leg person, which was me, would have to run a lot longer, and for the '64 Olympics, Mr. Temple felt that I was capable of doing that, so we moved the zone back and that's what I did.

When the gun went off, Willye White, as he predicted, didn't jump, didn't lose anything, and didn't gain anything. She passed the baton to me, and all I could hear was her saying, "Go, Tyus, go Tyus, go!!" And then I was running my butt off until I passed to Marilyn White. By that time, Willye had come up to where I was. "We're gonna get a gold!" she said.

I agreed with her. "We got away! We're gonna get a gold!"

Then Marilyn started to run into the curve, and up came Irena Kirszenstein, from Poland, who's five eleven or six feet, and then all I could see was Marilyn's little legs moving fast but with these little steps, while Kirszenstein was taking these huge, long, loping strides—taking over until all that lead was *gone*. Kirszenstein just ate up Marilyn in the curve.

When it came time for Marilyn to pass to Edith, Edith took off and put her hand back for the baton, but it wasn't there; she had to slow up to get the baton from Marilyn. At that point, we were in fifth place. Edith went from fifth to second, but she couldn't catch the other girl from Poland. And that was that for the relay.

Willye White and I just looked at each other: *No gold for us.*

If it had been up to me, it would have been me and Edie—

Edie running anchor and me the one passing to her. That way, if we were behind, we had two people to try to make it up. That was my thought. But no one asked me. Fortunately, I would get another chance to run the relay in 1968.

College As Usual

When we came back from the Games in Tokyo, we flew into New York and from there to Nashville. A bunch of Tennessee State students as well as the president of the university were at the airport to greet us—even the band was out—all cheering and happy that we'd won our medals. The *Nashville Tennessean* always wrote about the Tigerbelles—they had even hired Mr. Temple part-time to report on us when we were in Tokyo—so they set up things for us to do when we got back, interviews and personal appearances. We stayed in Nashville for about a week, going around with Mr. Temple and meeting the governor and having our pictures taken.

After that, Edith and I took the train back to Atlanta, where they gave us a parade—but only in the Black community. I'm not from Atlanta, so I didn't think anything about it at the time; when they said they were going to do this, I just thought, *Wow—a parade!* And even though we didn't get taken through the downtown area, I still thought it was great for the Black community to be able to see us and know what we had accomplished. My mom and my brothers were there, and I got to sit in a convertible with my mom and Edith's mom and Edith and wave to the crowds. I felt so proud. My mom never had the opportunity to see me run in person, not ever. She couldn't go to the Olympics—nobody was sending her, not to Tokyo nor to

Mexico City, either—and she never got a chance to come to any of the meets I had in the US because she was always working. So it was wonderful to have her there in the parade to receive some of the honor and recognition.

OLYMPIC STARS RETURN TO GEORGIA

After the 1964 Olympics, me and Edith with our mothers at a parade in Atlanta. (Photo by Charles Jackson/*Atlanta Daily World*.)

After the events in Atlanta, my mom, my brothers, and I went back to Griffin, where my high school, Fairmount High, had a social event for people to come and meet me. I had my medals with me, and I put them on for pictures, but mostly I just *had* them. In Griffin, they gave me a parade through the whole town, including downtown, and that was lovely too.

While all this was happening, however, I was kind of in shock. I was still that little girl who didn't know very much. Although I had grown in Tokyo, especially in understanding, I was still processing everything I had seen and done. It was great to see that people were so proud of me—they even said, "Can I touch you? Can I touch your medal! I never touched an Olympic medal before!" But I didn't really know how to respond. It never occurred to me that people would feel that way about me. "They're all so proud of you, Suster," my mom would tell me. "All you need to do is be happy."

"Okay," I would say, "I *am* happy, and I'm proud," and she would have to explain to people, "You know, she just doesn't say very much."

Mom and me at the reception in Griffin after the 1964 Olympics.

Probably the thing that thrilled my mom the most was when, on December 1, 1964, I got to have lunch at the White House with Lady Bird Johnson and Vice President Hubert Humphrey; the president himself didn't make it until after the lunch because he was in a meeting about Vietnam. I still have the card with the menu; it just says *The White House* at the top, and it lists everything we ate—or at least everything that they served: cream of spinach soup, breast of chicken Georgina, rice pilaf, eggplant Provençale, and Glace Olympic, whatever that was. The menu was signed by both Lady Bird and Mr. Humphrey, and my mom just treasured it.

I was pretty excited myself. I had gone to Washington, DC, as a school patrol, and that was about all I knew about that. But to have lunch at the White House? Who would ever think a little country girl from Griffin, Georgia, would go to the White House? There had never been a thought in my mind that this would happen to me. And to be able to *say* I had lunch in the White House—how many people can do that? I thought it was the best thing since sweet tea. It was just the medal winners and their coaches—although that was still quite a few people, more than a hundred, if I remember correctly. There were a lot of round tables, and we were in a huge room, and I sat with Edith and Mr. Temple.

We met Lady Bird, but of course I didn't talke to her. I passed her in line, and we shook hands. That's how that went. Humphrey said something, and Lady Bird spoke to all of us, but don't ask what they said. It's a blur after that. You have to remember that I was nineteen; you know how teenagers are when it comes to paying attention. And I had just won in the Olympics, so on the one hand I was very la-di-da, but on the other I was back to being quiet. It was kind of overwhelming when I really think about it. I was just a little teenager, going to the White House before heading back to school, learning to talk to people, and getting better at reading.

That's how I felt at the time. Looking back at it now, other things stand out to me. One was that they had never done it before—we were the first. Which seems contradictory: think about all that Cold War competition with the Soviet Union, how important that all seemed in the press, and this was the first time that the medal winners got any recognition from the president? My husband Duane recently found an article about it in "Sports of the Times"[17] where it explains that the lunch was the president's personal idea and that the White House didn't pay to get us all there; the US Olympic Committee did, to the tune of $30,000—in 1964. The article also pointed out that in the Soviet Union the government was a lot more appreciative of its athletes, gave them better apartments and TV sets and things like that. The final thing that I noticed about that article was that the only individual athletes they mentioned were men.

But I guess that set me up well for school, because going back to Tennessee State for the winter quarter, I got even less attention; Tennessee State was used to having Olympic champions. They had already had Wilma Rudolph and Ralph Boston, who had won gold in the long jump in 1960 and silver in '64 and was an honorary Tigerbelle. Not only that, Mr. Temple made sure that no matter how many gold medals you won or how many times you were honored, you knew that you were no better than any of the other Tigerbelles. We were all there for the same thing, everybody striving to do their best, whatever their best was. Not every Tigerbelle was going to win a medal, so Mr. Temple never made any exceptions for those who did; he never treated us any differently. I had to go to practice, be on time, put in the work, just like everybody else. Mr. Temple was still very strict about those things, as well as making sure we stayed on top of our education. His rules applied at all times to every girl on his team.

So when I went back to Tennessee State, it was just college as usual. I was thinking that I had to keep myself in shape for '68, but mostly I was just doing all the things I enjoyed doing. I tried to do everything I could do in college because I had come

---

17 The article, written by Arthur Daley and dated December 3, 1964, can be found in the *New York Times* 1964 archive at http://www.nytimes.com/1964/12/03/sports-of-the-times.html?_r=1.

from a place where I was never able to be on my own or alone with friends. I was always with my parents, with my family. You hear people say, "I did this when I was sixteen," or, "I did that when I was eighteen." For me, nothing much happened until I went to college, so when I got there, I wanted to go to parties and socialize. I may not have talked much in those days, but that didn't mean I wanted to be alone all the time. Mr. Temple kept a close eye on all of us, and like I said earlier, it wasn't just him; colleges at that time had curfews for women. If you were a freshman, you had to be in the dorms by nine o'clock on week-days; on weekends, you could stay out all the way to nine thirty. The latest that you could be out ever was eleven o'clock, and that was only if you were a senior. They even had room checks. And these were not Mr. Temple's rules; they were the college's rules. We were, after all, young women in the South.

But if you were like me, you learned that whatever you wanted to do at night, you could do in the daytime as long as you didn't have a class—which was good learning because oth-erwise I would have missed out on a lot of experiences. I didn't know anything about going to bars or parties because that was not a part of my life in high school, so that's what I wanted to do. We mostly went to clubs near campus—we were not allowed to go to the Grand Ol' Opry because it wasn't integrated—but there was plenty of other stuff to do and see in our own com-munity. Just being in Nashville was a big deal for me. I went to town, I went to parties, I went to more parties—I even learned a little bit more about libraries. And I ran.

When I look back, though, I spent most of my time in the dorms, sitting in people's rooms and playing cards and con-versing about everybody and everything. For me, that meant mostly listening and gathering information, taking it all in; I was still in my growth period. Although technically I was a half-sophomore, because I had missed the fall quarter for the Olympics, I was still feeling fresh. Also, in the year leading up to the Games, I hadn't taken a full course load because I was traveling so much. So in my mind I was just a freshman, happy to be in college and enjoying the things that freshmen do. It was a good time for me—going to class, doing better in school, getting a better hold of who I was, having a boyfriend—just enjoying being me, a college person who was growing on a college campus.

Mr. Temple was aware that we went out and partied because all his friends knew the Tigerbelles, and he had friends who owned clubs in Nashville. If you did something that he didn't want all of the Tigerbelles to know, he would call you into his office and talk to you, and if you did something that he wanted to make an example out of, he would talk to you in his office first and then say it all again in front of everybody. "We're going to present this to the Tigerbelles," he would say, "and let everybody know that this is something you should never do."

I had no trouble with that; it was something my father would do. He would say, "I didn't raise you that way, and you're not going to act like that," and I appreciated that kind of guidance. But as I mentioned earlier, even though Mr. Temple was like a surrogate father, I didn't agree with everything he said or do everything he wanted. For example, I dated a football player throughout my whole time at Tennessee State, even though Mr. Temple didn't want us to date football players, ever. He felt that the football players took all the scholarships, number one, and number two, half of them didn't graduate. Not only that, if you ever got famous, he would tell us, they were never going to be able to handle it. They always wanted to think they were better than everybody else. And that, in my mind, was pretty much true. At least to a certain extent, it was true of my boyfriend: he didn't graduate, and he had trouble with me being the person I am. I traveled a lot, and there were many things said that he didn't want to hear—some by Mr. Temple, specifically, in the *Nashville Tennessean* in '64, when he was writing for them about the Olympics. "Tyus and Hayes holding hands," he wrote, "looks like this is going to be a fast combination!"

That got printed in the paper, and I didn't know about it until we got back, but my boyfriend did. Bob Hayes and I were just friends, though I guess Mr. Temple needed something to write about—I have no idea. When I got back to the States, everybody was teasing my boyfriend, saying, "That woman—she doesn't want to be bothered with you!" Claude Humphrey, who later played football for the Atlanta Falcons, had classes with me, and he used to call me "Beep Beep," like the Roadrunner. Every time he passed my boyfriend, he would say, "Beep Beep! She's gone, buddy. You ain't got nothing there anymore."

And it wasn't just him; everybody used to tease my boyfriend, all the time, and that was part of what eventually broke up our relationship. We pretty much broke up before I even finished school after he got a contract with the San Francisco 49ers.

"These football players," Mr. Temple would say, "get these pro contracts, and they don't do anything with their money but buy a new car and clothes. They don't know how to save, they get the big head, and they think they're better than everybody else. The girlfriend they had, they don't want anymore the minute they see something better—something they *think* is better."

Since I was dating a football player and everybody knew it, we had to have some fun with the situation. Before Edith retired, she and I were the team captains—captain and cocaptain—and for team meetings, we would sit up in the front. There we'd be, right in the first row, when Mr. Temple would start in on one of his anti–football player speeches. "Everybody knows how I feel about these guys," he would say, "and you shouldn't be dating them—not any of them."

Edie would look at me, and we would both look back at the rest of the team with our eyebrows up, and say, "Who's dating football players? Who would *do* that? Is anyone back there dating any football players?"

Mr. Temple always spoke his mind—didn't care to whom or how he said it, and whatever else transpired, he didn't want his girls to get stuck in a bad place. So he didn't hold anything back. "You're not going to school to get an education to support somebody who's not going to do anything with their life," he would say, "somebody who thinks football's going to be their *whole* life—you need to think more of yourself."

Mr. Temple knew about my boyfriend, but as Edith put it, "What's he going to do? You're doing good at school, you're his best athlete—he can't put you off the team!"

Because that was another thing he would say: "You're going to get sent home if I see you ruining your life that way!"

And I would turn around and whisper, "Nobody wants to go home, do they? *Don't date football players!*"

And of course the other girls knew about my relationship—everybody on campus knew. The place was just that small—when I was in school, there were less than five thousand students there. And Mr. Temple knew too, but there was nothing he could do. Edie and I still laugh about that.

Dating a football player, despite Mr. Temple's objections, was just a part of my growth. Another part, a much more exciting part, was going to Africa. In the summer of 1966, the State Department sent us there—me, Edith, and Mr. Temple—to be Goodwill Ambassadors. We went over, believe it or not, to encourage African women to be involved in sports. That was pretty much the gist of our ambassadorship: to show that we were two women who had gone to the Olympics and won medals. Because women at that time, especially in Africa, were not encouraged to run or be a part of a team or anything like that. So we were over there doing that kind of goodwill. At least, that was our interpretation of what we were told.

The State Department had organized these types of ambassadorships for athletes before, but mainly for male athletes. Mal Whitfield, who won gold medals in the 800 meters and the 4x400 relay in the 1948 London Olympics, was there and had been there for years; he set up all of our tours and activities. For our ambassadorship, we went to East Africa—Ethiopia, Kenya, Tanzania, and Mozambique. When we got to Kenya, we stayed in the city of Nairobi, and every morning they would come and get us, and we would go out to the countryside and put on running exhibitions, teaching whoever wanted to run, not just the women but the men as well. There weren't that many women interested in running because they weren't encouraged to do so, which was both why we were there and kind of a catch-22.

There were always interpreters, but in a lot of the places we went, the people, especially the young people, could speak English. Of course, there were always young men who wanted to run against us, and there was one guy who felt particularly strongly about it; Mr. Temple loved this story. We had just finished doing a clinic, and Mr. Temple was talking about how fast we were, and this one guy stood up and said, "No girl could beat me. No woman could *ever* beat me!" And he just kept talking and talking like that. Although it wasn't really part of the clinic, we would sometimes run against people, and so of course we had to race him. The last thing he said before we started was, "If a girl beat me, I'd kill myself." We don't know if he's dead, because after we beat him, the guy just ran off. We never saw nor heard anything else from him ever again.

When we weren't running or teaching people to run, we would have conversations with the people in the villages. And once again my eating became an issue, because if you went to the villages, you got invited into their huts, and they would feed you. And Mr. Temple would say, "Well, don't send Tyus in there. She's not going to eat." But he was wrong—part wrong, anyway; there was always something I could taste—not so much eat, but taste. They would invite us in for tea, and I don't drink tea, but I learned to sip on it. I did a lot of things I wouldn't normally do. It was very enjoyable, very educational, very enlightening. Life-changing. You grow up and see pictures and hear things about Africa, and you think, *God, they do that?* And when I was growing up, part of the story about Africa was Tarzan. I knew it was nothing like that, of course, but still, just to be able to be there, to be in a place that you hear things about, and you just never know what's true, and then you see the people, especially in the cities, and you think: *Gosh, they're just like us.*

There's no difference when you think about it. It's just that they're black, pretty much all black. There were a lot of westernized Africans, people who dressed like us, as well as those in native dress—even in the city. To me, that was what Africa was all about, that mixture. Buildings and cars and men with big bundles of wood on their heads walking for miles, and women carrying the same kinds of loads but with their babies strapped onto them too. We saw a lot of that in the cities.

And then you go out into the countryside, into the different villages, and it's just a whole different way of life; they were always cooking, there was always something going on. It gave me a big appreciation for people, for my people, for people who look like me; they don't just live in America, and they don't all do the same kinds of things I do or live the way I live, but if they want to, they can just go live in the city. Just like us. And that was something, just that, being able to be there and understand that and, through that understanding, improve on who I was as a person.

Now that I look back on it, I kind of take it for granted, yet I am sure that at the time it was a shocker for me—although many of the villages would remind me of my grandmother, my dad's mother, because she and her son lived strictly on the land and by the land. They were people who ate red dirt, and they had that in Africa as well; you could buy dirt and eat it. So there were differences that were not that much of a difference because of my grandmother. I didn't eat dirt myself, but I ate a lot of bread, a hard, crusty type of bread—I can't say what kind it was—and the flatbread, injera; I tried that too. They would spread stuff on it and use it to pick up the food, like in a Moroccan place—or like you're in a Black American family and you're eating collard greens and you sop up the pot liquor with cornbread. We used to do that all the time. Because that was a big thing that my mom and my grandmother—both grandmothers, actually—would do: make a big pot of greens or cabbage and take cornbread and soak it and pick up the greens. We would eat with our fingers, and my mom would say, "We are *not* eating with our fingers—that's what forks and knives are for!" But it didn't mean you had to give it up. You could still do it at midnight when nobody was looking. Or you could just go to Africa.

Sometimes we went into villages and the kids older than me had on nothing but what looked like a diaper or a half-dress, and they did a lot of dances for us and put on shows and greetings, which were great. I remember one time we got stuck in a village during a big downpour, and we all had to go into one hut. Everybody just crowded in, and of course they want you to feel comfortable, so they offer you food and you're like, *Okay,* but the rain is coming down so hard you feel like it's just going to flood you out, and you're all tensed up, waiting for it to come. And then after a minute, it just stops. It reminded me of Georgia, where it just pours, and then it's gone, and everybody's back out and playing. Same thing. But with all the things that were the same and all the things that were different, I just had a good time.

"That's what you're here for," Mr. Temple told me, "to have a good time and put on these clinics, and to let women know that they can run too. They too could be a part of the sports world."

Our ambassadorship was supposed to last two months, but we only stayed for a month because the airlines were planning to go on strike, and Mr. Temple didn't want us to get stuck there. "Tyus has to get back to go to school!" he told us. "We can't stay." But Edith and I were thinking, *Well, we could just stay. If we're supposed to be here for two months, maybe the strike will be over by then.* But Mr. Temple said no; we had to get back.

In Kenya, serving as a Goodwill Ambassador. (Photo by Ed Temple.)

* * *

Another thing that contributed to my growth was learning about politics and the movements that were going on at that time. There was a lot of social unrest in America, and many of the students at Tennessee State knew people who were in the Civil Rights Movement. Stokely Carmichael came to our school and I went to listen to him, and as we were leaving the gym where he spoke, a lot of people were up in arms over who he was and all the things he had said. Some students and people who had come from off campus started rioting, and then someone called in the military—they brought in *tanks*. They brought tanks to *campus*. We were shocked. A dorm was being built at that time, and somebody fired a shot into that unoccupied building, and after that they shut us straight down—the whole campus. It was brutal.

Jefferson Boulevard runs through Nashville and right into Tennessee State, and there's a central area of campus where Jefferson ends, and all that was shut down. We couldn't go past a certain point unless we showed ID and had a reason for going there. You could always go in through the back parts if you knew the way, but you still had to face the military, walking around campus with guns, for a week or better.

One of the managers for the track team, Pam, was part of the movement; she was from Pennsylvania and she was always protesting. She was there when people started to riot and break things, and when the military began shooting into the air or doing whatever they did to disperse the crowd—she was a part of that crowd, and she ended up twisting her ankle very badly. Mr. Temple would tease her: "They started shooting, they knocked you down, and your buddies just ran off and left you. They didn't even think nothing about you! You were hurt, and they just left you to get arrested!" They didn't arrest her, fortunately.

Still, Mr. Temple would say, "That's Pam—my little rebel."

He liked to tease us like that, but it wasn't always funny; sometimes it was harsh. If you took it personally, though, you could never survive with him. So I would just laugh and think, *Hmm, okay*, and make up my own mind about Pam and what she did.

I was aware of what was going on in the movement, but I was not involved—because of Mr. Temple's teasing, but also because my parents had made it clear to me that you should not want to be with anybody who doesn't want you in their surroundings. They had taught us that you needed to know people in order to trust them, and if they didn't want to know you, there was no way you could trust them. Why would you want to be integrated with people like that?

Also, pacifism was not my strong suit. Not even my brothers could hit me and get away with it. I could never be a marcher or a sit-inner because nobody could hit me, spit on me, or anything like that, without my reacting in kind. My parents and their folks had suffered a lot of violence, and they did not think we should allow ourselves to suffer anymore. If there had been any other way for me to be a part, I would have done it, but I didn't see how I could fit in. I know there are people who can do that, and I take my hat off to them. It wasn't that I didn't agree with their goals, and if I had the power to say something, or felt that I was in a position to say something, I would do it—as I did later, in '68. But the nonviolent strategy did not work for me. I am not one to take a licking. That's what it involved at that time, and I felt that there were people who were put on earth to do that—like Dr. Martin Luther King Jr. Although I never saw him speak, I of course had an appreciation for him and the things he said. When he was talking about going to the mountaintop and seeing the glory, he reminded me of the Baptist preachers in Griffin. You could tell that he felt something big was going to happen to him, but also that he wasn't afraid because what he was doing was just much bigger than anything anybody could ever do to him.

It was like he was saying, "I'm not afraid of you. Whatever you do to me is going to help my cause." He would lay his life down for a cause, for his people—and by "his people," I feel he meant "all people." It didn't matter who believed in him and who didn't. He believed he was put here especially to do what he was doing and for whatever happened to him to take place; he was basically saying, "I have put my life on the line, and I'm not stepping back." Sometimes people will start something and then begin stepping back, but that was never him; he was more in the way of stepping forward, right up until the moment he was killed. I remember hearing that he had been shot as I was leaving the dining hall and not believing it, and then going to the TV in the lobby of the dorm and trying to see whatever news there was to see. Eventually there was a protest, but at first the campus just got very quiet, and that's what I remember most: the quiet.

I have always admired Dr. King and the people who followed him, but I wasn't one of them. In my mind, you have to know what your strengths are, what you can do, and what you can't, so that when it's time for you to play your part, you're ready. I was never the one to be out front, and I knew that. Sometimes you can speak, you can say things, and I knew I would have my chance, but at that point, in '65 and '66, I was not going to be the one talking. That silence was still a part of who I was.

That said, I supported the goals of the movement, absolutely, and when Stokely Carmichael came, I enjoyed hearing him, especially the way he talked. For me, to hear people from other parts of the country talk was something in itself. I was used to people with a long, slow drawl, but Carmichael was able to speak very quickly about many different issues, like nothing I had heard before. He was so clear about how things should be—so clear on what was right. He reminded us that we were human beings, that we were no longer slaves, and that we had to be more active. I heard in his speaking too that there were those of us who were going to be on the front lines and those of us who were not, and you couldn't hate your brother or sister because they weren't with you yet. They needed support, and they probably needed more support than anybody else. That may not be exactly what he said, but that's what I heard—that's how he came to me.

So my involvement at that time was always to know what was going on and to know in my heart how I felt about it. I also knew that not everybody would agree all the time on how things were supposed to be; one person will say this, and another will say that, so no one person can speak for a whole group of people. That was another thing that Mr. Temple taught us. You have to make your own decision about what each person says. Not everyone thinks this way. If something happens in a Black community, a lot of times people will say, "That's just what Black people do," and, "Why aren't you with them?" But every Black person was not raised the same way—we haven't all had the same experiences. You have to win people over in a lot of different ways. For Dr. King it was nonviolence, and a whole lot of people wanted to do things that way. But you also had a lot of people who said no. And I was one of those. "No, I can't." I had friends who went on the marches and sat at the counters and went to jail. That just wasn't me.

One thing I eventually became involved in was the Olympic Project for Human Rights—eventually, because the people in the project and I kind of got off to a bumpy start. I was defi-nitely aware of them and their plan to boycott the Olympics before I went to Mexico City in October of 1968. By that time, I was kind of dating my now ex-husband, Art Simburg, and he, Tommie Smith, John Carlos—we all called him Carlos—and Lee Evans were at San Jose State. Art was a journalism major there and one of the people who was instrumental in getting the whole "Speed City" thing started. He was a fanatic about all sports, not just running.

I had met Art at a party after a track meet in California; he talked to me all night because he's a real talker. Fortunately, since it was a party, I didn't have to listen to him the whole time; I would listen to him for a while and then a song would come on and I would say, "I just have to dance to this song," and I would go and dance, and when the song ended, there he was, wanting to talk some more. Later, when we talked about how we met, he would say, "You just kept going up there and doing all the dances you did, and then you would come back and talk, and then you would go and do another dance—all night!" And I would say to myself, *I was doing the dances so you would go away!*—not that it worked. He was a persistent man; I will give him that.

Art was involved in getting runners—including Tommie Smith, Lee Evans, and John Carlos—to San Jose State, and once they became involved in the Project for Human Rights, he thought I should be involved too. He would call me—I didn't have a phone in my own room; we had an old one in a phone booth at the end of the hall—and he was just amazed that the girls who would pick up the phone didn't always know who I was. The first time he tried to reach me, he called the dorm—I don't even know how he got the number, probably because he's very persistent at everything—but anyway, as he put it, "I must have talked to five women, and nobody in that dorm knows who you are."

And I thought, *Well, that's a good thing.*

"How could they not know who Wyomia Tyus is?"

"Because," I told him, "they don't give a damn. They're not here for that. They don't care if I won medals; that's over. That's done. We're all back to what real life is all about."

"But everybody knows you—I just can't believe it."

I tried to move him along: "But you finally got someone?"

"Oh. Yeah. The last person I talked to—I must have talked to this girl twenty minutes on the phone, and she eventually says, 'Oh yeah, I know who she is.' So I said, 'Well, could you go get her for me and tell her I'm on the phone?'"

And that's how I finally got to talk to Art. He called so often that everybody on the floor not only knew who I was, they also knew who *he* was. He kept me informed on what was happening at San Jose State, what Harry Edwards, the sociology professor, was saying, what they thought they might do. He would call and say, "They did this" and "They were talking about that" and "You need to know these things!"

"Well, okay," I would say, "but I'm in Nashville, Tennessee. And I don't see anybody coming down here to organize us."

That didn't bother Art. "They're talking about not going to the Olympics," he told me one day.

"Okay."

"Well, what do you think?"

"I don't understand," I said. "What do you mean, what do I think?"

"They're saying they're not going to go because of all the unrest and violations of human rights." He meant things like Jim Crow laws here in the US and apartheid in South Africa and all the other injustices that were going on at that time.

"Okay," I said.

"Well, are you going to join them? Because I could tell them if you're going to join them."

"No," I replied. "You can't tell them I'm going to join them because I don't think they can make those kinds of decisions right now. They need to make the *team*. If they don't make the team, they're not going to go anyway."

He didn't answer right away. Then he said, "Only *you* would say something like that. Only you. You put a damper on everything."

"That's not a damper. That's something to really think about."

"Have you been talking to Coach Temple?"

"Are you saying I don't have a brain? Because I have a brain." I didn't have to talk to Mr. Temple. I'd talked to Mr. Temple from the time I was fifteen; I knew what he would say, and on a lot of questions—not all—I believed the same things he did. He always said that you have to think things through before you speak out. Saying that you're going to boycott a party when you haven't even gotten an invitation wouldn't make much sense to Mr. Temple, and it didn't make much sense to me, either.

"Look," I told him, "Mr. Temple is not calling us into the office and saying, 'You can't do this,' or, 'You can't do that.'"

I didn't tell him that what Mr. Temple did do was hold a meeting, and at that meeting he said, "Look. They're talking about boycotting the Olympics. It is not something I would do, but if it's something you really feel strongly about doing, you know what you have to do. That is up to you. But I can tell you this: you can't boycott the Olympics until you make the team. And another thing I have to tell you is that the press is calling here and asking all these questions, but we don't know anything from the people involved. All we know is what the press tells us.

We don't know if they're quoting Smith right, or Evans right, or Carlos right. We just know what the press says they're saying. You have to make your own decisions. But if they call my office, I am not going to go get you out of class to talk to them. And you don't have to call them back. If they really want to talk to you, they can come down here and talk to you. If they really want to know how you feel and how you're thinking, they can come down here and ask."

Of course, Art was giving me information long before the press called and would tell me about the things that Professor Edwards and Tommie and Lee and Carlos said they were going to do. But none of them called any of us. They called each other. They talked to themselves. And I understand—kind of, sort of: you're there, and you're talking about what you want to do. But you can't make a statement for everybody: "This is what we're *all* doing."

According to Mr. Temple, one of the reporters who talked to him said, "This is what they said they're going to do, and they said the women are going along with it. Is that true?"

"You would have to talk to the women about that," Mr. Temple answered. "You would have to talk to them."

But that was the press. When it came to the people involved, no one even bothered to try to talk to us. I don't fault them for not calling, but I fault them for assuming that we would go along with whatever they wanted. Because that's not right. How can you speak for a group of people? You don't want anyone speaking for you—that was one of the reasons people were protesting, one of the reasons there was so much unrest: because some people were always speaking for everybody else. Maybe we would have supported their plans if we had known all the hows and whys. But that reaching out to us never happened. Mr. Temple was getting all the calls, and all those calls were from the press—except, of course, the calls I got from Art.

And then when we went to a meet, this is how the press would address us: "Smith, Carlos, and Edwards say the boycott is on. What do you think?" Sometimes they just said: "Are you going along with the plan?"

And I would say, "Well, no."

"You're not?!" They would act all surprised.

"No one has said anything to me. So I'm not going along with anything. I don't know what you're talking about."

"But they said the women would go along."

"Well, then that's what *they* said. No one here said that. And you need to talk to more women. I'm just one person. I can't speak for anybody else."

That was a big point of contention between Art and me. He would always say, "You know they're right. You know what they want to do is right."

"Yes," I would say, "I'm not saying they're not right. I'm just saying that nobody is talking to me. You're talking to me. You figured out how to contact me. But nobody else has." Contacting us women was the furthest thing from their minds. I know that. But that didn't make it right. It didn't give them the right to speak for me—or to think for me or to speak or think for any of us. I don't think they were very organized—not to the point that they could organize *us*. But I can't say; I shouldn't because I wasn't with them.

The other problem was that, according to Mr. Temple, most of the time the press would quote Harry Edwards, the professor, and *then* they would quote one of the athletes, Tommie or Lee or whoever. And the closer it got to the Olympics, the more urgently they would ask Mr. Temple, "What are you going to do? What are your girls going to do?"

"You'll have to talk to them, and you might as well wait until they go to the Olympic Trials and come back. Once they make the team, you should talk to them."

But, of course, even after we made the team, no one asked us anything. And that was not the only issue the women's Olympic track team had to deal with.

Spiders and Fires and Bombs

As much as I was not leading in the movement, I was leading on the track: 1965 was one of my best years for running, and I set most of my records then. On an indoor track at Madison Square Garden in New York City, I broke the record for the 60-yard dash and almost every other indoor record there was. I had a great year. Not that I was cocky; I just felt good every time I stepped on the track. I don't attribute that to the fact that I had won the Olympic medals but to where I was in my life and how I felt about my accomplishments—not just participating in the Olympics, but being able to come back and go to school and continue to grow as a human being. I grew even more than I had in '64—getting bigger, as Mr. Temple would say.

Which was good because, heading into the '68 Olympics, the pressure was *on.* No one—no *person,* man or woman, not in the seventy-two years the men had been competing at the Olympics or the forty years women had been competing in track and field at the Olympics—had ever gone back-to-back in the 100 meters before, and I was *not* thinking that I would be the first; that was not in my consciousness. Even Mr. Temple told me, "It's going to be hard. Everybody's gunning for you."

Not only that, but the year prior to '68, two things happened to me that made it seem like I might never go back to the Olympics at all. I'd never pulled a muscle or sprained an ankle or been injured in any way before '67, but in that year, when I was out in Los Angeles for a meet, I got bitten by a spider on the lower part of my leg. I didn't feel it when it happened, but after about two weeks I kept noticing a blister, and the blister kept getting larger and larger. Being the doctor that I am, I kept popping that blister, thinking that I must have burned myself somehow, maybe on one of the radiators in the dorms.

After about a month or so, though, it still hadn't healed. In fact, it had stopped being a blister and had become something else: a thin layer of skin had grown over it, and you could tell that underneath something was *happening*. We finally went to the doctor, and he said it was a spider bite that had turned into an ulcer and was eating its way in. I was horrified. I wondered what would happen if it ate all the way to the bone. But the doctor just said to stay off it—stay off it completely—not puncture it anymore, and quit trying to be the doctor that I was not.

It started off that I had to rest for two weeks, and then I went back to practice, but my leg had not healed, so we went back to the doctor, who said, "She needs to be completely off her leg *until it heals*. The only thing she can do is go to class. And when she's in class, she needs to have her leg elevated."

Mr. Temple was okay with that, but he kept asking, "How long is this going to be?" As it turned out, it took just over a month. That spider bite was ugly and kind of scary. I still have a scar, a circle where my skin is very thin. But eventually it healed. It took its time, but it did heal.

Then, when I was finally allowed to go back to practice, I had another mishap: I was taking a class in camping and outdoor education, and one night when we had a campfire, somebody threw a paper on it, and a wind came up, blew the paper onto my other leg—the one without the spider bite—and burned the whole front part of my ankle. Then *that* was blistering, and it was very difficult to move it, and it took a long time for it to heal and for me to be able to practice. Of course, I still had to *go* to practice, even with my injury; I had to show up to the track for moral support and all that, so I was out there with my foot up, watching the others train.

When I started running again, I was not my fast self. I was there, I was running, but I had kind of lost sight of the Olympics. I started thinking, *I already won my gold medal; why do I need to go to the Olympics again? Somebody else can have that spot.* Because going back knowing that you're not in top form is not something you want to do. And I wasn't anywhere near top form. At the trials for the '67 Pan American Games, I didn't even qualify for the 100. I ran so poorly that, after the race, Mr. Temple said to me, "We're going back to campus and we're just going to work and work and *work.*"

Oh no, I thought, *that's* not *going to happen.* Everyone else would either make the team and start practicing with the Pan American Games team coach or go home. If we went back to Tennessee State, it would be just him and me. He would be sitting under a shade tree, barking orders, and I would be out there running and sweating in that hot sun. *No way,* I told myself. *I am not going back there to practice alone with him and have him hold this race over me.*

So I said, "But Mr. Temple—I still have the 200."

"No. We're going to pull you out of the 200. You already look bad enough." You may remember that Mr. Temple had always wanted me to run the 200, but in '67, at the Pan American trials, he wanted to pull me out, and that gives you a sense of how badly I was running.

I didn't give up. "But I can make the team in the 200, Mr. Temple."

"It just doesn't make sense for you to run the 200. You can't get down the track in the 100. You've got next year to think about, and you need to get yourself together. We're just going to go back, and we're going to *work out.*"

"Okay, Mr. Temple," I said, "that sounds good, but could I just run in the 200? Don't pull me out. Can I just run in this race and see where I am? And then maybe we can see how much work I have to do?" I had finally found a reason to say more than just a few words.

Eventually, Mr. Temple agreed. "Okay, Tyus," he said. "But I think it's awful, watching you do that—that you even *want* anybody to see you running so badly. That 100 was enough."

"Okay, Mr. Temple. Just let me run it."

And he did. And I won. Because I said, to myself, *I am not going to return to Tennessee and run all summer with him like this.* That was not going to work out for me. So I just decided that things would go differently. The fact that I was mostly by myself and not talking—the fact that I talked to myself constantly, in my head, and was always thinking things through—helped me to have a psychological edge. I don't know exactly where it comes from. But for me, with most things, if I sit and think about it, I can talk myself into it. Now that I'm older, it comes much more slowly, but when I was young, it used to come to me right away, like: *This is it. This is how it should be, and this is how it is going to be.* And I'm usually right on it. I can make it happen. Not all the time. But usually.

That wasn't always enough for Mr. Temple, though. Even after I won that 200, he said, "You still didn't look that good."

"But I won something that I don't run, Mr. Temple. I don't even like the 200. So that means that I'm getting better. I just don't have the quick speed right now for the 100. And that's okay because I won't be running the 100 in the Pan American Games."

"I just don't know, Tyus. I just don't know."

"I can do it, Mr. Temple. I am telling you: I can do it."

I knew I *had* to do it, so I went to the Pan American Games in Winnipeg, Manitoba, and I won the 200—just like I told him I would do. It made a big mess of the 4x100 relay because, on a team like the Olympic team or the Pan American Games team, they can make up the relays in a couple of ways. They can say that the first four in the 100 will be the relay people. Or they can say one and two in the 100 and one and two in the 200 can make up the relay team. There are a lot of different ways, and it depends on the coach. Because I got fifth or something like that in the 100 at the trials, the Pan American team coach thought I shouldn't be on the relay team. I thought my winning the 200 might change that, but it didn't. *Okay,* I thought, *I'm all right with that.*

But Mr. Temple was not. "What kind of craziness is that? That's not how it's going to be," he said, and he went to bat for me even though I told him it was okay.

Then when we got to Winnipeg and were training, they could see that I was improving, and suddenly they wanted me for the relay. But I wouldn't do it. They were upset with me, and I didn't care. "No thank you," I said. "You have the four people who won the 100, and that's what you said you were going to do."

So I didn't run the relay; I was only there for the one race, so I just had fun. Mr. Temple supported me. "You should have nothing to do with them," he said. "They didn't want you in the beginning, they don't need you now. Let them run with the girls they chose. If they lose, they just lose."

They did lose, as it turned out. Barbara Ferrell won gold in the 100 and silver in the 200, but the relay team did not place; they got beaten by Cuba, Canada, and Jamaica.

All that was my prelude going into '68. But then, after all that, once it got to be '68, my thinking changed; I went from doubting myself to thinking I could win to *knowing* I could win. *I'm going back as the defending champion,* I thought. *I can do this.* First, I convinced myself that everybody else in the race should be afraid of me because I was returning; I had nothing to be scared of. Then I saw my competition at the meets leading up to the Olympics, and I didn't think any of those women could beat me. Of course, I had to keep myself on point because reporters and other people who talked to me would ask, "Don't you feel old?"

"I'm only twenty-three!" I would say. But I knew what they were thinking: twenty-three is old for a sprinter. Wilma Rudolph, you may recall, was twenty-three or twenty-four when Mr. Temple made her retire. Even so, part of that had nothing to do with running. When we were in college, Mr. Temple would stress that while you needed to do the things you needed to do on the track, you also needed to get your education, leave college, and get a job. Your time of competition was going to end, and you had to be prepared.

I was in a different position in that I was still only nineteen during the '64 Olympics and had not even completed a full year of college. After I won my gold medal, I went back to the same routine I'd always had: I was back in school, I had Mr. Temple there to guide me, and I was doing all the things that got me to the '64 Games—why wouldn't I get to the '68 Games?

Other athletes, ones who ran for clubs instead of schools, had to put themselves through college if they wanted a degree, and for many that meant that they also had to maintain a job and convince the person that they were working for to let them go on trips, to take four-day weekends for meets or even go to the Olympics for a month, which was not fashionable for companies to do at that time. So for club runners, retiring at an early age was a matter of economic necessity. And even for those who ran for schools, graduation meant that your life was going to change. You had to get yourself a full-time job, eight to five, figure out some way to continue to practice, and find someone who was going to be very understanding to work for. That was just not happening in the 1960s, especially not for women—and even less so for Black women. The support was just not there.

So I was lucky that I went to my first Olympics when I did, at the age that I was. I was in good shape—I could feel it—and I was beating not only the runners from other schools and clubs but also the other Tigerbelles. If you could beat a Tigerbelle, Mr. Temple would say, you could beat anybody—anybody in the world. Not that there was anybody else running sprints from Tennessee State in '68; it was just me. Edith was two years ahead of me in school, so she had graduated in '66.

As the Olympic Trials drew closer, I knew I was ready, both physically and mentally. I had a new way of walking, so to speak. My attitude was: *I am going to graduate from college, and I am going to go to the Olympics and win my last gold medal. And then I'll be done.* Those were my goals.

By August of '68, I had reached the first goal: I graduated from Tennessee State with a degree in recreation[18]—not that I ever used it in any direct way, although it was helpful when I worked in outdoor education. What I really wanted to do was become an athletic trainer. I've always been fascinated with biology, kinesiology—anything that has to do with observing the human body and analyzing how it works. I took a class called

18 In 1968, only 8 percent of the female population and 11 percent of the male population earned four-year college degrees in the United States; see "Percentage of the US population who have completed four years of college or more from 1940 to 2015, by gender," Statista.com, Statista Inc., August 26, 2016. Statista does not have completion rates sorted by race, but I think we can assume, based on the overall tenor of racial discrimination at the time, that the percentages would be even smaller.

"Care and Prevention of Athletic Injuries" and just loved it. But that kind of career was not available to me at that time; it was not something women were supposed to do. It probably would have been possible at one of the other schools, and it might have been possible for me at Tennessee State if someone had been encouraging me to take the extra classes and do it. But nobody was doing that. In fact, Mr. Temple just said, "You need to get out of school! Don't be trying to change your major. You need to get out of school *now*—that's what you need to do."

It's official! College graduation picture, 1968. (Photo courtesy of Tennessee State University.)

* * *

Although I knew many of the athletes from the US men's track-and-field team, I didn't see a lot of them in the run-up to '68. We rarely competed at the same time or in the same places—we had our Olympic Trials in one place, and they had their Olympic Trials somewhere else. I don't know why, but they never had us together. And when we went to our Olympic Trials, there would be nobody in the stands for the women, while the men's Trials were televised. But we never let that bother us. Being seen was not what we were there for; we had bigger fish to fry.

What did bother us in '68 were the separate and unequal locations of the men's and women's Olympic training camps. The 1968 Olympics were held in Mexico City, where the elevation is over seven thousand feet. So we needed to train at a high altitude, and they placed our camps accordingly. The men's Olympic training camp was in Lake Tahoe, California—a beautiful place. The women's Olympic training camp was in Los Alamos, New Mexico—*that* Los Alamos—where it's very hot, and where the government carried out all their nuclear weapons development and testing.

At first, we didn't know a lot about Los Alamos or the things that went on there[19]; our main objection was the isolation. When we got off the bus, we all looked around and said, "Wow, there's nothing here." Because there was *nothing* in that town—nothing but all the nuclear weapons development facilities. As time went on, we began to understand why it was so isolated. There was a long-distance runner who would just go off and run, and one day she headed into an area that she shouldn't

19 According to the United Nations Scientific Committee on the Effects of Atomic Radiation, three major nuclear-related accidents have occurred at Los Alamos nuclear laboratories. Critical accidents occurred in August 1945 and May 1946, and a third accident occurred during an annual physical inventory in December 1958. "Sources and Effects of Ionizing Radiation—2008 Report to the General Assembly," 2011, pp. 2–3.

have been in. That's when the coaches called us together and told us, "You should not be running anywhere but where you're told. For you long-distance runners, we have a place for you to run, and these are the areas you go to. Don't go off the beaten path." They didn't say it like that, exactly, but basically it was, "Stay where you're supposed to be. Don't go gallivanting off into places where there's no telling what might happen."

After that, even breathing seemed suspect. *What am I breathing in? Have I not adjusted yet? Is it the altitude? Or is it the chemicals?* Yet there was nothing we could do. As far as I could tell, nobody was concerned about our health. Nobody cared. And I think we talked about it more because we had nothing to do—nothing except touring the nuclear development facilities, which is one of the activities they arranged for us. *Okay, we're here. Let's go see these plants!* But I didn't want to be around those things.

In addition to taking us on tours of the facilities, they were doing all kinds of tests on us: measuring our body fat, putting us in tubs of water to see what got displaced. Basically, we were guinea pigs. We weren't thinking like that at the time, but that's what we were: experimental subjects. I don't know what they used the information for; that's something I wonder about to this day. Also, at that time they had started testing us to see if we were truly women. They would scrape around in your mouth, and if you had the wrong chromosomes, they would say, "Something's wrong. You're not a woman!"

We did get to learn a little about the Native American culture down there, and about making turquoise jewelry, and that was interesting. But other than that, there was absolutely nothing. Far, far away from everything—desolate. Nobody. Nothing. And we were there for at least three weeks, maybe four, with no choice in the matter at all, and nothing to do but stay in the motel the whole time. They had one movie house. That was it. It was horrible. And I would always wonder, *What are they trying to do, putting us down here with all this nuclear stuff, experimenting on us? What was going through the Olympic Committee's brain to put us here?* Getting acclimated to the altitude was the stated reason. But there are other places in the US at that altitude—Santa Fe, for example, which was not very far away. And I never understood why they didn't just put us with the men in Tahoe—that's where we should have been. But no. Separate-and-not-equal ruled the day. So that's where we spent our time.

The movement was still on the West Coast, and it stayed on the West Coast—and it was not, at that point, a women's movement.

B2B100m

Once we all were in Mexico City, we had to make a decision about whether or not to boycott. There were people for, people against, but nobody could really bring everybody together and say, "Okay, we're all going to do this." So we had lots of meetings.

The meetings were not just for Black athletes. They were for all the athletes who wanted to be involved, and that included white athletes. The movement had started with the idea of just a Black boycott of the Olympics, and that's how people thought about it: "This is what *the Blacks* are talking about. They're not going to the Games." But by the time we got to Mexico City, the organizers had decided to change the focus from Black Power to human rights, and that's how the Olympic Project for Human Rights was started. Because there were a lot of things happening in the world that were wrong. In addition to Black oppression in America, people were protesting the massacre of the student activists in Mexico City itself, in Tlatelolco. They were protesting apartheid in South Africa and the crackdown on the student uprising in France—not to mention what had gone on in Algeria, which only got its independence from France in 1962—and the war in Vietnam, although that was never one of the talking points. Human rights violations were not just happening to Black people in the United States. They were happening to people all over the world. All kinds of people's rights were being taken away or had always been denied.

The cause of human rights was broader than the cause of Black Power, and in my view, that's why the direction of the movement changed—it *had* to change, if you ask me, because I never felt that there would be enough people who would stand up just for Black rights. In any case, after it changed, there were a lot more people involved. They had buttons made and everything, and in Mexico City they were giving out those buttons to anyone who wanted them. Of course, as I have mentioned, neither I nor any of the other athletes on the women's track team were involved in the decision to change course or the button making. I guess that all happened up in Tahoe while we were down in lovely Los Alamos.

Two of the white athletes who were very involved were Hal and Olga Connolly. Hal was a hammer thrower for the US, and Olga threw the discus for what was then Czechoslovakia. They were in the 1956 Olympics together and fell in love, and when they got married, Olga came to live in the US. They were part of the Olympic Project for Human Rights right off the bat, and one of the things they did was keep in contact with the Harvard rowing team, who were also white. The Harvard rowers were all in support of the Project; they wore the buttons and came to the meetings and spoke out whenever they got the chance.

The meetings were in the Olympic Village gathering area, and there were some fifty or so athletes at most of the meetings, and when they left, most were wearing buttons. Pretty soon the people from the Olympic Committee started saying, "You can't wear those buttons, that's not part of the uniform." But the athletes would wear them anyway. They'd say, "What are you going to do? Put me off the team?" And at some point the Olympic Committee must have figured out that putting people off the team was going to attract more attention than us wearing the buttons. So we wore the buttons. I sure wore mine; at that point, I knew that I was going to be me, and whatever else was going to happen was going to happen.

Eventually, the Olympic Committee got so worried that they decided they would send in their gold medal troop to address us: Jesse Owens. At one of the meetings, he came in and started saying what a wonderful thing it is to be a part of the Games, and that we wouldn't get this opportunity every day, and we should think about what's going on and how we were affecting the world. I thought he was saying some of the right things—affecting the world was exactly what we wanted to do—but trying to bring us to the wrong conclusion. The Olympic Committee thought Jesse was going to be their Olympic savior. But when he finished his speech, we just looked at each other and thought, *Oh, please.* Nobody was interested in listening to Jesse. We pretty much waited for him to finish and then said to ourselves, *Get him out of here.*

This was both because he was representing the Olympic Committee and because of the way he was seen personally. He was respected as a runner, but not as someone who was ever part of a movement. We would all say that Jesse was their poster child. But when you really talked to Jesse and thought about what he did, you wondered why he let them make him be that. Because after he went to Germany and stood up to Hitler—represented the US and stood up to Hitler—he came back to the US and had to run against horses for money. How degrading must that be? To run against an animal? And I'm sure there were many other things that happened to him because of what life was like for Blacks back then that I don't know about. There was a time when Jesse had nothing—absolutely nothing. And then he comes in and tries to say to the group, "You shouldn't do this. This is America, and we should be proud of our country."

At a certain point, your country has to give you a reason to feel proud, has to recognize your accomplishments—not to mention your humanity. And remember that in '64 they didn't even give Edith and me a parade in downtown Atlanta. Just in the Black community. Which I was okay with because those are my people. But I was lucky that I had my life at Tennessee State to go back to because my country, which Jesse was telling us to be proud of, was not offering me anything in return for how well I had represented it. And after a while you start to look around you and think: *What's wrong with this picture?*

Not that the country didn't claim our victories—that's the reason you're allowed to be a part of the USA team: because they want to claim all that's good. So if I'm winning, of course they're claiming it. It's all about counting medals; it always has been and I think it always will be—even though the Cold War is over. And in the sixties, for women, particularly Black women, that's all you were: part of the count. Before the Olympics, they don't say anything about you, and then you win and they'll mention you in maybe a couple of articles: "Our girls are doing wonderful." Or "Our gals"—that's how they used to refer to us—"Our gals did great. Let's move on." *Grrr*. We weren't treated like the men, never saw articles that said we "came through for our country." But if we didn't do well, then: "You really let your country down"—like that Russia trip with Flamin' Mamie. Nobody ever asked whether the country let us down. That's the real question. Because the country did let us down. Many times. As Black people and as women. Not that that affected me because I had enough love and support from my family, Mr. Temple, and the Tigerbelles, and knowing that what I did was a good thing—for me, if nothing else.

I think that what had happened to Jesse Owens bothered him, but—from the way I see it—in '68 they needed him, so they were doing a lot for him then: giving him a cushiony job and all the respect he hadn't gotten in the forties and fifties. Maybe that allowed him to put the past behind him. But it didn't make us any more interested in what he had to say.

We had flown straight from New Mexico to Mexico City right before the Games started, about two weeks before we were supposed to compete. We didn't have an acclimation period in Mexico City like we did in Tokyo because there was no time zone difference, long flight, or altitude adjustment (since we had taken care of that in Los Alamos) to worry about. But it also meant that everything happened very quickly. The meeting with Jesse Owens occurred within two or three days of our arrival, and it was not the first meeting we went to. The first meeting didn't have very many people at it, and then at the second meeting there were a lot more, all saying different things. They couldn't reach agreement. They wanted to vote on what to do, but could never even get a majority of people to agree to vote. Whenever they asked for a vote, someone would say, "Why do we need to vote? The people who want to do something should just do something."

And that's what eventually came out of it. It was decided that the action was all up to the individual: whatever you wanted to do to support the movement, you should do. If you wanted to speak, if you wanted to wear something other than the assigned uniform—however you wanted to demonstrate, that's what you would do. I don't think anyone went home from the meeting thinking they were going to do anything specific. There wasn't that much direction. I don't think even Tommie Smith or John Carlos knew, at that point, what they were going to do.

At least from what I know, they didn't. How could you sit in a room and think of doing what they did? That's one of those things that I always felt was a spur-of-the-moment decision. But it was a great spur—an inspiration. It was a spur of the moment that lit a light—one that's still shining. It was one of those things.

Unlike Tokyo and the '64 Olympics, I had been to Mexico City before. They had invited the Tigerbelles down there to race, so I knew what to expect, running-wise. The pollution was not as bad there as it is now. It was bad, but I don't remember it being an issue. And the altitude didn't affect us sprinters in any negative way; the thinner air makes you run faster. So even with all the political conflict that was going on, I was still feeling good, physically and mentally. My goals were still the same, and looking back on it, I was pretty focused and hoping that whatever other things I was going to do would not interfere with those goals. But I was also open to anything. If the group had come to a consensus that we would not compete, if that's what it was going to be, then my goals might have changed. It wouldn't have been a big change for me, on the inside. It would have been something that I could do. Like I said before, I'm not the person who is going to go out and take their licks in a protest. But changing my goals to serve a purpose? That I could do. Because that wouldn't make me feel like I'd been stepped on, trod on, nothing like that.

In the discussions, I just listened; I was still not someone who was going to speak up. Part of it was that, as well as I knew Tommie and Carlos and Lee and all that, they never, even there, came to us and asked us to join them. I never thought of them as selfish personally, as selfish individuals. It was just that whole male thing that I always hated, that "Whatever we say, you're going to do." Not "Be a part of it." Not "Stand up with me."

But "Get behind me." That never appealed to me; my mom and dad did not raise me that way.

After the fact, when I talked to Tommie—and Tommie is not a big talker—he'd say, "I'm just a good old farm boy!" And I'd say, "Yes, you are." And eventually he realized, "Well, we're just the same—we have a lot in common."

"Yeah," I would say, "we do." But see, I had known that a long time before; I was just not on his radar in '68. None of us women were. It's no big thing. I feel that we are all always at different stages of our lives. And we all change, or we don't.

Another reason I had to sit and listen and think about what was being said and who was saying it was that, a lot of times, when I listened to people speak, they would say one thing in a big crowd, and then, when they were out of that crowd, they would be saying something else. That molded my mind. I had been with them and known them and known what they said and I had to ask, *How much of this is you and how much of this is Harry Edwards?* Harry was the one, to me, who always had things to say and knew how and why to say them. Not to take anything from Tommie or Lee or Carlos. I think they had things to say too, but Harry had a way of putting it together to make them say, *"That's* what I was thinking!" And that's good because it was needed, but in my regular conversations with the athletes, the things I needed to hear to make me feel a part of it—to make me feel won over—didn't always come out clearly.

It was also the case that Harry had a lot to gain from it in terms of publicity—because he was the professor, the one who would be invited to speak, the one who could get paid. Tommie and Lee and Carlos couldn't be paid because of the rules about amateur status. Or they could be paid, but under the table, not up front, and that was always a risk. "He has a lot to gain from it," Mr. Temple would say, "and I just hope that in his gaining,

Tommie and Carlos and Lee and all the others gain something too." Which of course they did, eventually, but back then nobody knew how it would turn out.

At any rate, my race came before theirs, and I was in the best possible frame of mind, despite all of the goings-on. You have to be able to multitask. And not only that: I had been there already. For me, the pressure of the Olympics was nothing. The pressure of, "What are we doing about human rights? Are we going to boycott or not?" *That* was a pressure for me. But not to the point that it was going to make me not be prepared for that 100.

There was a lot of rain in Mexico City, but my workouts were good, and I was running well in all the trials leading up to the finals. There were two other Americans running, Margaret Bailes and Barbara Ferrell, but they were not Tigerbelles. Barbara Ferrell was from the LA Mercurettes and Margaret Bailes was a teenager—she was seventeen—from Eugene, Oregon. She had been running really well, and before we went to the Olympic training camp, Mr. Temple asked me, "Did you see what Bailes was running?

"Yes, Mr. Temple."

"You're going to need some more practice."

No, I'm not, I thought, but I didn't say anything.

"They're running all these great times. Ferrell is running great, and Bailes is running great."

Well, yeah, I thought, *because they're on the West Coast. They've got good weather. We've got snow. We only get to compete in three meets a year. They get to compete all the time.*

Mr. Temple would read stuff about their times and have us running our butts off. Then we'd get to the meets, and we'd beat them. Everywhere. And we'd think, *We didn't have to work that hard!*

Also, I had my position about the competition, and it didn't involve worrying about Barbara Ferrell or Margaret Bailes. At the Olympic Trials, a *Sports Illustrated* reporter asked me what I thought about Bailes, and I told him, "I don't think about other people. I let them think about me."[20]

I knew how to keep my cool. One of my methods—one that they made a lot of fuss about in the press—was to do a little dance as part of my prerace ritual. Before the 100 meters in the Olympics, I was hanging out in the Village and talking to some of the Tigerbelles, and I told them, "When I get to the start of the 100 meters, I'm going to do a dance called the 'Tighten Up.'"

They all just looked at me. "You ain't going to do that."

"Yes, I am." In the trials, there were people from Jamaica in the stands right near the starting line playing the bongo drums, and that made me feel like dancing. "I'm just going to do the 'Tighten Up' before my race," I said, "so I won't tighten up during my race."

This was just a little conversation between Tigerbelles; I wasn't thinking of telling anybody else. But I must have mentioned it to a couple of guys or maybe one of the other Tigerbelles did, because after the race, one of the guys remarked, "You said you were going to do that. I never believed you would, but you did."

For me, it wasn't that much of a stretch. They were playing the music, and people were dancing in the stands, and when you're standing in front of the blocks, that's always kind of a

20 The article, by Bob Ottum, entitled "Dolls on the Move to Mexico," published on September 2, 1968, is a step forward from the 1964 article about the Bouffant Belles. Although the writer spends an inordinate amount of time discussing the female athletes' looks, including comments about "girls who look great in those warm-up suits, almost as though they were modeling them, for heaven sakes, instead of just keeping their muscles warm," he does discuss women who actually went to the Olympics.

dance anyway, all the shaking and wiggling you do, trying to stay loose. And the "Tighten Up" was not all that different from what I would normally do. It's kind of like a herky-jerky thing. People in the stands knew what it was; it was very popular at that time because of the Archie Bell & the Drells song. In any case, that was my thing, and I did it.

One of my competitors—Raelene Boyle, from Australia—was psyched out by it; she kept looking at me sideways while I was dancing, which was good.[21] I was hoping that it would psych out *someone*. But it was mostly a comfort thing, for me, to let people know: *Hey—this is me. Get in line because I'm feeling fine.* There was no way anyone could say to me that I was not going to win that 100 meters. I just felt so confident—in me. I wasn't saying it out loud to anyone else—except maybe through the dance. But I was thinking that they should be afraid of me because I had the gold medal, that experience, under my belt, and they had *nothing* on me. Everything Mr. Temple had taught us about experience playing a big part in success, that with experience you know how to handle pressure and do what you need to do to win—I felt all those things. I just thought: *I am in a place in my life where this is going to be mine.*

At the same time, I wasn't looking to break any records; I just wanted that gold medal and whatever came with it would come with it. When people ask me, "What records do you have? What records did you break?" I tell them the truth: "I don't know." To me, records don't matter. I could run the fastest time that I had ever run, which would be a record for me, and somebody could

21 Tyus's impression of Boyle's response is corroborated by Jimson Lee, who has reminded *Speed Endurance* readers more than once that it was not Usain Bolt or Michelle Jenneke who introduced prerace dancing to the Olympics, but Wyomia Tyus. See "Year in Review: Michelle Jenneke Pre-Race Dance? Wyomia Tyus Did It First!" (January 1, 2013) and "Wyomia Tyus: The Famous Pre-Race Dance to Out-Psych Everyone" (June 16, 2010) on speedendurance.com.

beat that time because on a different day in a different place they ran better. But to me it's not the time that you run that matters. Because time never crosses the tape. It's the person that crosses the tape. If I ran a twelve flat, I'm okay with that. Some people would say, "You were slow." And I would say, "You could say that, but what does this gold medal say? It says I'm fast. It says I was the fastest person in the world in that race on that day." And nothing will ever change that. So I was never a person about time, and that's why I don't know too much about my times. I just know that I ran, and that you always have to run as best as you can, and that's what I did. And in '68, I thought my best would be the best in the world. I didn't think anybody could beat me; I didn't think anybody else had that feeling. Or maybe they did—maybe they felt that same way too. But—oh well. I got the medal.

Other than Raelene Boyle, I couldn't tell if anyone reacted when I started doing the "Tighten Up"; the people up in the stands were already dancing and cheering and yelling. We had three Americans in the group, so the American fans were cheering for us all, and other people were cheering for the runners from other countries. Mainly, I remember the Jamaican group with the bongo drums; I knew a lot of the people who were part of that group, and they were dancing and having fun, right there at the start of the 100 meters. They were mostly athletes— they had a little section for athletes who wanted to watch the races, so that's where they were. And that's how I got to see what happened when Tommie Smith and John Carlos made their stand, from that section. But that was later.

When we were getting ready to start the 100, the weather changed, and it was clear that it was going to rain. *I really don't want to be running in any rain,* I thought. Not because I couldn't. The Tigerbelles trained in the rain all the time. Mr. Temple would look at the weather report in the summertime and he would tell us, "They say it's going to be raining at noon"—our practice wasn't until one—"so everybody on the track at twelve." Just so that we could be out in the rain. "You have to be able to run in all conditions," he'd say, "because you never know what it's going to be like when you race." So maybe *because* of all the practice in the rain, I didn't really want to run in the rain; I knew what it felt like, and it wasn't my favorite feeling. I wanted that race to be over before it really started to come down.

Then, when we were down at the start, Margaret Bailes jumped. And I thought, *Doggone it, it's going to rain before we get this 100 off.* It's not like today, when you jump and that person is out. Back then, you got three—one, two, and the third jump, you were out.

So we all got back in the blocks, including Margaret Bailes, and then Barbara Ferrell jumped. I was halfway down the track, and as I walked back I was thinking, *It is definitely going to rain. Why can't they just wait for the gun?!* That's all that was going through my head. But of course I couldn't say anything to anybody.

I was always pretty much the last person to get in my blocks. With or without the "Tighten Up," I had a fairly extensive prerace ritual. My husband Duane always says, "You cheating Tigerbelles. You were always cheating—stalling—in those starting blocks."

It is true that we Tigerbelles took our time getting into the blocks. I'd always been taught that you stand in front of your blocks and you shake your legs out—you shake and shake. Take deep breaths. Touch your toes and make sure you're still shaking while you do. Then you kick your legs out to put them in the blocks—you kick, kick, kick, and put that one in, and then you kick, kick, kick, and put the other one in. Then you sit there on your knees and you look down the track.

I wore a watch when I ran, and people would say, "You're going to time yourself?"

"Of course," I would reply, "I'm going to have more than enough time to look at my watch." The watch was too big for my wrist, so I would have to shake that down too, into the proper position, and then, and only then, would I take my time to get on my mark. I took *forever*; it's true.

Sometimes, they would call me out and say, "You're taking too long." But it was the same ritual that I always did, and it was nothing that broke any rules. Duane says, "You did that to make those people mad." But that's not true. We just did it because we did it. Although sometimes it was an advantage.

When we ran against the Russians in the US-versus-Russia meets, the starters would say, "Runners, take your mark," and the Russians would run *really fast,* and—just like that—they were in their blocks. And we hadn't even *started* our ritual yet. They would be there, all tensed up like that, forever. By the time we did get down, their little arms were tired. They were really ready to go and wondering, *What is taking them so long?* Sometimes they waited so long, they would have to raise their hands to get up off the blocks when we were just barely getting down. The Russian team people would get really upset, I know. So the judges would tell us that we needed to get in the blocks a little quicker. We could get in a little quicker, but we weren't going to be running into our blocks. It wasn't our fault that when they said to take our mark a second time, the Russians would just go and do the same thing again, running *really fast* and getting right into their blocks. Even when we got in a little quicker, the Russians ended up on their fingertips for a long time—not as long as the first time, but they were still there for a while. And nobody was supposed to be moving, but by the time we were ready to put our hands down, they would be moving. "The movement needs to stop," the starter would say. Then, finally, we would all come up to a set position, on our fingertips, all our weight there. The Russians would jerk up onto their fingertips, and they'd be ready to go, and we would slowly rise up to the point where you stop—and they couldn't shoot the gun until we stopped. So the Russians were under a little more pressure at the start, which is why Duane says we cheated. But I just thought we were smart.

In any case, despite or because of the "Tighten Up" and my typical Tigerbelle prerace ritual, there were two false starts in the 100 in '68, one by Margaret Bailes and the other by Barbara Ferrell. How bad a false start is depends on where you are on the track. If you're way over on one end, and the false start is a real burst, you can see it happen, but usually if you're at the far end, you don't really see it. Sometimes, even if you're in the middle, you won't see somebody jump if they're on the end. You only find out about the jump when the officials signal it with a second shot, and sometimes that shot is late—I mean, we're only talking about eleven seconds here—and you'll be thirty yards down the track, and at that point you're tired. And if there's a false start and you hear that second gun, you shouldn't just stop right quick; you have to run out so that you don't pull a muscle. But I didn't feel tired out after Margaret and Barbara jumped. I just thought Barbara had lost her best advantage, and Margaret Bailes too. Because she had a pretty decent start herself. She was young, though, and I think that the whole atmosphere of being in the Olympics had an effect on her.

So when we got back in the blocks, I was thinking, *Barbara jumped, so she's not going to be able to have that fast start she always has. She's got to sit and sit and sit and wait in those blocks. I could have that* one *step I need.* In my head, it was all just fitting right into what I thought it should be. Beyond that, I wasn't thinking of anyone—I wasn't even really thinking of Barbara. The only part of Barbara I was thinking about was the fact that she had a great start and it had, in the past, been hell for me to catch up to her, but maybe that great start wasn't going to be there for her on this particular day.

When the gun went off, I was *out.* The best start I've ever had, ever in my whole career, was in that Olympics in '68. The first thing I remember thinking was, *I got a good start! I got a good start! I'm out! I'm out front! I'm out front of Barbara!* And then I was like: *I know she's coming.* And I knew that Poland's Szewińska—who was Kirszenstein in the '64 Olympics; she had gotten married—was also in the race. And I thought: *She's going to be coming. But she's just as old as I am, and I'm faster.* All this was going through my head, yet I was running strong, and I never looked back. I didn't hear Margaret or Barbara or Szewińska—I didn't hear any of them. Even so, I wasn't really listening for them. If I was listening for anyone, it was Raelene Boyle, but I had psyched her out, so she was not going to beat me.

Now I was thinking, *Stay relaxed, lift your knees, stay relaxed, lift your knees. Don't forget to lean at the finish line!* And then it was over. Just like that.

As soon as I crossed the line, it poured. I mean, *poured*—like the sky almost fell out. And I thought, *Well, thank you.* Because it waited for me.

After the Deluge

Usually, as soon as you finish a race, the officials shoo you off the track so that the next race can start, but after the 100 in '68, Howard Cosell, the sportscaster, was running a live feed, and he grabbed my arm. "Wyomia," he said, "we want to talk to you about the 100 meters," and then he turned to the camera and said, "We have right here Wyomia Tyus, who just won her second—" But at that point one of the officials started practically pushing me, trying to get me off the track, and Howard shouted, "Leave her alone!"

"She has to get off the track so the next event can start!"

"Get your hands off of her! She's talking to her country!" Howard kept yelling at the officials until he finally got them away from me. At that point, I was shaking because it was cold, and I was soaking wet. "You're cold?" he asked.

"A little bit," I said.

He put his ABC coat around me, turned back to the camera, and said, "I just gave this fast young lady my jacket. She's shivering!" That was his lead-in. He was just too funny: "She's talking to her country—get away from her!" Go Howard! But he was a nice person, and I appreciated him giving me his jacket. When I got back from Mexico City, I bought a Paddington jacket—you know, for the bear, the little yellow one?—and I drew *ABC* on it. It was tiny, and I wanted to present it to him and say, "Look, here's your jacket back—after the rain in Mexico City." I never got to do it because the day I knew I was going to see him, I forgot it at home. It would have been a cute thing, but it didn't happen.

While I was talking to Howard—and my country—the officials confirmed who had won by going over all the tapes, checking to see that nobody had run out of the lanes, that I really had crossed the line first, things like that. (I don't think they were doing drug testing then; I don't remember having to pee in a cup, so if they were doing testing, they weren't testing the sprinters, or at least they didn't test me.) A very short time later—I assume it was a short time, because it was still pouring—I was out on the victory stand.

The rain was soaking us, and I was wiping it away from my eyes, and everybody who looks at the video thinks I was crying, but I wasn't; I'm not a crier, and I wasn't crying. The main thing I was feeling was relief—because I had accomplished all my goals. I had my degree. I had won my medal. *I am ready for the world!* I told myself. I was also thinking about how much my mother and brothers had sacrificed for me to get there and how proud they must have been at that moment. Being up on that stand was just *pleasant*—I felt the way you feel when everything falls into place, and your life is where you want it to be, and you know you're at the beginning of a new life—a new phase of your life. For me, at that moment, it meant no more running. I wasn't thinking of ever running again, after that. I was done. Then they played the national anthem, and I was good to go. I could have gone home that day.

In my mind, that would have been the perfect ending for my second Olympics—with me achieving the second of my two goals and becoming the first person to win back-to-back gold medals in the 100. But as it turned out, there were still some things I had to do—both on the track and off.

For one thing, I still had to run the relay and the 200, but those races were just not the same as the 100. That 200? I wasn't even thinking about it. Didn't care about it. That race was just something Mr. Temple wanted me to do. The relay meant more to me, but it was not the most important thing I had left to do, not by a long shot.

I was in the spectator area for athletes when Tommie Smith and John Carlos and Peter Norman, the Australian runner who got the silver in the men's 200, came out to get their medals. There was a rail between us and the track, and you could look down the chute where the athletes come out. There were a lot of us there, and we were all yelling our support.

When I saw Tommie and Carlos come out, the first thing that ran through my head was: *They don't have no shoes on.* I watched them walk onto the medal stand, and when "The Star-Spangled Banner" started to play, I watched them raise their fists. *Oh my!* I thought. The crowd was just quiet at first. Nothing. No sound. Then people started talking, a buzz rose up, people near me whispering, "Did you see what they did? Did you see what they did?"

"Yes, I did," I said, but I was also trying to see if there was anybody up above us trying to do anything else—anything retaliatory. Because while some people were cheering, some people were booing. They were angry. You could see it in their faces. And I kept thinking, *I just want to be out of here.* Because I didn't know what was going to happen. I thought: *That was so powerful* and *It's going to strike so many people the wrong way* and *I hope nobody hurts them.* That was one of my first thoughts: *I hope no one hurts them.* I wanted to get out of the stadium before something happened. There were too many people there, and we were in front and kind of below everybody, and there were just a few of us Black athletes. And I thought, *There are probably some Black people booing too.* It was a scary moment.

When they came off the stand, they walked right past us, and we were giving them back slaps and high fives and saying supportive things. After that, all hell broke loose—for them. Once we got back to the Olympic Village, there was a meeting of just about everybody, and everybody was saying that Tommie and Carlos were being sent home and that their medals would be taken away.

"Take their medals away?" I said. "How can they take their medals away? What are you talking about?"

"Yes, that's what's going to happen," more than one athlete responded. "That's what happens when you do things like that."

"Oh, please," I said, "Tommie and Carlos are not going to give up their medals."

Still, that was what most of the athletes believed: that their medals would be taken—because that was the propaganda that was put out, just that quick. And who would do it, other than the officials? The word all around was that the Olympic Committee was going to take their medals and put them out of the Village. And that's what came across to America too, in the papers: that they got their medals taken and they'd been put out of the Olympic Village for disgracing America.

But I was thinking, *They are not taking their medals.* And as it turned out, I was right, but if you were to search it online right now, you would still find sources that say they were "stripped of their medals" or "forced to return" their awards. In reality, that never happened, but the propaganda continues.

Tommie and Carlos were not at that meeting because it *was* true that they were banned from the Village—but in any case, they weren't going to go there because they figured the officials wanted to put them out of not only the Village but also the country. So they went to a hotel. Still, I don't see how anyone from the Olympic Committee could have put them out of the country; it wasn't their country. In my mind, these were all just the rumors that were spread to cause confusion among the other athletes and keep them from doing anything else.

Nevertheless, another meeting was called to talk about what other people were going to do in light of what happened to Tommie and Carlos. The outcome of that meeting was still: *You can do whatever you want. What they have done, that said everything right there.* And that's when people started getting ideas: some of the men on the relay teams wore berets, and there were black socks and black shorts and black armbands and things like that, and Ralph Boston was barefoot when he went on the stand to get his medal. I don't know how much of it came across on the television, but many athletes continued the protest despite all the threats to Tommie and Carlos, and I was one of them.

The next day, I ran the 4x100 relay. Even though I had achieved my goal of winning the 100 and felt satisfied, I had to think of my teammates—Barbara Ferrell, Margaret Bailes, and Mildred Netter. I knew we had the best team; the only thing we had to make sure of was that we didn't make any mistakes, like dropping the baton or running out of the passing zone. Barbara had gotten second in the 100, and even though Margaret was only seventeen, she ran well in the 100, placing fifth, and had really been setting the world on fire in the run-up to the Games. The relay was probably most significant for Mildred: the 4x100 was her first race in the Olympics; she didn't run anything else, so it was her only chance to get a medal.

Barbara ran the first leg; she had a good start and was out in front when she passed to Margaret, who ran really well and handed the lead over to Mildred. Mildred had a good race—

such a beautiful curve!—but I misjudged her speed coming up and was a little slow taking off. None of us were used to passing to each other, and even though we had practiced, three of us had to train for the 100 and the 200, so we didn't have that much time for the 4x100—unlike the Europeans, who kept their relay teams the same so they got to work together all year. Despite all that, Mildred and I still had a good pass, and with such a solid lead, the fact that she ran up on me didn't matter. Mildred ran after me almost all the way through the curve, yelling, "Go, Tyus! Go, Tyus! Go!" So I did, and we not only won but set both an Olympic and a world record with a time of 42.8 seconds.

As part of my contribution to the protest for human rights, I had worn black running shorts for the relay, rather than the regular white running shorts that were issued to us—although I'm not sure anyone noticed. But after we won and had been given our medals, we went into the pressroom, and they asked us what we thought about what Tommie and Carlos had done.

"What is there to think?" I said. "They made a statement. We all know that we're fighting for human rights. That's what they stood for on the victory stand—human rights for everyone, everywhere. And to support that and to support them, I'm dedicating my medal to them. I believe in what they did."

I don't remember planning it in advance. I was in support of what the whole movement was about, so I was ready to say something. It was not just what they did in that one moment, I told them. It was about human rights: what had happened to the students in Tlatelolco and what was happening to people all around the world. That's what the whole human rights project has always been about: we are all in this together. That's what I said to the reporters. But none of that got printed, of course, only the fact that I had dedicated my medal—that we all, the whole relay team, had dedicated our medals. That was okay with me—as long as the press understood why we did it.

Later, Mr. Temple asked me, "Did you think it through? Did you think it would have any consequences?"

"I don't think I really cared," I told him. Doing it was just a part of me. I surprise myself sometimes, but that wasn't one of those times. I had my medal. I had graduated. I was going to go and get a job—going to work eight to five, be shut off in some room someplace, and I knew that this Olympics was my opportunity—the moment when people might listen to me, the moment to speak.

Mr. Temple didn't ask me that until later because he wasn't in Mexico City. He had always told us, "Don't just go off doing things and then have to eat your way back home." But he never said whether he approved or disapproved, one way or the other, which to me seemed perfectly consistent with how he always was. I think that Mr. Temple felt that he had done his best to prepare us for the world. He always wanted us to be our own people even if it meant bumping heads with him. If he didn't agree, he wasn't going to say anything, and if he did agree, he might say one thing, but not much more. Because his main question was always, "Is this what *you* want? Is this what you believe in?" As long as you weighed it out and thought about the consequences—what else could he ask for?

Some people felt he could have said more, tried to have more influence, but that was not the man he was. If he ever had said more, I would have listened to him, but nothing would have changed. I was still going to be saying what I said. I would say, "That's me, Mr. Temple. You taught us to speak our minds."

Which to me meant he had been successful at doing the only thing that really mattered to him: making us feel comfortable being ourselves. He also tried to make it so we would enjoy that period in our lives—being in college, being able to travel, doing things that most people would never do. He wanted us to enjoy all of that. He wanted us to feel good about it, but he also didn't want us to just speak without thinking. That was his biggest thing. And it wasn't just about politics. It was about competition as well. Because he would say, "You hear athletes saying, *I'm going to do this,* or, *We're going to do this to this team or that person,* and it doesn't come out that way. Then they have to eat their words."

It makes great stories for reporters, though, when people brag and talk big. That's one of the reasons why I didn't get a lot of press. I was a nightmare for reporters because of my one-worders: "How do you feel?" "Good." "How do you feel about your medal?" "Good." Or "Great"—I changed it up sometimes. But that was me. When I said I was going to dedicate my medal to Tommie Smith and John Carlos, it was probably the longest thing I had ever said to a reporter.

I don't know for sure if there were any repercussions to me from that action. It's a difficult thing to measure. Mr. Temple felt that, because of the whole movement and what Tommie and Carlos did on the victory stand, no one ever really looked at all that I had done: back-to-back gold medals in the 100 and three gold medals total and breaking all kinds of records. But if it was that, it wasn't only that. It was also because I'm not only Black but a woman. Because you'll notice that no one—except Howard Cosell—was trying to notice me or give me a flag even when I had done something that no one else in the world had ever done—before Tommie and Carlos even ran their race and before I dedicated my medal to them. It was bigger than that. At the time, they were not about to bathe a Black woman in glory. It would give us too much power, wouldn't it? Because it would have been a moment, if you think about it: "She won back-to-back gold medals; nobody in the world has ever done that. Let's paint the US all over her—let's drape her in a flag!" You would think. But no. I would never see them hanging a flag on me. Because one thing the Olympics is not about is giving power to the powerless.

I think Mr. Temple would have agreed with that. Although one way I know that he was right about my being overshadowed by Tommie and Carlos is that when anyone wants to talk to me about what I've done, and they ask what Olympic team it was, and I say '68, they say, "Oh, you were with *them!* Those guys, those guys, those guys!" And I say, "No, I won my medal first, so they were with *me.*" I like teasing people. Because that's the first thing they bring up.

In some ways, I'm used to it. I came up in Wilma Rudolph's shadow, so I learned years ago that you have to know who's in the room with you. If the other person in the room is someone like Wilma Rudolph, there's nothing wrong with them getting the attention. And of course it's not just Wilma; if I go into a room and someone is talking to me, and then Serena Williams walks in, no one's going to be talking to me anymore, and my little story is no longer going to be on the page. I'm not offended by that. It's just the rule of the sports game.

So the way it gets talked about now is one thing. But the way it went down at the time, in terms of building the movement—that's a different matter. Sometimes I get asked if the movement would have been better at achieving its goals if it had included women. Of course I am going to say yes. We should have been included in the organizing, should have been consulted. It would have made a difference. But we weren't. Partly it was just a sign of the times, where we were as people, not just Black people but the world: women were expected to follow, to do what the men said. In '68, they weren't thinking about what women in general were saying or doing. No one was. Women's words and women's lives were not considered worthy of attention. That was not a Black thing; it was an all-race, worldwide sexist thing. Men know better, men are stronger. That's what most people thought. But I didn't grow up that way. My parents taught me that I'm just as good or better than anybody, male or female.

So for me, the fact that I and other female athletes were not included in the organizing before the 1968 Olympics was a problem. I can't speak for anybody else. But I felt that bringing us into the organizing would have been consistent with the whole idea of the movement, or at least what the movement came to be: a movement about everybody everywhere who was struggling for human rights. That message of inclusion was the reason I got more involved, started to read and think more about the movement. And considering that it was all about inclusion, it just would have made sense for women to be brought in, front and center.

I had somewhat of an inside source from talking with my ex-husband Art. He was always saying, "If we all band together, it should just work." And I was thinking, *No. It doesn't work that way. You have to include people. You have to include them actively.* No one asked me my opinion. No one asked me, "How do you feel about these things?" And I had feelings, feelings and thoughts, for sure, and if I had had the opportunity in the run-up to the Olympics, I would have shared them. Because I was in a situation that went like this: *I need to graduate from college, and I am trying to go to the Olympics again and be the best I can be when I get there.* Those parts were clear. Those were my goals. But on top of that, I had to think about this: *Once I leave college, what am I going to do with my life?*

That was the main thing going on in my head: *I have a life.*

And my life is getting ready to not be in college. My life is getting ready to be out on my own and trying to have a job. No one was knocking on my door saying, "Could you be the poster child for this or that?" I didn't see anybody asking me to do commercials, I didn't see a shoe company asking me to endorse their product—although I ran in their shoes, they never asked me—and I didn't see anyone trying to give me any money under the table like they did for a lot of the men. That definitely wasn't happening for me, and it wasn't happening for Black women in general. None of those things. So my goal was to graduate from college, go out, and find a job.

Up to that point, my environment had been protective, everything taken care of—my housing taken care of, my food taken care of, everything. But after the Olympics, I was going to be on my own; I had to get a job and find my own housing and put food on the table. I knew my family couldn't help me. And since no one was talking to me about the movement, I didn't know how to make the movement fit with all the things I had to do.

Once I got to Mexico City, it was different. I could be at the meetings and hear what everyone had to say and planned to do and decide if it was an approach that would work for me. One thing I felt the movement needed was a clearer plan. When Mr. Temple would talk to us, back then and even recently, before he passed away in September 2016, he would say, "There was no clear plan—nobody knew what was going to happen!"

And it was true. No one ever put anything down on paper, nothing was ever sent to us—airmail, special delivery, any old way—to say, "Listen, this is how we're thinking." That matters. Because not everyone is in the same place, not in their thinking and not in their needs. It's great when quite a few of us can see a way forward and feel like we can take risks. But a lot of people were looking at the Olympics as their salvation: "I'm going to go to the Olympics, I'm going to win, and it's going to propel me to do all these great things when I get back." That's hard to ask someone to give up. And the person you're asking to do that, if you have not talked to them, included them, you have not given them a chance to ask, "Well, what are we going to do when we get back? Do you have a map or any kind of clue about what's going to happen when you get back, if you do protest?" If they did have a plan, it wasn't shared.

Once they did what they did on the victory stand, I think it was bigger than they ever imagined. Because what Tommie and Carlos did made the world kind of stop. Everybody had to take a breath. And I'm sure they had things in their minds they wanted to say, but when people were throwing fifty questions at them, it was like they hadn't thought about how they were going to say them. They didn't have someone like Mr. Temple telling them all the time: "The press is going to ask questions to provoke you to say the things they want you to say—things that are going to follow you for the rest of your life, so always think before you talk."

I look at it now, and it occurs to me that Tommie and John were not that old; they were in their early twenties, same as me, which is actually very young. John grew up in New York—he had a brashness that Lee and Tommie didn't have, maybe because Tommie was born in Texas and grew up in Lemoore, California, cotton picking, with strict parents and all those kind of things, and Lee Evans grew up similarly, also in California, Madera, picking cotton and grapes. They hadn't had a lot of exposure. And then they were presented with this whole movement by Harry Edwards and some of the other people who were there. And you would have to talk to them to know how it all went down, because as I have said and said, I wasn't there and I wasn't told. But it seems like that must have been a factor.

In any case, in my mind, when you are trying to build a movement, if there are a lot of people who get left behind or are not spoken to, that's a weakness. My thinking is always: *Have we included everyone? Do you think we've talked to everybody?* Some people are going to say, "Well, they're not going to join in no matter what we say." My question is always, "But have you tried? Do you think we have tried enough?" Because everyone wants to be wanted and needed and feel like they're a part. And that wasn't there for us. I'm not upset with them. It's just more that, "How could you *not* think of us? It's the same thing that's being done to us by the powers-that-be. I mean, we're in Los Alamos, New Mexico, and you're in Lake Tahoe, California? No one was thinking of us. How could you not think of us?"

That's a demand that would have brought a lot of women in right there: have the men and women train for the Olympics in the same place. We never could understand why our Olympic Trials, our AAU championships, whatever, were never held together with the men. For what reason could that be? I mean, we were happy if there were twenty people in the stands for our Olympic Trials, but for the men, the stands were totally full. Why couldn't we be together? Didn't they want the women to be seen?

More thinking like that—more thinking about what would have brought more people into the movement—would have helped. When the movement started, its main goal was to make a better world for Black people. So what would have made the world better for Black people at the time? What did Black people need? They needed jobs and housing—same as now. Goals like that would have fit right into the things I was thinking about coming out of college. And I'm sure I wasn't the only one. We were all going to have to get jobs after the Olympics;

we were all going to need places to live. And we could have used our platform at the Olympics to move that forward, to bring more attention to it and gather forces behind it. If we had had those kinds of conversations, it would have made a difference for me. I probably would have spoken to reporters. I would have known what to say. And that would have been worth speaking about—those kind of things, which were already being said, but not by us, and here we had this platform, and we could be heard in a way others wouldn't. That would have been something I'd have totally been on board for. If we had had those kind of conversations, I would have been able to think it through, figure out a way to make it fit with my life.

I also think that it's always true that the more perspectives you have, the better your ideas are going to be—as long as everyone is on the same side. We had a perspective that was different from the Speed City crew. We were Black women, and they were Black men. We were in the East, and they were in the West—they were at San Jose State, and we were at Tennessee State. Like I said, Tommie Smith and Lee Evans grew up in California; they had a West Coast perspective. John Carlos was from New York, so he had a Northeastern perspective. But we were from the South, the Jim Crow South, and that's a very different perspective.

Then there are all the individual differences. I look back at being on a team with just women, and we had so many strong, opinionated women, and also those who were very talkative and boisterous and felt like, "If I stand up, then that's going to count." And then you had the ones who didn't talk, like me, who would sit and—after everybody had said whatever they needed to say—would say, "Well, I think we should look at it this way." And I look at that, and I think maybe that's what the movement needed. It needed someone who could do that—

someone who could listen and reflect. There had to be some people involved who were like that. And it didn't only have to be women; to me, Ralph Boston was one of those guys who is more quiet, more likely to think things through and say, "Well, have you looked at all these things?" And in '68 the question that needed to be asked—and it needed to be answered by as many people as possible—was this: "Do you think people really want to give up all the time they've worked? *Why* would they do that? What would inspire them to do that?" There had to be a good reason. They would have to see a future, one they could fight for.

It wasn't just the women who couldn't see that future. There were a lot of guys who weren't saying anything either. I guess sometimes people stay quiet if they feel like they're not going to be heard. But we really needed to hear from everyone. And if all those perspectives had come together from the start, we might have had a clearer idea of where we needed to go. We might have accomplished more. And—who knows? We might not have gone to the Olympics. There might have been a boycott of the whole Olympic Games. There could have been. I could see that.

But what actually went down was that not enough of the people who were speaking were thinking about what was going to happen *after* the Olympics. What's going to happen *then* if the athletes boycott? Who's going to help them? Because no company is going to want them. And we have to work in order to survive in this world. You can look at what happened to Tommie and John. I mean, things are happening for them *now.* Right after '68, they kind of vanished from the face of the earth. Nobody wanted to touch them at all. It was different for people like Harry Edwards. As Mr. Temple kept saying, "Edwards got his education. Nothing is going to stop him. He has a job." A lot of people say that's kind of Uncle Tom-ish, but I say that was Mr. Temple looking after his girls, because in saying that, he also said, "You have your own mind, you have your own thoughts, and you have to make your own decisions." He never told us not to do something—just before you do it, think it through.

It makes me wonder what would have happened if it had been turned around the other way, if women had been the ones leading from the beginning. I always feel that women in movements have a better understanding of the fact that you are stronger with everybody. If it was our movement, a women's movement, I can't help thinking that we would have been more like, "Let's make sure that we pull in as many people as we can and make them feel like they have a voice." If we are all moving together, wanting the same thing, we'll get it. For women—for Black women in particular—it's just clear: you can't go it alone. Not with everything we have to contend with. And I think also that we Tigerbelles understood very well what it meant to be a team, and what the benefits of teamwork were.

When I look at certain male athletes, it seems like that's less obvious to them. You have a lot of them for whom it's all about them—the individual: *I'm better than this, and I can do all this. Me, me, me.* But that's not what Mr. Temple taught the Tigerbelles. He knew track was an individual sport, but he also knew what worked: you have to be a team. And you have to be a team not only out on the track. You have to be a team in life, here, now. One of Mr. Temple's biggest things was that you had to find friends, friends who were not athletes, friends who were different from you. Because you are going to need help from all kinds of different people in the world.

That is what we were taught: the importance of mutual support. To me, that's what '68 should have been about. Not that

I was able to express it then, and not that anybody asked me, but looking back, that's how I feel, and I guess it's good to spell it out because maybe someone can learn something when they read this book. I don't take it personally that we weren't included, just like I don't take it personally that nobody made that big a deal of my winning the 100 meters back to back. I'm just happy that I got to be a pioneer. And I adhere to the idea that when you're a pioneer you don't necessarily get your day in the sun until the world is ready for you—but that doesn't change the fact that you did what you did. I won those races, and I dedicated my medal to Tommie and John—to the movement. No one can change that.

I say to a lot of young girls—in fact, I'll say it to anybody who asks: if you make history, there's no way they can not put you in it. It may not be the way I want, but every time they talk about the 100 meters, they have to mention my name. Maybe softly. Maybe just once. But they have to. They can't leave you out of history you've made. Somebody is going to find it and write about it and say something about it. If they want to talk about history and be taken seriously, they can't lie. Would I like for it to be more? Now, at this age? If it happens, it happens. If not, oh well. But getting this story told is making me happier than ever. So it is happening. And to me that's good enough.

Another Life to Live

When I came back home after winning in '68, there was another parade in Griffin. At that point, everybody knew who I was, and they were always coming up—Black, white, whatever—saying how proud they were of me, so I got all of that. But as far as what people get in this day and time in terms of attention from the media, there's no comparison. And I'm not even talking about money; I'm just talking about recognition from the press. The whole idea of a small-town person who went and made good—even winning back-to-back gold medals—is a story that could be told and retold. But it was never played up; it was like nobody ever thought about it—not until a male runner did somewhat the same thing some twenty years later.

Nevertheless, I felt that I had done all I could to be recognized as a runner. I had gone to the Olympics twice and won three gold medals and done something that no one else in the world had ever done before. How much further can you go to get on top? I felt at that time, and I still do, that you can't get any better than that. And Mr. Temple had told me just like he told all his girls: "If you can go out when you're on top, that's what you want to do: quit while you're ahead."

I was at that point in '68—and a good thing too, because it was still the sixties, and there was no one out there saying, "Hey, I have a job for you where you can continue to train and go back to the Olympics." Nothing like that was happening. No one ever said, "You can go another year—it would be great if you could win three times in a row." Because I could have gone to the '72 Olympics if I was in that frame of mind and track was still that important to me. And Mr. Temple had also told us we could come back and go to grad school. But I was through with school, and I was pretty much tired of running. I had always said to myself that when it gets to be a job, then it's time for me to end my career. Having Mr. Temple say, "You have to get out there and work, have that eight-to-five"—and thinking he was correct in thinking like that—made me ready to retire as well. Not in a disappointed way. I knew that track was always going to be a part of my life, but it was not going to *be* my life. I had other things to do, another life to live. I mostly thought, *I got to see what else the world has for me.*

I had already accomplished my two goals; I was ready to move on and see what else I could conquer—or not conquer. What I wanted most was to leave Griffin. I thought, *I've lived in Georgia, I've lived in Tennessee, I have not lived in California. I just want to see what California is all about.* I didn't need to travel; through running, I had traveled all over the world and seen a lot of things and learned a lot about myself and other people and what goes on in the world and in other cultures. I did all those things when I was really young, and it helped me to understand people, and I saw that as I got older. I appreciated it. But I was done. I just knew I was going to California, and that was it.

I didn't have a car, or any money, and I wasn't walking or taking the train, so I had to find a way to fly, which I did: I borrowed money from the bank, which to me said I was grown up, a college graduate, and taking on adult responsibilities. Matter of fact, the bank let me have the money just on my name. Five hundred bucks. That was one benefit I got from being an

Olympian: I left Georgia in December, and I had just won the medals in October, which is probably why I got the loan on nothing but my good name—you have to have a good name to borrow money, and at that moment, my name was very good in Griffin.

My family knew I was going to leave. I always said that I wouldn't stay in Griffin, that there was nothing there for me. My mom, of course, didn't want me to go, but I told her, "I'll be back! I'll come back to visit. But I have to go. Griffin is not for me." I couldn't see a way for myself in Griffin, and I didn't see too much change as far as how they treated people of color. I remember that when they integrated the town swimming pool, someone put cement in the water; that's how much they didn't want to share their pool with us. Of course, we got the last laugh because there was still a Black pool, and no one put any cement in that.

Getting to California was simple: I went to the bank, borrowed the money, and got on a plane. Getting a job once I arrived was more complicated. At first I thought I was going to work in Northern California at Foster City Parks and Recreation, but I ended up not taking that job and going to LA instead. LA was all I knew; I didn't know Foster City, I didn't know the Bay Area. So I went to LA, and I stayed with my roommate from college, Marcella Daniel—the one with the study skills. She was teaching at Bret Harte Junior High, and the assistant principal there went to Tennessee State, and his wife at that time used to be the manager of the track team at Tennessee State as well; I was well connected, and it wasn't long before the assistant principal offered me a job. "We could make you a long-term sub," he told me, "but you've got to enroll in school and get your teaching credential."

So even though I was an Olympic gold medalist, I got my first job offer out of college the same way many other people do: I knew someone who knew someone. I couldn't start right away, not until the following fall, because it was the middle of the school year. But at least I could look forward to future employment. I enrolled in school to get my credential and then all I had to do was support myself until it was time to start at Bret Harte.

My next job offer came out of name recognition: I got hired as an assistant research analyst for the Black Studies department at UCLA. They were creating a Black Studies library, and they had me looking up information and putting things in chronological order and making sure all the research got organized in the way they had decided to catalog it. It was nothing I had done before, so I think it's fair to say that they hired me because of who I was. But once I was there, it was never about my Olympic resume or even anything I had learned at school; I was just a research assistant, cataloging research.

I had a feeling I wouldn't be there long. Because I was thinking, *I know I need work, but I need something to grow on too. You can keep me here for six, seven months, then I have to go.* They were just starting to build the Black Studies center and the library, so it was a lot of research, and I could do that, and I knew I was going to grow from it and get something out of it. But I also knew that I was not going to be able to do it for a long period of time. There is only so much growth you can get from creating a card catalog.

It was pretty much the same thing in my next job at Universal Studios. That was when Universal was doing a lot in the Black community, sending people to meetings, listening, receiving suggestions on what they might do to benefit the community. You can't just stand there and give out money; you've got to have some idea of what's needed and wanted. And that was my job: to figure out what was needed and wanted. It was not so much that I was making the plan; the community had to come up with that. I could help tweak it and all, but that was about it. And once again I knew: I would not be doing that for the long term. I had to sit in that Black Tower[22] every day—on the eighteenth floor—whether there were meetings in the community or not. I would be sitting there, alone, in a big office with all these windows, trying to come up with ideas—about what, exactly, I don't know. I don't have that kind of creative mind; I need to have somebody to talk to. If someone came in and talked, or I could talk on the phone, that was fine, but otherwise I would just sit there and think, *There's no meeting in the community today, but I have to show up for work?*

Maybe there was room for growth there—maybe too much room—but I couldn't see it. And although they had hired me because they knew my name, once I was in the door, I was nobody special. Universal was giving money to the community, and I was doing the personal-appearance thing, which meant getting Universal's name out in the community—not "I'm Wyomia Tyus, Olympic athlete," but, "I'm here from Universal, and this is what they're doing." They never once encouraged me to play up the fact that I was an Olympic gold medalist. It was the same then as it is now: companies want to get as much as they can out of you for as little as possible. I didn't find it degrading or anything; I just needed a job, and that was the job I got.

Meanwhile, Art was working for Puma in Berkeley, and around

---

22 The "Black Tower" ("constructed," according to studiotour.com, "of black aluminum and glass") housed the executive offices of Universal Studios. The building was purchased by Comcast in 2013. See http:// articles.latimes.com/2013/ oct/02/entertainment/la-et-ct-comcast-purchases-10-universal-city-plaza-for-about-420-million-20131002.

the same time I came out to California, Puma asked him to move to LA because that's where all the runners were. He was still pursuing me, and his idea was that when he got to LA, we would move in together, get to know each other better, and figure out our relationship.

While I was running and the reporters would write stories about me, they would say Art was my fiancé, but that wasn't true; we had never declared what we were because what we were doing was something that was just not done at that time: we were dating if we saw each other. I was in Nashville and he was in California, and that meant we saw each other at meets or when he surprised me and showed up at Tennessee State. That's what that was. Art and I were not engaged, and I was not planning on marrying him. But for me, coming from my family, you didn't move in with someone unless you were married. If we were going to move in together, which seemed like a good idea at the time, we would have to get married, and that's how I ended up married to Art.

At first we lived in a tiny little bachelor apartment in Westwood, and then everything began to come together a little: Puma started to pay him, and I had my job, so we moved to a bigger place, still in Westwood but closer to UCLA. Art felt that people would be more liberal and more understanding of our relationship there. I didn't know what was going on with that; I just knew that I didn't want to be in a situation where I had to struggle to fit in, seeing that ours was a Black-white relationship. We're still talking the sixties, early seventies, so we knew some extra understanding would be needed. Little did we know that some people are not all that accepting no matter how close to a university they live.

The apartment in Westwood was in a very nice building, with a pool and everything—all the things you want when you're thinking of a place to live in LA—and quite expensive. But there was still racism and all that going on. I can remember getting on the elevator in the evenings after work, and this one man would say, "You're working late tonight."

It seemed like he was saying that to me almost every time I got on the elevator; we must have gotten off work at the same time. "I work late every night," I would tell him at first, but he just could not get his head around the fact that I lived there, and after a while I would say crazy things. "*Mm-hm.* That man of mine works me late *every night.*"

He would just look at me. He didn't know what to think. "Well, how much do you charge to clean and such?"

"You couldn't pay it. You don't have the money to pay what I charge."

"But you're always here *late.*"

"Yes I am—I'm here all night, believe it or not." And then I would just get off the elevator.

You would think it would be different in that area, in a nice place—but it doesn't matter where you go. And I could never get Art to see all that. He would hear people talking and get completely outraged. But I used to tell him all the time: "It doesn't matter where you live or how much money you have. They're not going to change." For me, it was enough that I could humiliate them and maybe make them feel stupid for talking to me like that. But he would stomp and rage, start yelling, sit down, stand up, keep talking all about it, until I said, "I don't have time for that. People going to be stupid, people going to be ignorant, and we have a lot of other things that we need to be concerned about."

Around that same time, I started working at Bret Harte, and I taught there until I was pregnant with my daughter Simone. After she was born, the question came up again: *Where* *are we going to live and get some acceptance?* We were still in the same building, and Art would often be out in the pool swimming with Simone, and one time I was out there with them and somebody from off the street came up to the fence and said, "There's that n***** in the pool!"

Art jumped out of the water—he wanted to fight, but I knew he could not. His fighting was always with his words. I was the fighter in that family, and I wasn't going to be bothered. "See?" I said. "I told you. It doesn't matter where we live. It's not going to be any different."

We lived there for a while, and then in Mar Vista, until we finally bought a house in Laurel Canyon—just a small house. Nothing like you would typically think of when you think of Laurel Canyon. Things were a bit better there when it came to acceptance, but by that time it was clear we had other problems. For one thing, Simone contracted spinal meningitis when she was three. I was on a trip, and she was visiting with my mother for a few days when she got sick, and they called and said I needed to come home. They didn't think she was going to live. It was bad.

She pulled through, but she had a hard road after that. She had to learn to do some things all over again as if she was a newborn. We had to teach her to crawl and then to walk, which took months. And we were constantly with doctors, always with doctors, especially neurologists, and they were never sure how bad it was going to be because spinal meningitis can take effect in so many different ways. Simone was lucky because the only permanent damage she had was hearing loss in one ear. But it took years and a lot of work for her to recover, doing things like taking gymnastics just so she could relearn how to balance.

Art's mom was helpful; she knew some of the best doctors in the world—at least it seemed like they were the best to me because they were helping to care for my child. "You *need* to get this person," she would say, and she was always looking things up and writing things down and trying to find out who was the best. So we had some great neurologists, and I was thankful for that. But Simone's illness took a toll on my marriage because I had no time for Art; I was all about my child.

It was not only that, though; we were just too different. Somehow I could never see our marriage, not even when I was in it. I mean, I knew I cared for him, I knew he cared for me, but there was always going to be a divide no matter where we were or what we did—even if we were only doing simple things. We would go to a movie, and afterward, if he had his way, we would have to go and talk about it. And I would be thinking, *Oh gosh, no. Oh no. Another talker.* And these were not just any movies, either; they were foreign movies. Art loved foreign movies, and I had to sit there and read those subtitles *forever,* and I just felt punished. But I did it. It was torture, but it gave me a better understanding and appreciation for a lot of good things that I would never have had time for in any other way. It let me know that I could do "cultured" things, things that would supposedly make me grow to be a better person. And that's how I started looking at it, kind of like how Mr. Temple would tell us to be when we went on trips. I knew that it was not going to hurt me, that it was going to help me gain knowledge—somehow. Not that I was ever going to use the knowledge I got from reading subtitles. But still. It gave me a flavor for languages, and that was the key.

Art encouraged me to see it that way. "Wyomia," he would say, "you need to grow."

But I knew all about growing, and I was in charge of my own growth. "You can't change me," I would tell him. "I'm still going to be who I was when you met me: a Black girl from a small town in the Deep South."

He accepted that, but over time it became clear that the person he cared for and loved so much was also a person he kind of disliked. Because I was someone who spoke my mind, and if he did something that I didn't like, I didn't try to clean it up. I would just say it.

For example, when I was in Mexico in 1968, Art was there too; I was running the race of my life, and he was being thrown in jail for trying to get Puma shoes into Mexico City even though Adidas had signed contracts for exclusive rights. When he got out of jail, he claimed it was Adidas that put him there. "You can't wear Adidas shoes!" he told me. "How is that going to look once we're married? I work for Puma, and you run in Adidas!"

"I don't care how it's going to look," I said. "I don't know what you want me to do."

"I brought you some Puma shoes. You need to wear them in the final for the 100."

"I do? Just like that? I'm just supposed to wear them because you said it? And because they . . . I don't even know who threw you in jail. It really doesn't matter because I'm here letting you know: I'm not going to wear Puma shoes. I'm going to wear Adidas."

"How is it going to look?! What will I say to my boss?"

"I couldn't care less about your boss. And evidently you don't care too much for me. It's the day before the final for the 100, and you're busy talking to me about a damn pair of shoes. I could give a . . . I don't understand. So I suggest you go somewhere else and think about what you have said to me because I don't think we even need to talk anymore. I'm done."

We got past it, but we never really made up. Because years later he would still say, "Someone is going to come up to you and ask, 'What shoe did you wear in the Olympics?'"

"And I will say to them, 'The one that won. The shoe that won. On the woman who won.' Who's going to care?"

Those were the kinds of problems we had; we just had different priorities and ways of looking at the world. And eventually we both understood: *This is not going to work.*

"We need to get out of this," I told him, "before we fully dislike each other. We have a child, and it doesn't make sense for her to come up under this. You went through that with your parents. I'm not going through that with my kid."

His parents—both highly educated people, good people—had divorced early, so he had some experience with that. But I didn't know anything about divorce. I came from a family where my dad and my mom were always there, and if they did fight or have arguments, guess what? We never heard it. We never knew nothing about it. Letting your children listen to you fight was not what married life was supposed to be. And that's all I knew.

So I told him: "I don't want my child growing up hearing me yelling at you or you yelling at me. I just want her to know that she has two loving parents. And these two loving parents—it's not that they don't love her; they're just not in love with each other anymore. We just have to split."

So that's what we did.

Making a Way

I have always felt that athletes should be paid—you could say that was a kind of a life goal of mine—so when I heard about the International Track Association (ITA) paying track athletes to compete against each other, I knew I was going to give it a try. I used to say all the time that if they had professional track, I would come out of retirement, and I had had my kid so it seemed like a good time. I started biking and running—not as much running as I used to, but we lived maybe two miles from the beach, and I used to bike to the beach and back home, and that started getting me in shape.

When the ITA started, they only had one event for women, which was the 60. *Well,* I thought, *at least you're going to have an event for women.* I was hoping that if I took this opportunity, maybe it could help propel things forward and there would be more events for women and more opportunities for female athletes to get paid for doing what they do best. In the beginning I was hopeful. There were three other women racing, generally, and one alternate, so there were five of us: Barbara Ferrell, Lacey O'Neal, Mable Ferguson, Vilma Charlton, and myself. All five of us ran the 60 because the 60 was all they had.

From the start, it wasn't everything I had hoped. We had to travel a lot—from LA to New York to Texas to Tokyo and Montreal—and they paid travel and hotel for the whole team, meaning four of us women and a full roster of men. Because, of course, there was more than one event for the men. They claimed that men and women got the same money, but I never believed it. They paid by the race, and if you placed, they paid more. If you were a woman you always placed, but you just had that one chance to run. So for all kinds of reasons, it wasn't a lot of money, but at least we got paid.

When the ITA started, it was mostly indoors because lots of people like indoor track; it's a closer arena, and you can kind of catch hold of it, really see the athletes. Unfortunately, the league never took off, partly because the whole idea was at odds with the amateur track-and-field associations. And then the ITA officials added another race for women, but it wasn't what I was hoping for at all: they started hosting events where they had women race against men just so the women could lose—for "entertainment." To "bring in the crowds." I guess, at that time, it was considered entertainment—just not the kind of entertainment I liked. But I still thought: *If this is going to get athletes paid* . . . That was my only reason for participating, and I only raced against the men a few times.

The first time, we were at a meet in Atlanta and ran 100 yards, the women sprinters against the men sprinters. We had a head start—if I remember correctly, we had ten yards on them—because otherwise we would have been beat right out of the blocks. I already knew that. It would have been different if I had still been running under Mr. Temple. If I had gotten a ten-yard start in my heyday, they would have never caught me. But not at that time. I was in shape, but I was not in shape to beat them. So they won. I also raced against Brian Oldfield, who was a shot putter. We ran 60 yards, and I think I had a two-yard, maybe a five-yard start ahead of him. And he won too.

Needless to say, it wasn't long before I didn't want to have anything to do with that. It didn't seem to me like something that was going to promote female athletes. First of all, the males were always going to win—always. Maybe if you have not such a great male athlete running against a great female athlete, then that would be a good contest, maybe the photo-finish kind. That's what they were thinking, I'm guessing. But the way the races were set up, that was never going to be the case. For one thing, there was the fact that someone like Brian Oldfield was never just a shot putter: he also played football, so he had some speed, and he also had that kind of training and competition even after the Olympics.

Then there was the distance: 60 yards. In 60 yards, I'm really just getting started. It might have been different if they'd had us running other races; over long distances, women have a better chance. But in sprints it's quite different. The men are always going to beat me in a sprint. I know for a fact that's going to happen—unless I'm ten and the boy is also ten. I can beat him at ten. I can beat him at twelve. But when you get to be older, unless the male athlete is not that good, or he's not a sprinter, he's going to win. I was running the 100 meters in eleven flat, and the men at the time were running it in ten something. If you give me ten yards, all you're doing is breaking it even. They're still going to beat me. And where's the entertainment in that?

In the beginning, women running against guys was never a part of it, but when the league started having trouble making money, they wanted to do it more and more often. We wouldn't go for that—*I* wouldn't go for that; that was not my cup of tea. But the "entertainment" events weren't the only problem: I had decided after '68 that I was done with running, and my experience with the ITA helped me to see that I had made the right decision—despite the fact that in the second year I won every race I entered. I had come out of retirement to see if I could grow and make some money out of it, but as it turned out, it was not a growth experience; it wasn't even a very good way of making a living, which was and had to be my main concern at the time. I stayed in the league until it shut down, which means I didn't stay for very long: they couldn't sign up anybody new after the Montreal Olympics and called it quits in '76.

The next opportunity I saw to make a way for women in sports was through the Women's Sports Foundation (WSF). The WSF started around the same time as the Women's Superstars, another sports "entertainment" enterprise that I was involved with in the seventies. For the Superstars, they had different competitions: running, cycling, basketball, bowling, tennis, and an obstacle course, to name a few. The first year, I didn't complete the competition because that was when Simone got sick, but the second year I was there the whole time. What started out as a game, a fun way to make some money, gave me a way to get to know other women athletes and ended up as a launch pad for something much bigger.

For Superstars, you could choose seven out of a total of ten events to compete in, but you were not allowed to be in any events related to your specialty. This meant I couldn't be in any of the running events, which was not fair, I felt, because I was a sprinter; I should have been able to run the longer distances. Those were the rules, though, so I did other things. I was a good bowler—not a 300 bowler, but I could keep a score of 180, 200—so I bowled, and I learned to play tennis, and I even tried cycling. That was a little too strenuous, but I tried it. I tried everything; I just wanted to stay in the mix.

At the Superstars, you got paid even if you didn't win; everybody got points, and everybody got money for the points they earned. At least, I know they paid the first five all right, and then the money went down and down and down. You also got some publicity because it was televised. In addition to all that, I just enjoyed it—trying to tackle all those new sports and be good at them, knowing that I couldn't be good at all of them, but making it my goal to at least finish in the top two or three. I also enjoyed just sitting around with the other women after each event and talking about our issues. Because, of course, at the same time as the Women's Superstars, they were having the Men's Superstars, and the men were getting bigger bucks than us. So all that was being talked about the whole time we were there.

Not that they brought the Superstar women together to have a meeting of the minds; it just happened: one minute we were competing against each other, and the next minute we were talking about what we could do if we worked together. It was Billie Jean King, the tennis player, Micki King, a diver, Donna de Varona, a swimmer, Mary Jo Peppler, a volleyball player, Sheila Young, a speed skater and cyclist, Joan Joyce, a softball player, and myself. There were other women, even early on, but those were the ones I remember talking with at the Superstars. We decided we should do whatever we could to get women more involved in sports and get people to recognize the women who were already in sports.

At that time, Billie Jean King was getting a lot of publicity, so she was able to say more about that aspect of her professional life than anybody else. She always had the right attitude for bringing people together—no "I'm Billie Jean King, and I need to be over here while you stay over there" type of thing. Very down-to-earth. She never wanted anyone to feel like they were different from her even when she was very well-known. You felt like you were just hanging out. Even now, when I see her or go to a place where she is, she's always trying to talk to everyone and make them feel comfortable.

And even though none of us others had ever gotten as much notice as Billie Jean King, we all had experiences, and we all learned from sharing them. That's what led to the Women's Sports Foundation: us all sitting around talking about the things that had happened to us, things that had *not* happened to us, and how we could get things to change. What could we do *as* women athletes *for* women athletes? We would have meetings here and there, especially on the West Coast because I think Billie Jean King was living in Palo Alto at the time. The other women knew a lot more people than I ever would, but everybody brought something, and we all agreed: "We need to do something."

We started hosting Women's Sports Foundation dinners, where the core people, those of us who started it, would all be introduced, and companies would pay for tables and for an athlete to come and sit at their table. It just started out very small and then began to grow. I think the first one was here in California, but it didn't catch on that much until they moved it to New York. Then it was like a snowball that kept rolling and rolling and getting bigger and bigger. The more we spoke up, the more women in general started to talk about it, and soon lots of different women were saying the same thing: "I always wanted to be involved in sports, but there was never an avenue for me. So I gave up."

We wanted equal rights for women—not just for women to have a playing field, but also for women to have the motivation and leadership to do well on that field. By that time, they had passed Title IX,[23] which made it so that programs with federal funding had to take steps to make sure that girls and women

---

23 Title IX was signed into law in 1972 by none other than Richard Nixon. You can read more about Title IX—and the Women's Sports Foundation—at https://www.womenssportsfoundation.org/advocate/title-ix-issues/history-title-ix/history-title-ix/.

were not discriminated against when it came to playing sports. For me, this never meant that, for example, a school should have a women's baseball team even if there were no women who could play or wanted to play, because that would just lead to more negative stereotypes about women and sports. There has to be merit to what is going on. I think everybody pretty much felt that way, but in my mind that was the main thing. So if they asked me about it, I would say, "I'm not here to demand that just because you're a woman and you're at a school and they have a men's baseball team, then you've got to have a women's team." Why would you use resources for that? But there are plenty of sports that women want to be involved in, and the money should be there for them. They should have the opportunity to train and play and learn to excel even if they're not turning out the crowds. Because there are a lot of men's teams that, when they started to play, couldn't play well either. Nobody came to see them, but they still got that chance.

As time went on, I was amazed by how many people spoke up about it. And I noticed that, for many people, it wasn't so much, "I couldn't do it," but more, "I didn't do it because no one encouraged me" or "No one ever wanted to see what I could do" or "There was never a program there for me." And however it had gone down for them, for people my age and even younger, they were all together on one thing: "That's not going to happen to my daughter." That's what made the Women's Sports Foundation grow and grow: "I'm not going to let this happen to my child. And I'm not going to let it happen to my grandkids or my neighbor's child, either."

Slowly, slowly, people's minds started to change, at least partly thanks to our work. I was at an event recently, and one of the sponsors, a woman, came right up to the podium and said, "I just want to thank Wyomia Tyus because the Women's Sports

Foundation and the passing of Title IX helped me so much." She was like many of the women I had talked to since starting the WSF: there had been no sports opportunities for her, and she was never encouraged, so she did her best on her own. Then, by the time she got some encouragement, it was too late for her dreams and desires, and she couldn't continue. But just knowing about the organization had affected her.

I cannot tell you how many women came to me afterward to tell me similar stories. And I kept thinking, *Gosh, that was so many years ago, but how they remember*. That feeling of being cheated. It made me think about how many women could never finish their dreams or do what they wanted to do. And it also made me appreciate how amazing it was for me and the other Tigerbelles to be able to have done what we did when it was truly not fashionable, not at all encouraged, particularly for Black women.

Living it, you don't think about it; you just do it. I was one of those people who, when facing obstacles, thought, *No, that doesn't apply to me*. And I have had several women say to me, even recently: "If I could have been as strong as you and just not cared—just kept on doing what I loved and cared for—things would have been so different." I believe them. And it makes me feel grateful—for my father, always encouraging me to be myself and be comfortable with myself; for my mother, understanding what I was capable of and not letting me come home that first summer; for my brothers, pulling together to support my mom and support me and leave me free to go to Tennessee State; and for Mr. Temple, seeing my potential at that meet in Fort Valley, Georgia, back when I was fifteen, and always making me believe I had something to contribute. Trying to make it so that every woman has that kind of support is what the WSF is all about.

I am still committed to the work of the WSF, and there is still plenty of work to be done. These days, the WSF gives out a lot of scholarships and puts on a lot of events so that young girls can be introduced to and become involved in all different kinds of sports. It has gotten very big, and I'm not involved in it as much as I used to be because I appreciate the fact that they need new blood. They need the people of today, people who can travel, young people who young women can identify with. That's what's supposed to happen, in my opinion. I figure it's enough to be the pioneer, get something started, and then, as long as they don't forget you, let it fly.

When the WSF first began, I was very involved, both because of what I wanted to do for others and because of what the WSF did for me. It let me know that I was not alone, that the fact that I had accomplished all that I had accomplished and wasn't getting much recognition wasn't about me. It wasn't personal. It was bigger than any one person—much bigger.

And of course it's not true that I didn't get *any* recognition. I got gigs here and there that honored my achievements and let me show off what I knew—like in 1976 when I worked as an announcer for the Olympics in Montreal. That was very different from the experience of being at a track-and-field meet as a participant. For one thing, they didn't present the events in the order that they happened; it was all about highlights, all about television. At that time, the announcers were people like Keith Jackson, O.J. Simpson, Frank Gifford, Bill Russell, George Foreman, and Chris Schenkel, and they would work with athletes to add expert commentary to their reporting of each event. The athlete was never the lead; there was always someone else with you. You would go in the studio after the event was over—someone else would have called it live—and then they would edit your comments into the tape. They would guide you, ask you what you thought about something they had noticed. And this was not just for me—not something that they did to make up for the fact that I was so quiet. They did it with everybody, and I was glad because I never thought it could happen—I was shocked they even asked me because of my reputation of not being much of a talker. But I guess that showed that I can talk when I have to, if it's part of a job. I mean, at least I knew what I was *supposed* to do. Nowadays, I'm more in tune with the fact that you've got to speak up if you want to do that kind of work, but back then I was still comfortable with being quiet.

I also had one or two people in my corner, so to speak, for the long haul. One was Howard Cosell. He was always backing me, trying to get me involved, trying to get my name out there. He was the one who would always announce—any time he had an opportunity to anyone who would listen: "This young lady has won back-to-back 100 meters!" He knew his stuff. So he was one of the people who helped me out.

I can remember in 1984, when they had the Olympic Games in Los Angeles, they had Olympians bring in the Olympic flag, and I was one of them. But Howard had pushed for me to be the person who passed the torch to Rafer Johnson, who won the gold for the decathlon in 1960 and was chosen to light the cauldron at the opening ceremony. The people in charge didn't want to commit to using me. They wanted me to try out first. "We have to know," they told me, "that you can run around the track."

That was a bit much for me. I mean, can I run around a track and carry a torch? I don't understand. But Howard said, "Just do it. Just let them see that you can do it because I'm pushing for you to be the one."

Anyone could see that I could do it; I was only thirty-nine.

If I had to prove that I could do it, to me that meant that they were saying, "We're not going to let you do it." Because I never thought they would let a Black person pass to a Black person. That was my first thought, anyway, but I was wrong. In the end, they got Gina Hemphill-Strachan, the granddaughter of Jesse Owens, who wasn't even a runner, which made me feel like they *really* didn't want me. But Howard kept pushing for me to do it because even though I already had the spot for the flag, he thought that would be the best thing to do—the most prominent thing. I did eventually get to carry an Olympic torch many years later when it came through Griffin before the Summer Olympics in Atlanta in 1996, but that was not until after Howard had passed away.

Howard Cosell was someone who understood what I had done and wanted me to get my accolades, and he tried to set things up so I could get them. But most of the time it was a lot more random than that. There were so many jobs! Although I didn't get to carry the torch at the 1984 Olympics, I did work for *Sports Illustrated* during the LA Games. They hired athletes to sit in the stands with their biggest patrons and fill them in on what was interesting about the athletes, what the main rivalries were, answering any questions they might have, and improving their experience of the events. *Sports Illustrated* had rented a ship that was moored in San Pedro, just outside of LA, and we all stayed on the ship, the athletes as well as the patrons, and every three days or so they would take us out onto the ocean for wining and dining. It was good work—I got to meet a lot of different people and had a lot of fun—but it wasn't long-term.

Around that same time I also did work for Coca-Cola; they hired Nancy Thies Marshall, who was a gymnast, Jennifer Chandler, a diver, and myself to do a women's tour, traveling around and talking about our experiences and encouraging women to get involved in sports. We would go into a city, and they would book us on as many TV and morning radio shows as they could. Also, if a big sports event was happening, they would book us just to show up, be seen, talk to young girls about sports, and speak with the press if the opportunity arose.

I appreciated those kinds of jobs as experiences—not to mention the fact that they helped to put food on the table— but I knew that I had still not found my place. I had so many different jobs, and at each new job I would meet new people, and later those people—and this still happens—would call and say, "I heard you do this or that. Can you do that for us?" A lot of my jobs came that way, from word of mouth, through chance encounters: you meet people, they offer you work, you analyze the job, and if the job is not something that's going to intrude on your values, you take it. So I did all kinds of things. I even coached track for a school year at Beverly Hills High. After that, every time I sent out my resume, the people who saw it would say, "Oh, you were at Beverly Hills High! How was that?" And I would have to say that it was not much: I was not a teacher, and I was not in the classroom. I went there at three o'clock every day and helped them work out at the track. It was an after-school program, and I wasn't even making a full salary. It didn't matter to them that I was an Olympic champion; they weren't going to give me any more money to stay there. I was only doing it because I had bills to pay, and I could never figure out why everyone thought it was so great. But I guess it did look good on a resume. And that was a good thing, because I needed work.

Although being an Olympic champion didn't lead to steady employment, I was recognized in other ways, like when I was inducted into the US Track and Field Hall of Fame in 1980 and then into the US Olympic Hall of Fame in 1985. I'm proud of all my inductions; they all have special meaning even if they didn't change the course of my life. They were just moments: you go to wherever it is, introduce yourself, tell what you have done, and then they give you your plaque and send you about your merry way.

These days, they may do some more hoopla for some people, but not at that time. I mean, they really want to honor the athletes; that's genuine. They respect the athletes and want to show that they appreciate them. But it's not as if they see the events as a way to launch people into new careers or boost their old ones. And even if the organizers saw things that way, they can't force the companies to take anyone on.

But if being an Olympic champion did not make my life easier—or at least not very much easier—I'm okay with that. Because at the end of the day, I got to have that experience. I got to see things that I never would have seen otherwise and meet people I never would have met and try to understand who they were, their culture, their ethnicity. I got to go to the Olympics twice, and grow as a person, as a human being, into who I am today. And I am very appreciative of that.

And I got to run. The running was wonderful. In some ways, it was a means to an end, but I still enjoyed it, all of it, the whole process, the part of winning and the part of losing. The part of practicing was not my favorite: the preparation, the drills, all the stuff leading up to the running. But there were times when I really enjoyed that too. I liked to sweat, and I liked to see the progress I was making. For example, I didn't always have a great start—'68 was an exception—so if one day I did have a great start, I would feel very good about it. It was almost like I had little mind games I would play so that I could always notice what I did well.

I have never thought of myself as someone who needs things to be perfect, who needs for things to always work out, but people keep telling me I'm like that, so I guess I am. I used to argue with people, used to say, "It doesn't have to be perfect; it just has to be right for me." And I would think: *I just want to get out of the blocks like everybody else. That's not perfect. That's just being there with them. I don't want to be left behind. It's all about being there with them.*

11

Getting Out of the Blocks (Like Everybody Else)

Proud to be recognized by my hometown. (Photo by Duane Tillman.)

One way or the other, I was able to make ends meet— because I worked hard at it. Because I was always out there. Sometimes I took jobs I did not want, and sometimes I took jobs that I shouldn't have taken because they set the wrong precedent. For example, in the beginning when I would do speeches and appearances, I would do them for free, thinking that would be a way to get in the door. As it turns out, when people hear that you've done something for free, they don't want to pay you to do it ever again. And if they do pay you, they only want to give you a little bit of money. That was not going to work for me. I was not living high on the hog, ever, but I had to live. And after my divorce, I still had to live, and I had a kid to raise, and although I got child support, that money wasn't for me; that was for Simone to do things that she needed to do, to go to the school that she wanted to go to, to do whatever was best for her.

So I did the work I needed to do. I didn't do things that would harm me or that I would hate later on in life; I always tried to look at each job as a step in the right direction: if I do this, then it will get me closer to someone who's going to see that I can be an asset to them, a person of value. It's very difficult, promoting yourself, and by nature I am not the one to do it. But there was nobody else willing to promote me, no one who wanted to say, "Hey, look, I could represent you. We could do this." I was just flying by the seat of my pants. But I was also always trying to learn. When I went to an awards dinner or a WSF event, I would listen to people and think, *I need to be a little more outgoing. I should be saying that.* I remember being at one dinner, sitting around a table with three or four people just talking about a lot of different kinds of things, and after a while this one lady said, "Those women, those other athletes, are all trying to figure out how to get ahead, and you're just sitting here talking to the common people. You need to be over there talking to *those* folks!"

And I thought: *I like it here. I don't want to be over there.* And that was another growth lesson: That was just not going to be me. I was not going to be the person talking to people I didn't want to know just to get ahead. The corporate world was not the place for me. And once I figured out what I wasn't going to do and who I didn't want to be, I needed to find where I *should* be. Around that same time, I also decided that if anyone wanted me to speak or make an appearance, they would have to pay me.

But since no one was tripping over themselves trying to get me to do either of those things, I had to find more regular work, and that's how I came to be employed by the Los Angeles Unified School District. The first job I had with LA Unified was as a facilitator in a student integration program that started after they ended mandatory busing. At that time, LA had a so-called Black area and a Latino area, a white area and an Asian or Pacific Islander area; although all of them were actually pretty mixed, the schools were not fully integrated. The student integration program would pull schools from as many of the different areas as they could to make it as diverse as possible. Four schools would come to the camp—high schoolers, junior high schoolers, and elementary school kids, but not all at the same time—and they would stay for two and a half days, doing hikes and, if they were high school or middle school kids, talking about racism and sexism and what they thought their roles were in making change.

When the kids first came, we would split them up into racially mixed hiking groups and cabin groups. Then we would spend the better part of the first day and the next morning doing team-building activities. Once we had done all that work bringing everybody together with people who were different from them, we would divide them back up for a discussion about racism: white here, Black there, however they classified themselves—although if you were a white person you couldn't say, "I'm Black and I'm going to sit here in the Black group." But people of mixed heritage could choose where they wanted to go. When they were all in their groups, we would spend a whole hour just talking about them, asking them questions like: "How do you feel about being who you are? What's it like to be a member of your group?" And we would write everything they said down on a chart.

After that chart was done, we would say: "Okay, that's how you feel about yourselves. How do you think society sees you? When people see you, what do you think they think of you?" And then all the stereotypes would come out, and we would write those down too. We wouldn't have enough *paper*.

Once they were done charting what they thought about themselves and what they thought others thought about them, we would ask them about each of the other groups: the Black group and the white group and the Latino group and the Asian/Pacific Islander group and so on: "How do you view people who are different from you? How do you view white people? How do you view Latinos?" And again, all the stereotypes would come out.

Everything anyone said was written down, and at the end of the allotted time, we put the charts up on the walls and everybody walked around and viewed them. And oh, the fury, the anger, the people sitting down with *big* spaces between themselves and the other groups. They're not sitting with their friends anymore. They're asking, "How could you say that? How could you allow *anyone* to say these things?" And then we would have to diffuse all that.

To me, it was interesting that, when talking about negative stereotypes, no one ever looked at it as what *they* thought. They would say, "Well, we don't think that; that's what other people think!"

And we would come back at them: "You must think it too because you put it up there. We didn't make you say it; we just asked the question. You could have just said that you had no comment or made it clear that that was not how you feel."

The main thing was that once you've opened it up, it's a can of worms, so to speak, and you have to sit there with them and bring it back together. All the students who stayed the two and a half days could see that people view others differently, that they attach stereotypes to you, that they look at you and the first thing they look at isn't necessarily what you want them to see. But then, how do you look at others? Are you looking for what they truly are or just confirming what you've heard about them? It could be very humbling, but it could also be very equalizing: *everybody* gets stereotyped and *nobody* likes it. And then you just go from there.

I enjoyed that job because it was something I didn't know much about—an opportunity to learn, a step in a new direction. They gave us training, which not only helped a lot with the camps but also gave me tools to use in my own life. Some people have written that I participated in the student integration program as a form of activism, as a way of helping Black youth, but that is not true; it was never something I did as activism. I was doing it as work, and the camp was open to all the students in LA Unified, not just the Black students.

I worked at the student integration program for six or seven years, but then they ended the program, and I was looking at not having a job again. Fortunately, there were other things going on in my life.

Before I started working on student integration, I met my current husband, Duane Tillman, at the wedding of one of my best friends, Cora, who went to Tennessee State but was not a Tigerbelle. Like I said, Mr. Temple always preached that you need all kinds of friends: you need people who are smarter than you in your life because you can always learn from them, and people who are not involved in sports so that everyone you know is not having the exact same experiences as you. You don't want to have to talk about sports every time you sit down. You want to be able to talk about the whole wide world. Cora and another friend of mine, Clara, play that role in my life.

I was separated from Art and going through my divorce then, and considering that and my responsibilities as a bridesmaid, finding a date was not on the top of my mind. Duane was also in the wedding party; he worked for LA County with Ken, the groom, and I got to know him over several days because we had rehearsals and all that. At one point, I took Cora aside and said, "Ken's friend Duane? He's nice-looking."

"You got too much on your plate," she told me, "to be talking about anyone like that."

"Well, yes, but he's still good-looking."

"Yes. And that's his girlfriend over there."

"Oh. Okay." And that was the end of that.

Then Duane and his girlfriend broke up, and Cora and her husband broke up, but Ken and Duane were still friends, and Ken and I were still friends, and we used to talk all the time. To make a long story short, one night some years after their divorce, we were talking, and I said, "Where's your friend Duane? I think he's nice-looking. I should go out with him one day."

"Yeah, you should," said Ken. "You want me to give you his number?"

"I can't do that!"

"*You* can't do that?" he said. "You? The one who believes that women can do anything?"

"It's not that. I just don't think he even knows I'm around."

"Oh," said Ken, "don't worry. He likes you too."

"Were you *talking* about me?"

"I didn't say that. I just said he likes you. I'm going to give you his number. You always say that if you see something you want, you have to go get it. That's what you believe. Call him."

"Yeah, but—I don't know. I have to think about this." Because

I could still remember Cora saying, "You got to get your life together!" At that point, it was about three years after I had first met Duane at the wedding, and my life was still only somewhat together. At least I was divorced; that was one step in the right direction.

Anyway, I called him—I called him that night because Ken would not let me go without doing so. We didn't go anywhere that first time I asked him out. He had said he would stop by at nine, but it wasn't until ten thirty that I got the call: "You have a visitor."

I lived in a gated community, so Duane had to get past the guard. I also came from a school that said when you tell some-one you are going to be someplace, you are there *on time.* So when Duane wasn't there at nine fifteen, I put my pajamas on. I was in the mood to watch television and do nothing. But still, when I got that call from the gatehouse, I said, "Well, yes, you can let him in. Tell him where to park."

When Duane came up, I still had my pajamas on. I wasn't going anywhere. "I didn't think you were coming," I told him. "You didn't call."

He didn't have much of an excuse for being late—there's no excuse, unless you call—but we sat and talked, and when he left, around twelve, he said, "Maybe we could try this again."

"Maybe. We'll see."

He called a couple of days later. He and Cora were going to a New Year's Eve party; I went with them, and after that, Duane and I were together. We didn't get married right away, but now we've been together for what seems like forever. Duane is the type of person who just says, "If that's what you want to do, then do it," which has always worked for me. He doesn't like to fly, so most of the time when I go on trips, he stays home. He has always been very supportive of me, and he has always given me space; he's very giving in general. When I worked for ABC in 1976, he came to the Olympics in Montreal, despite the fact that he doesn't like to travel, just so we could bring Simone. So right from the beginning, the three of us made a nice little family.

To me, it's important for children to know both sides of the family. Every summer, Simone would go to my mom's in Georgia for a month, and then she would go to see Art's mom Pearlie in Berkeley. Pearlie is from Montreal, and her family is there, so Simone sometimes went to Canada in between Georgia and Berkeley to see that side of the family too.

Before Simone would go to Georgia, she would practice trying to talk Southern, because when she first went there, her cousins sat her down and said, "Talk." They liked the way she spoke. Which was not Southern. "She speaks so proper!" they would say, and then they would just sit there and look at her. "Just talk! Say something! Say anything!"

She hated it. "They just want me to talk all the time!" So she conjured up in her head that, before going to Georgia, she would practice saying *y'all* and all that. And then she would come to me to see how she was doing.

"You got to talk a little slower," I would tell her.

"Mommy, *you* don't talk that way."

"I did, and I still do sometimes. You can hear the twang."

After a year, she had gotten it down, talking like that, and then she would leave there and go to Canada, or go to Pearlie's in Berkeley, and it was a whole different accent and a whole different culture.

My mom was always saying things to Simone like, "You can't do this, you can't do that—nothing can happen on my watch!" Strict. And then in Berkeley, Pearlie would have her enrolled in everything, from tennis to art classes, whether she wanted them or not, or Simone would go off to Canada for a week and that would be a whole other lesson, because they were outdoor people and they would swim in lakes and travel to all different parts of the country. It was really good for her. She learned a lot, and I was happy for her.

My son Tyus came into our lives in 1979, and from the time he was a little boy, he had those thick Tyus eyebrows, just like my father. One time we were in a store in Griffin, and some of my relatives saw him, but they didn't know that he was my child. They went right up to him and said, "You must be a Tyus. You got those eyebrows—those Tyus eyebrows."

In addition to the Tyus eyebrows, Tyus has the Tillman height—and the Tillman asthma. When he was little, I was in a doctor's office every week and the emergency room at least once or twice a month—not just stopping in but staying over. It seemed that it would only happen late at night. His regular doctors worked out of UCLA, and I used to drive very fast to get him there, pass through every red light, just flying. He had been going to UCLA forever, so they knew him, which made things much easier. They would say, "Oh Tyus, you're here again?" And they would make him feel comfortable even though he could hardly breathe.

Not that he ever let his illness take over his life. He's a fighter that way. He was always the kid who wanted to do what all the other kids were doing even when it was not the best thing for him—like when he decided that he needed to play flag football. He's allergic to grass and pollen and weeds, so he would have to put on gloves and a long-sleeved shirt and have his legs completely covered. That way, if he fell in the grass, he wouldn't have such a bad reaction. But no matter how many attacks he had, he would always find a way to do whatever he wanted. He has a lot of his mama in him. When Tyus was eight or nine, I let him sit in on an interview I was doing, and the reporter asked him, "What do you think about your mom? About the fact that she has won gold medals and can run really fast?"

"She's not very fast," Tyus told him. "I can beat her. I beat her all the time. She's not fast at all. Matter of fact, she's very slow."

That was the last time I ever let him beat me—who's slow now?—and the last time I let him sit in on an interview. Because he told things out of school. By that time, he had become quite a talker, and he's still a talker to this day. You wouldn't think that such a big talker could come from such quiet parents, but he did.

A lot of people send their children "back South," and I sent mine east and north as well because I wanted them to know their families, and their families' cultures, which can be very different from what we have in California. Family is one of the most important things to me, and I wanted them to see the difference in how people live. My great-aunts—the ones who used to tell me that I shouldn't be running?—they were twins, and I wanted my children to know all about them: the way they talked and the crazy things they said and the fact that they dipped snuff. My kids did not know anybody in LA who dipped snuff. They didn't necessarily like it, not any more than I did, but there were their aunties, trying to kiss them, saying, "Don't be scared of me, I'm your family!"

Knowing that someone who is so different from you is also a part of you makes you a stronger person. It helps you to be able to appreciate life, to really laugh at life, to see the things that people do as part of a culture. I wanted my kids to know that my dad's side of the family is different from my mom's side, and both are different from Duane's family in Ohio and his grandmother who grew up in Tennessee. This is your family. This is part of you, so you should appreciate difference and not put other people down. You might find yourself ten years from now doing the kinds of things your great-grandmother used to do, so you should know: This is the blood that is running through you. This was also a part of my life. And for them to really know me, they have to understand that part. On top of that, when we went to Georgia, they got to see the people I grew up with, and some of my close friends had kids their age, so that's another family for them right there. You can't buy that.

Now that my kids are grown, we're carrying on that same tradition: every summer, Tyus's three children—Tyus Junior, Amare, and Sukari—visit with me and Duane for two whole months. Tyus Junior—we call him TJ—comes to us from Hanford, California, so we see him a lot throughout the year, but Amare and Sukari stay in St. Louis, and the summers give them an opportunity to learn what our California culture is like. Simone's kids, Damani and Anika, live right here in LA, but they come around a lot more when their cousins are in town, and they get the other side of the picture from them. Because family should know family, and when you know your family, you know yourself.

Me, my kids, and my grandkids. (Photo by Leslie Penn.)

* * *

Tyus was in middle school when I found my last job—the job I had before I retired. The way I got there was through one of the people who worked with me at the student integration program—we called him Bear, but his name is Mark. When that job ended, he went on to work at the Clear Creek Outdoor Education Center, which was another program through LA Unified. After a while, Bear got to be assistant director, and when he heard I was out of work, he convinced me to come work with him as a naturalist.

It was not the perfect job in the beginning. For the first six months, it rained every day because of El Niño, and it was an outdoor program, so we had to be out in the rain most of the time. And I just kept thinking, *I must be out of my mind.* But I enjoyed it—even a lot of the rains, I enjoyed. The hardest part was that when you came off the trails, if you didn't have a break right away you just stayed wet until your break time rolled around. We also had to do a lot of indoor games, and I guess that's where my education came in, my degree in recreation, because I kind of knew all those things. Over time, it got to be something that I really wanted to do, and it gave me a way not only to build off my education but also to build off of what I had been doing with the student integration program.

We worked mainly with fifth and sixth graders, but during the summer we had high school students as well. There would be two different schools at a time, and we would try to get them from two different neighborhoods, around forty kids from each school. There were four naturalists, so we each had eighteen or twenty kids in our groups. We did a lot of team building; we had to get the kids to believe that we were a real team because we were together for a full week. All the students had to stay in the groups they were assigned; they couldn't change groups, which meant that the first thing I had to do was get them to like me and believe in me as a leader. Then I had to get them to work well with kids they didn't know.

Not just at the beginning, but for a while, I was thinking that I was a little too old for all that. I mean, I had two kids of my own. And it was like camping although we didn't sleep outside; we got to sleep in cabins, and we didn't have to sleep in the cabins with the kids. We got our own, but still. It's just that whole thing you get yourself into whenever you work with kids—the constant supervision, constant interaction. We had the kids from eight in the morning until noon; we got them again from two o'clock until five; and then we got them one last time after dinner for a night hike or a campfire. So when you were on, you were on pretty much nonstop.

But I accepted it, and it was one of the best things that could have happened for me because there was so much about it that I loved. Just the mere fact of being able to work with students from all different backgrounds was one thing—seeing them get off the bus that first day, all wide-eyed and a little queasy from driving up those twisty mountain roads. Then, a few hours later, they would be mad because you didn't put them with their friends. And then they would think they got put in the "wrong" group: "I want to be in that group because that group seems to have more fun."

"They do have more fun," I would tell them. "In my group, there's no fun; it's all about the learning." And then by the time they had to leave, they didn't want to go; they would have enjoyed it all that much. It was wonderful to see how they had learned to appreciate nature and being outdoors.

I also liked being outside, walking on the trails and being under the trees, just like when I was walking the farm as a child with my father. And all the teaching, all my teaching, I did outside, kind of like my dad. The only time I wasn't teaching outside was when it was raining very hard, but if it was misting or scattered rain, we could sit under the trees and stay dry. And I enjoyed getting to know the children—even the ones who liked to complain and the ones who could always figure out a way to have a problem: "My mom told me I better not mess up my new shoes!"

"But we told you not to bring new shoes. So what are you going to do?"

"I can't, I can't . . . I don't know."

"Okay. We have a lost-and-found. We can find you some shoes."

"I'm not wearing someone else's shoes!"

"Well, one or the other. Let's figure it out." So it was all about problem-solving and thinking things through. Those kinds of things. The things I had learned to do not only in the student integration program but also from all those years of working with Mr. Temple: thinking things through and working as a team, everybody making a contribution. And it was fun, kidding them, bothering them about this or that, and watching them grow.

One of the things we would do when the kids first arrived was bring them into our museum, which had a geology section and pelts from different animals that they could touch, as well as living creature like newts and turtles and cockroaches and hamsters and snakes. Outside the museum there were other creatures, ones that we could not touch: a red-tailed hawk, a turkey vulture, an owl, and a bobcat. The snakes in the museum were gopher snakes, and I'm not a snake person, but I learned to like them, and I loved to watch the kids warm up to them, to go from being afraid of being eaten to touching them—even if it was only with one finger.

So they got to learn, and I got to see it. For me, teaching young people, showing them things they'd never seen, was wonderful. It was their moment of discovery, and I was there with them. My discovery had been totally different; it came through track and through travel, but I guess they were traveling too, in a nature kind of way. There is so much to learn in nature; it's like a journey all by itself. And like I said, it brought me back to my own childhood, and how my dad would tell us that you had to step out and see what was there, what you could find in the woods if you looked.

The team building and trust building—getting them to look out for each other—was also meaningful to me. I had to help them to understand that just because you were raised a certain way doesn't mean your feelings are any different from anyone else's. People get hurt by the things you say and how you look at them just like you do. We taught the kids that no one has any cooties. Because they could understand that. And it's amazing what you can do in a couple of days. You can see that kids—no matter what they've been told—can figure out how to work as a team if they're in an environment where they're all pretty much treated equal and going through a process together. Of course, there are going to be kids who know a lot more, and some of them will make fun of the kids who don't—like that kid who thinks that a snake can eat them. "Why would you think that?" the know-it-all kids would say. "That's stupid."

So I had to teach them that no one is stupid; some people just come from limited experience. "Think about what you just said," I would tell them, "about how hurtful it is to call someone that. And think about how you know the things you know. Maybe it's because someone helped you. And now we are going on a hike, and let's say you're falling off a cliff, and that person you made fun of is the only person who can save you. So you need to think in terms of who has helped you and who's going to have to help you and who you're going to have to help."

That was my teaching, and I don't know if everybody taught that way, but as it turned out, it was something I was perfectly prepared to do, first by my father and then by Mr. Temple and the Tigerbelles.

It was while I was at Clear Creek that I learned one of the most important lessons of my life: if you try, if you stay open to growth and keep looking for ways to grow, you end up where you're supposed to be, and you get the recognition you deserve—maybe not all that you deserve, but enough. That was made clear to me while I was working as a naturalist, and even clearer when some folks in Griffin decided to build me a park.

When I first heard about it, I thought, *Yeah, right. Griffin is going to name a park after me? The people who live in Griffin? Please.* And then they started contacting me, but not in a way that made me think I should take them seriously. I know the business, and if you're going to honor somebody, there are *t*'s that you have to cross and *i*'s that you have to dot. You should be calling that person on a monthly basis and making sure they're available for certain dates and prepared to do certain things. That wasn't happening, and at first it made me think that *nothing* was happening. But then I remembered: *I'm from Griffin. They do things their own way.* And they sure did. Because while they were not checking in with me to make sure I was available, they thought nothing of knocking on my mom's door and talking to her like she was still in charge of me. And then she turned around and said, "They want to do this for you. Don't you want them to do it?"

"Hmm," I said. "Who's *they?*"

And as it started to come closer to actually happening, they finally did call to ask me who I wanted to invite.

"Well, Mr. Temple will have to be there!" I said. I didn't know who else to ask. I told Evelyn, Cynthia, and Cantrell, who are all Tigerbelles, as well as Gloria, who ran with me that first year in the summer program. Edith was going to be out of the country and she didn't know if she'd be back in time.

Maybe they kept me out of the loop for a reason. I'm not sure. Maybe they wanted to surprise me—show me what they were willing to do *for* me without any help *from* me. But at that point, all I could think was, *They just need to hurry up and do this. Why does it have to be such a big deal?* I thought it would just be a little park because I know Griffin, and I figured it would be in the Black neighborhood, which would mean there wasn't much space for it.

After a while, though, I started to get the feeling something more was going on. "Well, you know, sis," my brother Junior kept saying, "they're going to give you a pretty big park."

"Did you see where it is?" my brother Jackie asked me.

"No. Where is it?" And when they said where it was going to be, all I could say was, *"Really?!"*

When the time came, I went to Griffin—all of us went, my whole family, Duane and Tyus, Simone and her husband Nyaniso and their son Damani; they lived in Atlanta at the time, so they didn't have that far to travel. I was still partly thinking: *It's not like I'm just going for this park thing, whatever that is. I always go back home anyway in the summer.*

But on the day of the dedication, I was totally floored. I didn't know it was going to be *that* big. I was just in shock. We drove out there, and when I saw it for the first time, it was like, *"Okay!"*

First, they had this white fence leading up to the entrance, and then, when we got to the entrance, we saw this huge brick wall, and on one side it says, *Wyomia Tyus Olympic Park,* and on the other side, going the other way, it says the same thing. Then we went in, and they did a whole torch-run ceremony and passed the torch to me. It was clear that they had put a lot of time and energy into making it happen. I was speechless, to tell you the truth. I was shocked and pleased and didn't know that people cared so much. It was great.

The entrance to my namesake park—164 acres in Griffin, GA. (Photo by Duane Tillman.)

Everyone I had invited came, as well as a bunch of people I didn't think to invite. Edie was there; she and her husband had gone to Africa, and she had just gotten back and told them not to tell me she was coming. Then there were some other good friends of mine who went to Tennessee State, seven or eight people from school, and whether they ran track or not, they were there.

After the dedication, I spoke with some of the people who were instrumental in making it happen. Bill Beck, who has passed on now, was the first person to talk about it with me and my mom, but he was ill at the time and couldn't be there. Martha McDaniel was there, though, and held the ribbon while my mom cut it. I was so overwhelmed that day that I can't remember all their names. At one point, one of the people from Parks and Recreation came up to me and said, "You know, we really didn't do very much for you when you came back from the Olympics, and this is to show you how much we appreciate what you did."

Ribbon cutting at the grand opening of the park. (Photo by Duane Tillman.)

And I thought, *What?! White people talking to me like that?* Because that is something to be said, when you think about it. To confess, "We know that we did not honor you properly," is a big thing in and of itself. But then to actually do something about it, to be able to say, "We hope that this does it. We hope this makes you feel appreciated." That is something else again. And I did feel appreciated. It was totally over the top and way beyond. We're talking 164 acres of park with soccer fields and baseball fields—they're even getting ready to put in an Olympic-sized pool. And they have hiking trails and a pond that you can fish out of with some swans on it and a fountain, and you can have picnics there. And now, whenever people go to Griffin, they tell me, "I was at your park!"

It's just amazing. Oh my goodness. I never, ever thought a day in my life that something like that could happen. I still can't find the right words to express my true feelings. It's such an honor. One of the best honors I have ever received. And they did it. My little town of Griffin, Georgia. It seems there were people there who supported me the whole time. And I guess I knew that, but you still don't put it all together—until someone builds you a park.

Having a happy time at the Wyomia Tyus Olympic Park opening: Mr. and Mrs. Temple with me and my husband Duane.

Mr. Temple's Legacy

A statue in honor of Mr. Temple on the greenway next to First Tennessee Park in Nashville, TN. (Photo by Duane Tillman.)

Edward Stanley Temple
September 20, 1927–September 22, 2016

When I think about what made the Tigerbelles successful, I think about the relationships that Mr. Temple encouraged us to build. For starters, you have the tried-and-true friendships like the one I have with Edith. We developed a special bond from the beginning, and I am very thankful and grateful to have had her as my teammate, my friend, my sister. You name it, and she's there at the top of my list.

Some people just can't believe that Edith and I have been such good friends—we talk on the phone almost every day—for close to sixty years. They think it's a big deal that we stayed friends after I won the gold in the 100 in the '64 Olympics—a medal that everyone expected her to win. But I think they misunderstand what it means to be on a team and have teammates. We both knew why we were there. Whether you're a champion or not, if you're in a race, you want to win. If you don't want to win, then why did you train? Why did you go? You didn't have to go. If you wanted someone else to win, you could have stayed home. That's something that Edith and I both understand. It never mattered to us if we were running in the same event because once they said, "Take your mark," I didn't know her, and she didn't know me. We were competitors—both there to win. And once it was over, we were friends again—two friends who had just done their best at what both of them came to do.

So running has never come between us—which is not to say we agree on everything. We don't. But if we disagree, we have a conversation about it. I'm that way with anybody I would call a friend. I feel that you should be able to at least talk things through. You won't always settle everything, but you give people respect if they deserve it, and respecting someone means knowing that everyone has their own mind.

Although not all the Tigerbelles are as close as Edith and me, everybody has a crew, and all the crews stick together. There are several different generations of Tigerbelles, and each one has a different personality—a group chemistry. The crew that Wilma was a part of got along, and they would always help each other, but there was also a lot of wolftalking between them—who's better, who could whip who, that type of thing—which brought a lot of liveliness to the whole process and sometimes still does. They were a bit different from our generation, and Mr. Temple had to treat them a little differently than he treated us. Or at least he tried.

Our group didn't so much talk about each other; we didn't boast a lot. Matter of fact, we didn't boast at all. We were very quiet, and pretty much whatever Mr. Temple said, we were going to try to do. Pretty much. With some exceptions, of course. We were just a little bit more—I'm not sure what the right word is—reserved, maybe? Some of the mood was set by whoever was captain of the team. That was the whole point of naming captains. Being top on the list speed-wise wasn't enough for Mr. Temple; if you weren't respected, you would never be captain.

With our group it was more—at least, I like to think—that we were all equal, despite the fact that Edith and I were captain and cocaptain. Nobody was bothered by us having those positions. And there wasn't very much for us to say to them. "You need to follow Mr. Temple's rules," we would tell them, "and if you're not going to follow his rules, you should not bring attention to yourself so that he is *knowing* that you're not following them."

Funny thing is, I feel that Mr. Temple knew that we were going to get into some trouble, but that it wasn't going to be bad trouble. He wanted each of us to grow to be our own person, and that meant finding the limits to what we wanted to do. But he was also a good judge of character, and he respected us; he knew that we respected him, and that as a group we respected our families—that we were a crew that was going to be thinking about what our parents had taught us, and if we were going to do anything, we would be thinking about how it would look to our families. He knew we wouldn't want to do anything to disgrace them, let alone something that would get us sent home.

That was true for me, and I think it was true for a lot of the young girls who were there. Most of us came from families where you were not encouraged to question what your elders told you to do—or you could question things, but how you questioned them mattered. You had to really think before you started talking. I believe our whole team got along because we were all coming from that same kind of place—not to say that the older crew was not like that, but they were a little more rambunctious.

Of course, when we saw them, at fifteen, sixteen, we never knew there were any ruffles between them because that didn't come through—not to us. To us, they were just Tigerbelles, people we looked up to—the ones who taught us whatever we needed to know, to be good on the track and at school, how to talk to Mr. Temple. They taught us how to play cards—how to play Bid Whist and Tonk and Spades. We would get together after the five a.m. practice and play until it was time to go back to practice at nine. We would play all day long and half of the night and talk junk and just have a good time, and the older girls made sure of it. Because however rambunctious they were, they took their roles seriously. That was part of being a Tigerbelle. You're supposed to help teach the younger ones. And that attitude of mutual support is some of the glue that holds us together to this day.

Even at the time, young as we were, we were all very conscious of the need to take care of each other. Some people may have come from cities—from Atlanta or from one of the bigger towns in Alabama or Mississippi, maybe even been on a college campus before—but a lot of us came from small towns, and for us, just being able to get on a train and get to Tennessee State was an adventure in itself. So from the moment we arrived, support was something we wanted to give and to get.

All the different generations are like that—supportive. And even though our generation was a little quieter, we spoke our minds when we needed to. Edith, for one, has no trouble saying what she thinks, but never in a bad way. If things have to be said, she is the one to say them—which is good for me because you know I don't want to have to do it. When we were captain and cocaptain, Edith did all the talking; she would want me to talk, and I would say, "You have to tell them. You're the captain." Even recently, before Mr. Temple passed, he would say that if someone wanted to talk to him or to the Tigerbelles, "Everything needs to go through McGuire and Tyus."

And I would tell Edith, "Your name came first. It has to go through *you*." Because Edith is just better at talking than I am. She's diplomatic. I'm not.

Edith was about two years ahead of me, and the girls who were with her—Vivian, Lorraine, Marcella, and Flossie—and the girls who came in with me—Evelyn, Essie, and Cynthia— all became friends, although I'm closest with Edith. Flossie and I don't talk all the time, but every now and then one of us will call. And I still see Gloria, who only ran one year in the summer program; she lives in Atlanta, so we never completely lose sight of each other. Cynthia lived in LA until she also moved to Atlanta, and we have always stayed in contact. Same with Evelyn, who was my roommate at Tennessee State after Marcella; I went to Florida to celebrate her seventieth birthday in 2016, and she and I talk often. Carrie, who was one of the team managers, lives right down the street from me, so it's easy for us to be in touch.

But it's not only those Tigerbelles who are friends who stay in contact and help each other out. People's personal likes and dislikes are less important than the fact that, even to this day, we know how to work as a team. Although the different groups, the different generations, are tighter with each other than they are with the others, all the Tigerbelles have a support network. When something happens, good, bad, or indifferent, you make it your business to know, or if you can be at someone's event, you try to make sure you're there. If someone is coming to LA, I find out where they're going to be and figure out if we can get together. We also see each other at meets, and if any Tiger-belle gets sick, we will call her and each other, get everybody on top of what's going on, and see what we can do to help. When Mamie Rallins passed away, we were all on the phone until we knew that somebody from the Tigerbelles was able to go to the funeral and represent us. The support comes through us from the Tigerbelles who came before and goes past us to the Tigerbelles who came after. That was what Mr. Temple always wanted us to know: that everyone is an important link in the chain. I almost don't know how to convey how I feel about the Tigerbelles. You can leave home and still feel at home, and that means a lot to me.

Up until he passed in 2016, Mr. Temple was a crucial part of that network. Edith and I used to talk to him all the time, espe-cially when he reached his eighties, and he was still very attuned to whatever was happening to his Tigerbelles and giving a lot of his self—just like he always did. Back in the day, he had a wife and two children, he taught sociology at Tennessee State, he ran the post office on campus, and he was our coach, so he was always traveling, yet he managed to not only hold all of that to-gether but also see beyond. He knew that Black women wanted something other than just a sedentary-type life, that track gave us an opportunity to do extraordinary things, and that there was more for us to do than be a teacher or a nurse—although if that was what you wanted to do, he would encourage you to do it. I never thought a Black woman with some schooling could have an occupation other than those two until I went to Tennessee State and got to talk to Tigerbelles who had gone places and done things—things I had just heard about or maybe read in a book. Mr. Temple got us to see beyond what society expected for us at the time, and if he had done nothing else, that would still have been enough.

But of course there was more. There was something about him that made it possible for us as women to accept him, to let him be a part of our lives. Even with some of his antiquated ideas—and you know we disagreed with some of them—we still allowed him to be who he was and accepted what his program was about. Because we all had to give a little so that we could work together to get what we wanted. If I had gone in and said, "You can't tell me who to date!" I would have been home the next day—on the train with the comic book and the apple. But as strong-headed as I am, I knew I wanted more than a boyfriend, and I knew that I could get a boyfriend all by myself. But to get the things I really wanted, I needed help. I needed support. And Mr. Temple was the key to that support.

Some of the girls would say, "I just don't *like* this. I'm going to go talk to him." It's difficult when you're young; you know what you want to say or do, and you know it so *hard*. But you can also *not* say certain things, and that's not going to kill your pride either—although sometimes it takes a minute to figure out which things you might not want to say. One example was when we were pledging to be in sororities, and Mr. Temple took us off the line two or three times because he heard that some crazy stuff was going on and didn't want the Tigerbelles to be involved. So we couldn't pledge for a week. Edith was a Delta, and she didn't like that, so she went into his office and said, "Mr. Temple, I need to talk to you." And then she said what she had to say about Tigerbelles not being able to be on the line for a week.

After she finished, Mr. Temple told her what he thought about what the Deltas were doing.

"Mr. Temple," she said, "that is *Delta* business."

When Mr. Temple told the story in later years, he would always say: "I let her finish"—he never once told the story without saying that. "I let her finish," he would say, "and when she finished, I told her, 'If it wasn't for the Tigerbelles, you wouldn't have no Delta business. So this is Tigerbelle business, which is my business. Deltas don't have no business! You would not be sitting up here too long telling me about Delta business if it wasn't for Tigerbelle business. You can just go on out of this office.'"

Edith talks on this all the time, now that we're older, and she has some perspective. "I don't know what I was thinking," she'll say, "going into his office and telling him, 'That's Delta business!' Like, who was I?" But at the time, she didn't see it that way.

Edith and I made the decision years ago that we would go back to Tennessee State every year at homecoming. That way, we not only got to see Mr. Temple, but also a lot of the people who we went to school with—although we mainly went to see him. And when we went back for homecoming, we would sit and talk with Mr. Temple for hours and not even know half the things we'd talked about; just the mere fact of talking to him made the time go by so fast. He mellowed a lot over the years, and I gave myself the opportunity to enjoy that, to enjoy the best part of him, not just the whole coach thing, which was really great because I never got to have that with my father as an adult. And I got to see him recognizing *me* as an adult, as an equal.

Because you know, with Mr. Temple, whatever he thought was going to come right on out of his mouth. Once, we were in Sacramento, and Kathy McMillan, who won a silver medal in the long jump in 1976, came up and was hugging him, but Mr. Temple didn't recognize her. "Who are you?" he said.

"Mr. Temple," we said, "that's Kathy."

Now, Kathy had always been thin, but she had gotten older and wasn't as thin anymore. And Mr. Temple just looked at her and said, "Kathy McMillan? Shoot. You look like a shot putter. You need to go out there and put that shot around. You make a team, putting the shot."

And we were like, *Oh my God, did he really say that?*

But Kathy just laughed. And after he left, she told us, "Don't worry, I know him."

And knowing him meant knowing that he would say any word that came into his head—unless it was a curse word. When we were young, he would never use any profanity when we were around. And then one time, several years before he passed, Edith and I were visiting, and when we left his room we could barely keep ourselves from laughing, and as soon as we got out the door, Edith said, "Did you *hear* him? He used the word *shit.*"

He would never, ever, *ever* say anything like that when we were younger. There we were, nearly seventy years old, with our hands over our mouths, saying, "Oh my God, he used a *curse* word. Did you hear him *say* that?!" We got in the car and just laughed all the way back to the hotel. Because we knew he finally saw as adults—people he could cuss around. That is the kind of thing we will remember.

But there was also the pleasure of just sitting there and talking about how he saw the Tigerbelles, and realizing that through all those years, and with all these different women, the reason he could put up with all of us was that he *understood* us. He had a perspective on every girl. I believe he understood each and every one of us, that he understood each and every one of our needs. Can you imagine the energy that must have taken? To have so many girls and women come in and out of his life and still have time and attention for each of us?

Of course, when it came down to discipline and things like that, he did it all the same way across the board, so no one would feel that there was favoritism. That's just who he was, and you couldn't fault him for that. But for him to be able to do what he did for hundreds of Black women in such a way that most of them appreciate it—and I think all of them do, really deep down—is just incredible to me. I am always speechless when it comes to describing how I feel about what he did. For me. For so many of us. How do you say thank you? How did he ever come up with the whole idea that I could do what I did? How did he know I could make it work? How did he build trust in the parents who let their daughters come to Tennessee State at such a young age? Where did he get the strength to assure them, "Your daughter's going to be safe"? And he did keep us safe. In that place. At that time. For him to do that, I mean, I look at that, and I'm just—wow. Speechless.

And even when things were hard, he was not a complainer—or a boaster. He never wanted to take credit for anything he did. When he talked about it, he would say, "All that stuff fell in my lap, pretty much; I was just flying by the seat of my pants, doing the things that I felt were right." He just wanted to make sure that the team stayed on top, that people respected us, and that, more than anything, we respected ourselves. In the later years he would tell us, "You know, I may not have done all the things I should have done or could have done for you all, but my way of doing things was the only way I knew to do it. It didn't work for some of them, and some of them had to go. You know how young people are. I lost a lot of good ones, probably, but I will never know because they're gone. But I know the ones who stayed are the pure at heart, and that it worked then, and it still works, because look what I have now: all of you, out of school and doing well for yourselves."

And it was good to hear that, to know that he had some sense that there were people who couldn't understand why he did things the way he did or thought he was crazy. It wasn't ever that he couldn't see other perspectives. He was very self-aware, which made me respect him even more.

At first, after Mr. Temple passed, I didn't think I would be able to talk about it. When I came back from the memorial, Duane said, "You've got to get in a better frame of mind." And I said, "I know. I've got to talk about this for the book. I owe it to Mr. Temple." So I have worked on myself. I even had to take some time away from Edith because we were both struggling, and every time we'd talk about it, she would cry. *I'm not going to be able to finish this book like this,* I said to myself. *If I'm going to end it where I'm the best that I can be, I'm going to have to just do nothing but work on myself.* So I did.

In some ways, it was like losing my father all over again. But in others it was also a lot different in that I knew he was sick. It wasn't sudden, wasn't a surprise. The last couple of years, whenever we tried to make plans for the future, he'd always say, "I'm not going to be around." When I talked to my friend Cora about it and told her how it made me feel that he was always saying that, she said, "Well, he's just trying to prepare you. He knows what kind of time you had with your dad."

And she was right: he had been trying to prepare me—trying to prepare all of us—for years. After we had the fifty-year anniversaries—for the 1960 team in 2010 and the 1964 team in 2014—he told me, "Tyus, I won't be here for '68. I was here for '64. You had your fifty years!"

We were in Nashville at the time, at a luncheon. "Well, you know I like those doubles," I told him. "You have to do it again—four more years!"

But he was right. And when I truly look back, I know he said it in all the ways he could. But he was also saying: "You guys should keep on keeping on, doing what you do. I'm just so glad I got to see you do so many wonderful things, see you get your lives back together even though they were not so together at times. You turned out to be great young ladies."

So I started to prepare myself. I mean, when my dad died, I was not prepared. I was fifteen. I had had very little experience with life and no experience with death; when my dad passed, he was the only person besides his own mother who had died in my family since I was born. That was difficult.

But going through that at fifteen and then growing helped me to realize that, you know, people are going to go. You just don't want them to go before you think it's their time. For my father, I never thought that it was his time. That it could be his time was nowhere in my head. But with Mr. Temple, because of the maturity that had come in, the experience I'd had of so many people passing in my life, it was possible for me to see that he was ready.

The whole process of going through death and being around people who are dying forces you to grow in a different way from any other kind of growth I have experienced. My mom died in 2008, and then my brother Jackie in 2013. Jimmy Lee had died many years before that, back in the seventies. I don't want to say you get used to it, but you know the signs, and you have to say to yourself, *There's not too much I can really do about that; I've just got to get my mind wrapped around it.* That's kind of how I felt with Mr. Temple. And he did what he could to help me, which was the opposite of what my mom did: Mr. Temple kept saying he was leaving, and my mom kept saying she wasn't going to go—that she was going to hang on until there was nothing left that she could do. She would lie in her hospital bed and say, "I can't seem to remember anybody's name—can you still remember names?"

"Yeah, I can still remember names."

"Well, you live long enough, and you're not going to be able to remember names." She was a stone believer: just keep on living, and eventually you won't be able to do anything. There were still a lot of things that she could do, which to her meant she wasn't going to go. She was eighty-nine when she died, just like Mr. Temple, and whatever else I could say about what she did or what she said, she taught me a good lesson and one that I will always remember. Because I was there when all the doctors said, "We can't do anything. It's over." But it wasn't over. She was still funny and crazy. She was who she was, right up to the end, and that is something to know.

Me and my mama after the park reception. (Photo by Duane Tillman.)

The saddest part for me about Mr. Temple's death is that I didn't get there before he passed away. I would talk to him and say, "I'll see you at homecoming"—and we're only talking three weeks: three weeks between when he died and when I was planning to arrive. I should have made a better effort, but I kept thinking: *He's going to be there; he'll be okay.*

Back in the day I would call him once a month, but later I started calling him once a week. And I knew, just in the way he was speaking to me, that he was ready to go. That prepared me some more. So I put it in perspective in my heart, although I didn't know how I was going to handle it. In one way, he was just like my mom, totally himself the whole way. He laughed and talked; he was so clear of mind. It was just that his body was failing him. When I called him for his birthday, he told me, "Tyus, they doing everything they can to keep me alive, but I'm not going to be here."

"Why you saying that? You know I can't come now. I'll be there in October, so you just got to hang on."

"I'm not going to be here in October, Tyus. You need to understand that. All right?"

He died two days later. Edith was there, and he was really happy that she was with him. His daughter Edwina was also there; she had taken off work, and she stayed with him in the hospital for about two weeks. She went home at night, but other than that, she was there the whole time. I wish I could have been there too.

Both the church service and the memorial program for Mr. Temple were uplifting. According to Edwina, Mr. Temple had said: "I don't want no foolishness at my memorial. I don't want people I don't know speaking over me."

People kept telling her, "You should let this or that person talk."

But Edwina would say, "No, I'm not having my daddy coming back here shaking my house. He said what he wanted, and I'm doing exactly what he said."

I think the fact that he had it all planned was another sign he was ready. He chose the people he wanted to speak ahead of time. He had Lucinda from Wilma's era, and of course he had to have his Gold Dust Twins, so both Edith and I got to speak—he had us in order: Lucinda, then Edith, then me. And then Cheese—Chandra Cheeseborough-Guice—who took over coaching the Tigerbelles after Mr. Temple retired. We were the four Tigerbelles he chose to speak. I don't even remember what I said. I just spoke from how I felt. And I felt a lot.

Other people did other things: Ralph Boston was the master of ceremonies and Madeline Manning Mims—who won the gold medal in the 800 meters at the 1968 Olympics and was the first American woman ever to do so—sang a gospel song. The best thing about the memorial was that you could really see his legacy. Tigerbelles came from all the generations, not only the women that Mr. Temple had coached but from Cheese's era as well. The women from Mr. Temple's last team before he retired are especially dedicated to him. There's one in particular whose name is Rhonda, but we call her Baby Belle because she's one of the last of Mr. Temple's "products." She's also one of the nicest people I have ever met, and she would have fit in well during our era. I really felt for Baby Belle because in one of the quiet times she told us, "You know, since I've been here, I keep going to his house, and I just sit out in front and look at it because I can't believe he's gone."

I am still grieving, of course. I mean, I have my days. One thing that continues to sadden me is the lack of press around his passing. His memorial service was at the school, and I was disappointed that the press didn't do anything for him. The *Tennessean* did, as usual; I'm talking about national press and the sportscasters. There was an obituary in the *New York Times,* and the Ohio Valley Conference livestreamed his memorial service, but that was about it. I don't understand it. Here was this man who had done things that no other coach had ever done or is likely ever to do, who was known around the world. And we've got all these sportscasters, all these sportspeople, who are such fans of the Tigerbelles. But they never spoke about his death. When other coaches have passed and gone, there was something every half hour about how they had passed away, or how they had lived, or how they had settled their affairs. But for Mr. Temple? Nothing. There were some exceptions, of course; sports journalist Dave Zirin, for example, wrote a wonderful article. But why is that all? This icon, this man who did so much and gave so much to this country, passes with barely a notice. That sat with me for a while.

But then it occurred to me that it was just like being a Tigerbelle—just like he had warned us it would be: we would go out into the world and perhaps do amazing things, but because we were Black women, we better do them because that was what we wanted to do; we shouldn't expect to get honored for it, not by the powers-that-be. I guess that turned out to be true for him as a Black man as well. And I think he would be okay with that. "I want my flowers when I'm living," he used to say. "When I'm dead, I can't smell 'em."

Regardless of the press or lack thereof, he's just going to be missed. I'm not the funeral type, but when I go back to Griffin, I visit my mom's grave and talk to her like she can hear. And because my mom and my brother Jackie are not too far from each other, I talk to him too, and then I'm done with that. Maybe it will be the same with Mr. Temple. It's just that I'm not too depressed because I feel that I've been totally fulfilled by having him in my life and being able to see the changes he made in my life—the way he helped to make me who I am today, gave me the tools to work with, made me believe that I had a lot to offer and a lot to give, even if he never quite put it that way.

Sometimes when I feel sad, I start thinking about the crazy things: "You can't date a football player! You can't do this! You can't do that!" Edith and I were talking the other day, and I said, "He told us we shouldn't do these things, and we just kept on doing them because we knew he couldn't see us. But now he can see us, Edith. He can *see* us."

And that's a good thing. I'm in a real good place with Mr. Temple, more so than I would have thought. It's probably because of his philosophy, the philosophy that he passed down to us. He wanted so much for us. He wanted us to do well, and continue to do well, and to think of others. "Don't be selfish with your doing well," he would tell us. "You have to think of other people too."

There are no words that I can find to describe him that would truly do him justice. He was just a great man, with so much pride and integrity. Who would ever think that in the fifties and sixties he could pull off what he did? Have all these Black women go on to be not just Olympic champions but champions in whatever work they did? We always talk about the medal winners, but he also gave a lot to young women who never broke a tape, never made an international team—women he kept on the team so that they could get an education. And he never did it to try to bathe himself in glory. He did it because he had a vision that Black girls and women could do and be more.

I'm just glad that he was part of my life, especially that he was a part of my young life, because I don't know what I would have done without him. He was a gift to me, a gift to my life.

Thank you, Mr. Temple. Again.

My last walk on the track with Mr. Temple. (Photo by Duane Tillman.)

13

Black Women in Sports: Then and Now

At the time that I was competing, there were two main obstacles to my becoming an athlete: being Black and being female. There were others, but just those two would have been plenty, and not just for me: Black women and Black girls in general got no encouragement from the community, let alone the wider society. I was lucky; I was a person who had opportunities. I was supported when it counted by the people in my high school, and I was always encouraged by my family. My family wanted more—not just for me, but for all of us. When I was a young girl, my parents made me feel that whatever I wanted to do, I should be able to do. And I think that was different from what most girls were hearing at the time—it might even be different from what most girls are hearing now.

When you listen to guys coach their sons or coach other people's sons, you hear them saying, "If you want to win, you've got to be the best. Somebody knock you down, you got to get up." I think a lot of girls were not taught that way—to get up and fight back, to not let yourself get punished, to not let somebody keep you down—but I was taught that at a very early age. Having older brothers and playing with guys all the time backed up the lesson, so I knew: I have to be able to fight, and scrap, and do everything I need to do to win. If I'm going to cry, I cry in my pillow; I don't cry in front of you. We were all that way: if you want to cry, you got to go inside the house to sit and mope, and if you do that, you're not going to have anybody to play with—*and* you're going to have to go back to them someday. So you have to start somewhere to develop that strength from within, and I got to start real early.

We were also taught that it's important to feel good about what you're doing. If something makes you feel happy, then that makes that your life, pretty much. You do what makes you happy if it's possible, if it doesn't infringe on other people—what makes *you* happy. Not what society thinks you should be, thinks you should do. So when my great-aunts would tell me that muscles are ugly, I didn't mind. I heard them, but what I heard in my head was: *What your body looks like is good. Your body lets you do what you feel good doing.* And when they said that I was never going to have a husband, that I was never going to have children, I would think: *Like I really care at this point in my life. Not looking for a man. Not looking for a boyfriend or a husband or to have children. I'm enjoying what I'm doing.* I couldn't say that to them, of course, but it was always in my mind. I was a carefree type of child. That's what my parents wanted for me. Grow up being a kid, be who you are, and enjoy what you do. And who I was was strong and fast. And I got to feel good about the whole thing.

It wasn't just my parents who helped me to feel that way. My brothers really appreciated how strong I was, and the other guys we played with appreciated it too, especially when I had to be on their team because my brothers were mad at me or whatever. Some girls have to grow up with people saying, "Girls can't do this, girls can't do that." But when I look back, I don't think we heard, "She's a girl, she shouldn't play with us," more than once or twice. We probably heard it in the beginning, with new people, but after a while, it just went away. I was never the last one picked, I can tell you that. Sometimes people would even tease my brothers: "Your sister can beat you! She's faster than you!" But they didn't care what people said. They just wanted me to be my best. So when I think about my brothers, I think about the part they played in my being able to be the person I was as a kid, being able to go off to college, and being able to go to the Olympics.

Because of all that, when I was competing, I was competing for me and my family. I really wasn't thinking very much about representing my country because the country hadn't done anything for me. It kept me—really, it *tried* to keep me—down. Not just me as an athlete. Me as a person. The whole Jim Crow era was about *not* celebrating me or people like me, and I brought that with me to every race. It was not like nowadays, when Black athletes are all running for the country and draped in flags. That flag hadn't done anything to prepare me for the Olympics, and when I came back, it still didn't do anything for me—not that I was ever the type to drape myself in a flag anyway. First and foremost, I was out there for my family, then Mr. Temple, then Tennessee State, and then friends—the people who encouraged me, and all the people who helped my mom.

I guess you could say I did represent the US in some ways—I can't deny where I'm from, and there's not another country that I would like to live in. As bad as things have been, and as not-so-great as they still are, to me this is the country to be in to make change and have a voice and not be totally shut out, or shut down, or put away. So the country came in at some point, but it was later—much later. Because unlike the country, my family was always there for me. And when I look at the big picture, it's easy to see that not everybody had the type of family I have, so they needed support from country and community more than I did. But most women just weren't encouraged to go out and do well—to be *really* good at something—except maybe taking care of a family. So say you liked playing softball and wanted to be very good at it. That was on you—you, alone. No support from anyone. You had to be that strong.

Another part of the problem when I was coming up was a lack of coaching for women, especially in the small towns. Maybe it was different in larger cities, but in small towns you would have a teacher who taught physical education who might know enough to be a coach, and that was it. I was lucky that the women who coached me in both junior high and high school had gotten their degrees in physical education. They knew what to do—up to a point. But there was really no reason for most women to take it any further. Women coaches were not only not rewarded; they weren't recognized, which meant that you just didn't hear anything about them, so you couldn't even aspire to be a female coach of female athletes, really. You would have to be a visionary—like Mr. Temple—to even think of such a thing.

Meanwhile, the men were not coaching women, not even a little bit. At my school, the female PE teachers coached the women's teams and the male PE teachers coached the men's teams. There was one male teacher who did try to support us, but he wasn't a coach. He just happened to be the son of Miss Jessie Lee, the woman who was with me and my mom that first time we got a visit from Mr. Temple. He was my social studies teacher, and he had graduated from high school when he was fifteen or so and then came back to teach after he went to college, even though he was just a little older than we were. He knew a lot about sports just out of personal interest, and he was one of the people who drove the station wagons to the meets. He always thought I could run. But he came from a family that was all about going places and changing things. Where and when I was born, there just weren't enough people like that, not enough teachers, not enough programs for all the girls who might have been interested in participating. And even if you really wanted it, even if you were really strong, you only had two choices: you had track, and you had basketball, and that was it.

Most people's attitude was simple: women are not supposed to do these things. They were not to be athletes—not great athletes, at least. If you wanted to run, if you wanted to compete, then that was cute: "Oh, you want to play? Oh, go play! Stay out of trouble!" That was the attitude then. Don't be serious. Don't be good. And I think there were a lot of women who fell by the wayside who were just as good if not better than I was at either running or playing basketball but just couldn't see a way to make it work for them. Who is going to work hard—and being an athlete is hard work—at something that has no chance of going anywhere? Your hard work has to go *somewhere*. I played basketball throughout high school, but I knew I was not going to go anywhere with basketball because there was nowhere to go. And I continued track because of Mr. Temple—because he gave me a place to go. But he couldn't see every girl, and I feel very lucky that he did see me, saw my potential, and thought that I could make that potential grow.

Yet I often wonder: What if I hadn't gone to the Fort Valley meet? What if he hadn't seen me? What if any little thing had gone differently? On that one day. And what did he see that I didn't see? Because I was just out there having fun and enjoying it while still wanting to be the best and wanting to win; I did have that winning attitude. But there were other girls out there with that attitude too—I know because they were beating me. Mr. Temple saw something in me that he didn't see in those other girls; I don't know what it was, but he had the eye for it. Still, I wonder: what if there had been other coaches looking for a way to compete with Mr. Temple? What would they have seen? Who would they have chosen? We will never know because that just wasn't there. None of it. There were only two sports, and only one of them could go anywhere, and at first "going somewhere" meant going to Tennessee State or Tuskegee—small Historically Black Universities that could only take so many women. Sure, Texas Southern University and University of Hawaii started programs after a while. But how many people from the Deep South were going to go to Hawaii at that time?

And remember that this was the Jim Crow South, which means that all the people I've been talking about so far were Black people. So on the one hand, Black women and girls faced different obstacles than Black men and boys. But then there were also obstacles that were based on Black and white. For example, when the schools got integrated, all our records—all the records of all the Black athletes in all the Black schools at all the Black meets, all our times and trophies and accomplishments— they just threw them out the back door. My husband Duane has asked me, "What kind of times did you run in high school?" And all I have is my memory. You could go all the way to Georgia and look through all the archives, and you wouldn't find any records of what we'd done, the times we ran, the games we won in basketball, nothing. When they integrated the schools, they cleaned the slate—started over, like we were never there.

When talking about what needs to change today, I think it's important to remember what it was like back then. I suspect it's difficult for someone who came up after Title IX to truly imagine it. But you have to understand where we came from and how far we have come. Because things have definitely changed— not enough, but they have changed. You think about what Mr. Temple did—he did it all without Title IX. He *was* Title IX, so to speak—a one-man Title IX. He was *it*. So Title IX was big in and of itself, but I think things had started to change long before that. Women started to speak out, which gave momentum to the work of the Women's Sports Foundation as I mentioned before. By the time Title IX was being discussed, women were already comfortable speaking out about why it was necessary. The feeling was that girls should be able to play sports. Period.

Now, it's not only women's minds that have changed. There are a lot of men out there who are rooting for their daughters, who want to make sure their daughters have equal access to the playing field. You see it in soccer and softball, in baseball and volleyball. A lot more coaches, male coaches, are becoming involved in young women's lives and pushing for young girls to participate in sports. At the 2016 Olympic Trials for track and field in Eugene, Oregon, I noticed that there were professional football players not just cheering on but coaching their daughters. One was Randall Cunningham, a retired star NFL quarterback, whose daughter, Vashti Cunningham, made the team in the high jump. And then there's Michael Carter, who was an Olympian and played football for the San Francisco 49ers. His daughter, Michelle Carter, won the gold medal for the shot put in the Rio Olympics. Football players encouraging their daughters to compete? *Coaching* their daughters? Back in the day, men might coach their sons if they thought they had potential. But that was not happening for women when I was competing. That, to me, is a big change.

But for those of us who want more change and more growth, I think it's important to look into what makes change happen. I know competition had to have a lot to do with it; sports fans, the ones who really care, want to see the best. But it's also about what America wants as a nation, particularly when it comes to the Games. The people at the top want us to come home with all the medals. They want to be the best—even if it doesn't really have anything to do with them and they don't want to have anything to do with us, the athletes, present or past. More than anything, I think the Olympic Games are a spectacle, a showcase of national power, and when I was competing it was even clearer than it is today: we had to go out there and beat those Russians!

Some people try to say that's not what it's about. They say it's all about bringing different countries together and building the world community. I think that's a great idea. That's certainly what the Olympics did for me in '64. But I don't think that's what the people in charge are looking to accomplish, and every so often those true colors come right out—like when Jimmy Carter called for a boycott of the 1980 Olympics in the USSR.[24] That year it was very obvious, but it seems to me that it's always about coming out on top—and the US *better* come out on top.[25] Because whatever people say about global togetherness, many are actually more concerned with national competition, which

24 The boycott, intended to punish the USSR for invading Afghanistan, was popular with voters but opposed by Olympians. According to Politico.com, Julian Roosevelt, an American member of the International Olympic Committee (IOC), had this to say: "I'm as patriotic as the next guy, but the patriotic thing to do is for us to send a team over there and whip their ass.' Al Oerter, a four-time gold medalist in the discus who was trying to make a comeback at age 42, agreed: 'The only way to compete against Moscow is to stuff it down their throats in their own backyard.'" See http://www.politico.com/magazine/story/2014/02/ carter-olympic-boycott-1980-103308.

25 And, in fact, it generally has. The IOC does not keep records, but Wikipedia and Topendsports.com do, based on information released by the IOC. The US has won twice as many medals as its closest competitor, the former Soviet Union (which, Topend points out, will not be getting any more). The position of the US and USSR at the top of the all-time Olympic chart is a standing testament to the Cold War—and to the interrelatedness of sports and politics. US dominance in the Olympics is staggering, although the nation's glory is more vigorously upheld in the summer events; the US trails Norway for most medals won in the Winter Olympics. Also telling is the list of countries that have never won any medals—countries, for the most part, that are either in danger of inundation or famine due to global warming or are currently being bombed. See http://www.topendsports.com/events/ summer/medal-tally/all-time.htm, https://en.wikipedia.org/wiki/United_States_at_the_Olympics, and https://en.wikipedia.org/wiki/All-time_Olympic_Games_medal_table.

is obvious in the fact that as soon as countries are brought together, they are split apart again by all the medal counting that goes on. First it was the US against the Soviet Union, now it's the US against Russia and China. It's never going to be just: *Everybody go out there and run for it—run free!* I don't think most people would appreciate that. It would be more like, "Great, great, they won, but what country are they from?" Because it's so ingrained.

And all that together means that if the US needs Black women athletes to win, then opportunities are going to open up for Black women athletes, and they are going to keep opening up as long as Black women keep excelling at sports—because the US just *has* to stay on top. Sometimes the good can sneak in with the bad. And because of the Olympics, because of what we "did for our country," past athletes get at least some recognition every four years. I always know when the Olympics are coming around because it's amazing how many phone calls I get. If you look at my job records, you'll see that the sports-promoting gigs came pretty much every four years. All the in-between years were very lean. And a lot of the time, they aren't even offering money for those "jobs." They just want you to show up.

That's something else that has changed for the better: you can make a living off of track in a way that you just couldn't do when I was competing, especially on the European circuit—although there's money in the US for track athletes too. You can compete in five or six meets, and if you win all or most of the races, you get a big bonus. And you don't have to wait until you're done with the Olympics anymore; you can do it all: get paid for competing, for breaking records, for winning races, for wearing some company's shoes. You couldn't do any of that in my day, and to me that's a huge improvement because I think everybody should get paid.

I remember the Seoul Olympics in 1988 when the USA men's basketball team lost the gold medal to Russia.[26] After that, pro athletes could play basketball in the Olympics, and in my opinion that's pretty much what broke it all open. Before that, the American officials would say, "Professionals in the Olympics? That's so wrong! Olympians should be amateurs. Only the Europeans pay their athletes—those cheaters!" But if the USA doesn't want to lose, and the state doesn't want to support the athletes, what are they going to do but go pro? And it took something like that—for the US to lose in men's basketball, which they had always won—to make it happen. After that, the officials were saying: "Oh no! We can't have that! We need to send our best athletes to the Games! Something must change!"

Of course, it wasn't like that for me or anyone else from my generation, and like I've said, that's what happens when you're a pioneer; you don't get the same benefits as those who come after. But I'm still grateful that it has happened. Because athletes work so hard—it's a *job*. You have to train, you have to stay strong in mind and body, you have to risk injury. There's a lot to being an Olympic athlete that most people never see. So I am all for athletes getting paid, and I think the same thing should happen for college football. I feel very strongly about that. Most college teams are highly exploited. The schools can make a lot of money off them—tons! And the players get nothing. They just use them up—especially in football. Because in football you can mess yourself up forever and make yourself no good for anything.[27] They should be paid.

---

26 The USA women's team did a bit better, beating Yugoslavia in the finals 77–70 and bringing home the gold. http://www.nytimes.com/1988/09/29/sports/the-seou-olympics-women-s-basketball-us-women-beat-yugoslavia-for-gold.html.

27 See "110 NFL Brains" at https://www.nytimes.com/interactive/2017/07/25/sports/football/nfl-cte.html?emc=edit_nn_20170726&nl=morning-briefing&n-lid=73209967&te=1&_r=0.

In addition to the possibility—not a guarantee, but at least a chance—for athletes to earn a living doing what they love, there are also a lot more opportunities for women in general and for women of color in particular to compete in a wider variety of sports. While I was competing and for many years after I stopped, the number of people of color on American Olympic teams other than track was very, very small. If you looked at figure skating or gymnastics or swimming, there were very few people of color. And everybody would say, "It costs too much to train in those sports. People of color are too poor." That may be one factor, but I know it's not the only factor. Because you could find a way—if you had encouragement, if you had role models, if there were programs. There was always a way. So it was never just about money. Race—racism—was also a part of it.[28]

And that has also changed—it's not perfect, but it's different.[29] Look at the 2016 Olympics gymnastics team: there were two Black women and a Latina. And then you look at swimming—who would have thought we would have a Simone in gymnastics and a Simone in swimming, both Black? Isn't that something? You're seeing women of color in sports that they just wouldn't have been in at the time I was competing. It had to happen, that progress; you just can't stop it. It shows that

28 The suppression of Black history in general and the contributions of Black women in particular is part of the problem. The history of Black women in tennis goes back almost one hundred years: Ora Washington and Althea Gibson were champions in the early decades of the twentieth century. Meanwhile, in track, Aubrey Patterson, who was a Tigerbelle before Mr. Temple's time, won the bronze medal for the 200 meters in the 1948 Olympics. See *A Spectacular Leap: Black Women Athletes in Twentieth-Century America* by Jennifer H. Lansbury for more information on the hidden history of Black women in sports.

29 Evidence of both the differences and the persistent challenges can be found in a *Philadelphia Daily News* story about gymnastics at the 2016 Rio Olympics: a photograph of Simone Biles misidentified and illustrating a column about Gabby Douglas. Both Douglas and Biles are Black. http://www.nbcphiladelphia.com/news/local/Philadelphia-Daily-News-Mistakes-Simone-Biles-for-Gabby-Douglas-390449411.html.

people are in a different frame of mind, that Black women and girls are getting more opportunities. The more Black girls are encouraged to compete, the more they succeed; the more they succeed, the more role models there are, and that starts raising the expectations of young women of color when it comes to what they can do and who they can be.

Another sign that things are moving forward is the opening up of opportunities for women as sports commentators. When I did the commentary at the 1976 Olympics in Montreal, it was pretty much unheard of in track for any woman, let alone a Black woman, to be doing that kind of thing. You think back on the time when I was running—who was doing it? Nobody—except maybe in gymnastics. Now they have women commentators not just in track and field but in almost all the sports. They don't use a wide variety of people, but they do have women, and I think it's because society is demanding it, asking, "If women can do these things, why can't they talk about them?" I also think there is less tolerance for some of the more antiquated ways men have of talking about female athletes—as was shown by people's responses to some of the reporting on the Rio Olympics.[30]

First off, though, I have to say that the female athletes in Rio did a magnificent job—they did *such* a magnificent job that the press could not do anything *but* report on them—and I think that's going to mean a really big boost for women's sports in general. It shows the world that it's okay for women to be strong, to be competitive, to be the best. It also shows that the more you put into women's sports—the more encouragement women are given, the more opportunities they have—the more you get out of them, not just for the women or their countries but for the world.

---

30 Sexism in the coverage of the 2016 Olympics was a story in itself: see Introduction.

Even so, there were things said that didn't need to be said—like calling the women's judo final a "catfight" or giving a man credit for his wife's medal. And in general, it seems like they always have to say something about the woman being beautiful rather than just saying that she is good. That's the tone that comes through most of the time with reporters as well as some male athletes. Either women are good-looking, or if they're *really* good, then they're like men.[31] I don't know if these guys simply don't know how to do better or if they are actively trying to keep women down—keep them convinced of the idea that men are always going to be better, so they might as well not even try. Despite all that, what the women did was great, and the publicity they got was better than nothing, better than the teeny-weeny bits they have gotten in years past.

But don't get me wrong: women athletes still need more publicity and they need *better* publicity.[32] To me, that's the biggest issue, and it's an issue with a lot of different aspects. For one thing, there needs to be an attitude change around strong teams. I remember listening to a sports commentary program as recently as 2016, and they were talking about the UConn women's basketball team and how—because they're so dominant—they're hurting the sport. And I thought, *What are you talking*

31 During the 2016 Rio Olympics, two American male swimmers' comments that Team USA's Katie Ledecky does "respectable times for guys" and "swims like a man" were widely circulated—as positive praise—until someone pointed out how sexist this was. See https://www.si.com/olympics/2016/06/01/olympics-2016-road-to-rio-katie-ledecky-swimming for the latter and http://www.espn.com/espnw/voices/article/17251015/why-frame-katie-ledecky-dominance-terms-women-sports-not-mens for the former.

32 For example, the press could stop "forgetting" about women's achievements, as BBC reporter John Inverdale did in 2016 when he praised tennis player Andy Murray for being the "first person" ever to win two Olympic medals in tennis. Murray's quick reply, "I think Venus and Serena [Williams] have won about four each," set the record straight, but isn't it the press, and not the athletes, who are responsible for keeping track of such things? https://mic.com/articles/151530/ andy-murray-was-lauded-for-having-achieved-a-first-the-williams-sisters-already-claimed#.yLYCob69e.

about?! They kept saying things like, "Oh God, they are *dominant.* Nobody can win because they're just that good," like it was a *problem*—a problem for UConn! They would *never* say that about a men's team. When UCLA's basketball team had that string of victories during Kareem Abdul-Jabbar's era, or when Duke had a winning streak more recently, it was just so wonderful, and it helped the sport *so much.* And they said nothing about football getting ruined when the Cowboys were always winning, or anyone hurting the sport when certain teams dominated baseball for years. If a men's team were to be as dominant as the UConn women's basketball team, the sporting news would be all about how the rest of the league needs to step up: how everybody else has to play better, how they have to recruit better, how they need better coaches, all those kinds of things.

It was the same when I was running with the Tigerbelles; people were always saying, "Why do you guys have to win all the time? We're so tired of you winning." And now they're pulling this again with women's basketball? I feel like I'm back in the sixties. You would think that in the twenty-first century, it wouldn't be this way anymore, but there it is. And that is no way to get the public invested in a sport—to act like the dominant team can never be beaten—and it's not even true! UConn did get beaten not a year later. But that's beside the point. You need to get people thinking about what other players and other coaches and other teams could be doing. To make the competition better. To make the sport more exciting. Once you get the public involved in looking at a sport, and they see that all different groups and ethnicities can be a part of it, and they see that everyone is invested in being the best, that's when the stereotypes start to come down—and that's when more people will get excited about women's sports, all kinds of women's sports.

Publicity also plays into questions around money. At Tennessee State, one of the problems we had to contend with was that the women's track team didn't bring in the revenue; we didn't bring in "the crowds" was the way it was put. Because of that, the administration only gave us two, maybe three new scholarships a year—and this was work aid, which is not really a scholarship at all. Still, even with that very little support, Tigerbelles would go to the Olympics every four years and bring back gold medals for their country and all that recognition for the school. But we didn't bring in any money, so the football team got the scholarships. For the people in charge, it's a very simple equation—they bring in the money, so they get the money. That's all there is to it.

Maybe it's the good-ol'-boys thing. I don't know. But this was happening in the fifties and sixties, and you would think that people would change in thought and mind—all these so-called brilliant people we have now, how could they still think that way? How could they not figure out that the people who get the crowds are the people who are marketed and promoted? That if they were as committed to promoting women's sports as they are to promoting men's, the numbers would look very different? Apparently, they are not going to reach those conclusions by themselves. We have to make them see. Look at tennis. That same thing was happening with tennis until women started fighting it back in the seventies, and now they get equal pay—at least in most of the bigger tournaments.[33] It's so simple, and it would cost them nothing to think about it and come to

---

33 According to the *New York Times*, "Although men and women are compensated more comparably in tennis than in any other major sport, the annual prize money paid to the top 100 earners on the WTA and ATP tours roughly matches the general pay gap in American workplaces, with female tennis players earning 80 cents on each dollar men earn." https://www.nytimes.com/2016/04/13/sports/tennis/equal-pay-gender-gap-grand-slam-majors-wta-atp.html?_r=0.

the conclusion that, hey, they could make more money if they marketed women's sports alongside men's sports. And it's not like all the men's teams draw giant crowds or are even any good at what they do. But no one with the power to just go ahead and make things equal is looking to do so. Which means the athletes need to fight.

Even fighting won't get you too far too fast, though. It takes years—it may be ten, it may be twenty, but nothing happens right away. You have to think about that, and you have to persevere. If you look at soccer, in 2016, women players sued the league for equal pay, but they haven't won yet, even though, to me, they have the league pretty much where they want them. You have to do something noticeable, and the US Women's National Soccer Team has done that—the same way the female tennis players did. The women were outshining the men, and they were winning, and you had these great matches, and everybody was coming out to see the women play and cheering on the individual athletes.[34] That's another difference between when I was competing and now: people are more into not just looking at the athletes on the field but also what they're doing with their lives outside of sports. They still like a winner, though, and the US Women's National Soccer Team has been dominant for years. What has the men's team done? They keep trying to bring people in to boost them up and all of that, but they certainly aren't winning any championships.[35] And they

34 "For the 2015 [World Cup] final, an estimated thirty million people watched on TV in the US as Carli Lloyd's three goals sealed a huge win against Japan. It was and remains the highest-rated soccer match in American history including games played by the US men." http://www.cbsnews.com/news/60-minutes-women-soccer-team-usa-gender-discrimination-equal-pay/.

35 The story of the American men's soccer team is instructive; it demonstrates the US Soccer Federation's long-term commitment to building the team. For example, head coach Bruce Arena thinks that the US men's team has a chance to win the World Cup—in 2026. http://www.nhregister.com/sports/20170413/us-mens-soccer-coach-bruce-arena-thinks-americans-could-win-2026-world-cup.

still deserve to be paid more? Where is the sense in that?

So the issue of publicity and the issue of money are all tied up together. And it's not just whether women's sports are promoted, it's also which sports get publicity and what that publicity looks like. There are some sports in which women have had an easier time getting their accolades, maybe because people think of them as "feminine," like gymnastics and figure skating—those same sports that were mostly dominated by white women—although I don't mean to pick on figure skaters or gymnasts, just the press. So if you were good at figure skating, and you were white, you got all the recognition in the world; your choice of sport dictated your chances for acknowledgment. And not only the sport—the world dictated what it wanted to see. So every time they talked about figure skating, it was all about "the queen of figure skating," something the public and all the little girls who might want to figure skate could understand and feel good about. The same thing is true with gymnastics: when gymnastics started to change, and the girls were not so prim and so dainty but began to be more athletic, with more muscles and more power and showing, *This is what it takes to be the best,* the press didn't lose interest in them because they were "too masculine" or whatever, so people looked at them quite differently than they did women in other sports, like track. Even when we had someone like Florence Griffith Joyner with the nails and the outfits and the long, flowing hair—and they gave her a lot of attention because of all that—they still didn't call her "the queen of track." How they publicize the different sports, and how they portray the people participating in those sports, has to change if women are ever going to get all the opportunities we deserve.

I feel that it is still the case that women athletes have to be a certain type to get attention. Being fast or being the best doesn't hurt—of course, people want you to be the best—but they also want you to have that dainty side, that "feminine" side. I am not faulting the athletes; sometimes the athletes themselves have the personality and style that the press wants, and if they were like that before they came onto the field, then that's just who they are. But if they come onto the field and feel they have to change, then that's a different story. Even then I don't blame *them;* why shouldn't they try to get noticed? But why can't the press just notice women athletes for being great athletes?

This is one of the things that hasn't changed very much from my days traveling with the Tigerbelles. Mr. Temple wanted us to be what society said ladies were supposed to be, to the point that we had to fly in high-heeled shoes and stockings. And that worked for some of the Tigerbelles—Wilma, for example; that was just right for her. It fit her charisma, her attitude, who she was. But then you had Earlene Brown, the shot putter—the one they wouldn't let have a men's sweat suit at the Tokyo Olympics. She was a big woman, and I remember people saying, "You need to make her look a little more feminine." But Earlene couldn't have cared less about any of that; she was part of the whole roller derby thing after the Olympics. And she was fine with who she was: "This is me!" she was always saying, with her actions and her words. Yet society didn't want that, and if you ask me, it still doesn't.

There's more freedom now, of course. The women in track and field nowadays are different than we were in a lot of ways. For one thing, the Tigerbelles didn't do weight training—the closest thing we did to that was to run a lot of hills, do high knee drills, and run cross-country with weights in our shoes. That looked like weight training to me, at the time, even though I know it was not. I'm glad I ran when I did because doing what they do in this day and time—weight training and being in major competitions every week when the season is on—does not seem like something I would enjoy. But it does mean that female runners are a lot more muscular now, which also means that the whole ladylike thing is not what it was. Still, I think there's pressure to be something other than just an athlete. Otherwise, why would women running track be made up to the hilt? It's fine, of course; they should do what they want, but they shouldn't feel like they have to. And the shorts they have now? We thought our shorts were short, but they weren't really; I mean, they had the rubber in the legs, and you could pull them up as high as you wanted to, but our shirts were so durn big that when you were running you'd get this big puff of air in the back. Maybe you do run faster in more aerodynamic clothing. Maybe it cuts down the wind resistance, kind of like in swimming, but the opposite: male Olympic swimmers used to wear tiny little swimsuits and now their suits cover more. So maybe there's a similar but opposite argument about track clothes. I don't know. But I do know that the men's track shorts are still almost to their knees. So I have to wonder: is it about aerodynamics or is it about something else?

And it's not just the outfits. Lots of people still have a problem with women being strong. Depending on what part of the country you're from, you still have people who can't get over Michelle Obama's arms. I was in Georgia for a month, and I was with some people talking about our former first lady, and one of them said, "Did you see her? Her arms are so—" And then she just stopped, like there was something about her arms that is unspeakable.

So I said, "Yeah, I've seen her arms. They look good."

"No. That's just not a good look for a woman. And not only that, she doesn't wear stockings!"

I wanted to scream, *And what's wrong with that?!*

But they went on and on: "I mean, her legs were just . . .

There's nothing like a nice pair of stockings! She would look so much better." And when they finally got the message that that's not how I think, that they should not even be talking to me about that, that the conversation just needed to *end*, one of them said, "Well, that's just because you've been on that West Coast for so long."

No. That's not why. It's because I'm okay with women being strong. Women should be strong. Women need to be strong. Like I said, that was one of the life lessons I learned growing up. Also that no one could tell me what to do, that I had a mind of my own. But there are still a lot of people in our society who don't want to see women that way: strong for themselves and thinking for themselves. If they can't have women dainty and proper, they want them to be sexy.

To me, that's society. That's what some people want to see, and if you don't give them what they want, then you're not going to get seen. That's not going to change in sports until it changes in the rest of society. And for that kind of change to happen, there needs to be a movement—not just for equity in women's sports but equity for women in general. What women want—and we want it now, because it has not only not been given to us but actively taken away—is equity. That's all. All these years, we've been fighting for what we should have had anyway. You could look at the situation and say, "Well, why are we even here? We should be on another step." But that's not how it works, that's not where society is, that's not where the powers-that-be are or where they want to go. For them to move, we have to *make* them move, and when they move, they move at a snail's pace. You might like for the pace to be picked up and feel we shouldn't have to start from where we are, but too often we don't get to choose.

So we need a movement, and to make a movement, there

have to be people in the trenches working, people speaking out and saying the things that need to be said, and those people need to be constantly refreshed—you can't expect the same people down in the trenches to keep doing all the work. You've got to bring in more people, to help them, to relieve them, but also to build numbers. I don't know exactly how you do that in this day and time, but I know that this is what is very much needed.

In any type of movement, you've got to have people continuously supporting each other and feeding their spirits and trying to change other people's minds so that they want to join the movement too. And to convince the people whose minds are not wanting to change, you have to show them how your movement helps not only women but society as a whole. Because some people don't care whether women get help or not; at least, they don't care about women as women. But maybe they care about their daughters or their granddaughters or their great-aunt who always wanted to run a marathon and is now ninety years old. We have to figure out how to appeal to those people and show them that what's good for women is good for people—for all people.

But that also means that the society has to care more about people in general. Because what I said earlier about the football players being used until they're all used up—that's not just true about football players. That's true about pretty much everyone who works. We need to care more about people. We just do. And that's not what we're all about right now. Right now, it's more like, *Hey, I'm on top, and you're down there, and I'm going to try to make sure you stay there.* Not everybody, of course. But that's the mood. The country is going through a whole lot of changes, and it will always go through changes, and when you have an attitude like the one I'm describing, there's always going to be a response to it, from the movements that were happening when I was growing up and the Olympic Project for Human Rights to the professional athletes who are using their positions to remind people that Black lives matter.

When I look at the football players taking a knee or linking arms and getting all that attention, positive and negative, I sometimes wonder what it will take for women to be in a position to have that effect. What woman do they ever publicize anyway, when it comes to a sport or when it comes to a movement—unless that woman started the movement? I think about when we started the Women's Sports Foundation. The only reason we got any attention at first was because Billie Jean King had enough money to do the promotion herself. Then she had enough women who were well known to be a part of it— you're talking about eight of us who people knew and could say, "They're the greatest female athletes on earth at this time." That moment was key because when the whole concept of promoting women in sports came about, there was also a movement saying we needed a change for women in general. We need a movement like that today.

I look around and I am not sure where that movement is going to come from, but maybe it will grow out of another movement, like women's liberation in the seventies followed civil rights in the sixties—maybe the next movement for women's equality will come out of #BlackLivesMatter. There was never a time when they didn't matter, in my mind, but right now people are looking at the situation and saying enough is enough. We're not back in slavery when people could get away with acting like Black people's lives meant nothing

Even if it feels sometimes like things are moving backward, you can't give up and you can't lose faith. You have to start the fire again, gather up all the little sparks and hope that, this time, the sparks come together—not just because Black people or women speak on it, but because everyone is speaking on it, everyone is at that point, everyone can see that the situation is totally wrong.

14 *Blacks Lives Have Always Mattered*

The fight for racial justice is like the fight for women's equality: there has been change, but that change has not been enough. And sometimes that change isn't for the better; it's just change. For example, when I was growing up in Griffin, you could still see people—Black and white—working on chain gangs. They would be out there at five o'clock in the morning, and my dad and mom and grandmother would draw our attention to them. "That is what happens," they would say, "when you get in trouble. Stay out of trouble, or you'll get on that chain gang. You'll get on that chain gang, and you'll have nothing to say. You'll be chained to someone you know nothing about. You'll be out there working from sunup to sundown. They'll tell you when you can have a drink of water, when you can go to the bathroom, when you can stand, and when you can sit. Only thing you'll be able to do is what they tell you to do."

They used to preach that to us, and we could sit on our porch and look and see it was true. Because they were right out there on the roads—they paved the roads, they cleaned the roads, they dug the ditches, they did everything. They would work *hard*—when it was so hot we couldn't even play. We would play ball or tag and games like that in the morning, but by twelve o'clock the sun was too hot, and we would sit on the porch with our board games—*Monopoly*, checkers, and *Sorry!*

And if my parents were around they would look out at the people on the chain gang and say, "That's such-and-such's child. He did this or that. How could that boy *do* that?"

We kids would look at them and think, *God, I don't ever want that to be me.*

"You better not do anything bad!" my parents would say.

"We are *never* going to do anything bad!" we would tell them. "Never!" Because that was quite a visual: *This is what happens to you when you do not obey the law.* Of course, when I got older I also knew: *You can obey the law and this can happen to you anyway.* But the adults never said that part.

That's one of the areas where there's been change, but not enough change—change, but not necessarily change for the better. Because now they have a lot of people locked up in prison for decades doing work in tiny cells; they're not out on the roads anymore—at least, not where I live. That's different. But is it better? And if you're Black—or Latino, or from any other group of oppressed people—you can still obey the law and end up treated like a criminal, end up hurt, end up dead. So that's some change that still needs to happen.

There are lots of things like that. When I think back about growing up, I can also remember how my parents always wanted us to be very aware of what was going on in the world and to be very protective of ourselves and conscious of the things we said and where we were. I remember them making sure we knew that we should try not to get ourselves into situations where we were going to be harmed by anyone. I think about my brothers and how my parents always wanted to keep them secure because of all the things that would happen to Black men, especially young men, in those days. Today you might think of Tamir Rice, but back then you would think of Emmett Till, who was murdered three days after I turned ten. When people talk about the fact that Black lives matter, that's the first thing I think about: Black lives have always mattered. That's been from day one. Now, it has been said out loud, in the streets, so to speak, but it's always been in my life, all my life, because my parents taught me so hard how to take care of myself—and how to stand up for myself. That is something that hasn't changed.

But what also hasn't changed is that Black parents still have to teach their children that lesson. Even my son, who was born long after the Civil Rights Movement ended, had to learn that lesson. He is six feet five inches tall, and he was never a small child, so when he was seven, eight, nine, I started telling him: "You have to be aware of who you are, but you also have to be aware of what people see when they look at you." And when he started driving, I told him: "If the police pull you over, you need to keep your hands on the wheel, you need to say 'Yes sir' and 'No sir,' and you need to say everything you're going to do before you do it. You need to say: 'Can I roll my window down?' You need to say, 'I am reaching for my wallet now.' And you need to tell them which hand you are going to use to do it."

"I just can't believe I have to do this," my son would respond. "Why do I have to do this?"

"To stay alive," I'd tell him. "And it's not just you. We all have to. All people of color have to do that."

One thing that I found to be true, growing up in Georgia, was that I *knew* when I was not welcome, where I should not go. It was quite obvious. And I could deal with that. But then I moved to California and it got to be unclear—until I realized that I *still* was not really welcome. At first I was taken aback by that. Before I came out west, I thought it would be different— lots of people in the South thought that. To this day, people in Griffin will say to me, "California? Oh, you could have it so free there!" And before I moved, I agreed. *California's so open, I* thought. But no. It's not. Things are just more subtle than they are in the South. Because a lot of the people in California came from the South. And moving to California didn't necessarily change their ideas. It just meant that they were surrounded by change and maybe they had to bend a little bit.

So whether you're in the South or in the West, you still have to figure out who you're going to socialize with, and you still have to have "the talk"—not that it was ever one talk; it was something we always talked about. That was a part of growing up in my family—both the family that I came from and the family I made. I talked about it with my son, and I talked about it with my daughter too. Because even though it may seem like most of the bad things happen to young Black men, plenty of bad things happen to Black women as well, and more Black women than ever are in prison these days—though they are almost never talked about—and she needed to understand that.

As a Black person, you are aware of this danger, and I don't feel like you can ever really let your guard down. I don't care who you are, how much money you have, or who you hang out with, you're still going to be viewed the way the larger society sees you, and the first thing they see is your skin color—whether people say it out loud or not. This is nothing new. I turned seventy-two in 2017, and I have lived it for all these years and lived it continuously. What's going on now is that more people see that it's wrong, so it's getting a lot more press and a lot more recognition. Which is as it should be, when you think about what is happening to so many young Black people. One of the impacts of that recognition is that people feel a little better now to speak on the subject than they did years ago. Years ago, if you sat in Black people's living rooms, you would hear pretty much what people are saying out in the streets right now. But back then, most people did not feel comfortable enough to speak out

about it—I don't know if *comfortable* is even the right word—
safe is better. They didn't feel safe enough to speak out about it.
That's a problem. And if only a couple of people are speaking
out, they can shut them up right away, which is one reason
why numbers are important—why it's important now to try to
include as many people as possible in making change, just like
it was in the sixties.

It's hard for me to talk about all the murders that have happened, but I know every day that all of that is still going on,
and so are all the subtler things. When I was a naturalist at
the Clear Creek Outdoor Education Center, I worked above
La Cañada, a pretty much all-white community—and a very
exclusive community at that. On my way to work, I would be
driving on an isolated mountain road. You don't see too many
Black people up there, driving on that lonesome road, and I was
always extremely aware of the fact that I was a Black woman,
and that most white people who saw me would want to know
why I was up there.

And it wasn't just on the road that people thought they
needed to pay special attention to me. I remember going into
a market early in the morning in that neighborhood—I would
shop there before work so that when I got off work and drove
out of the hills, I could just go home and cook—and it was
that whole thing of people following you around the store. That
kind of thing has never ended; it never stops. To me, though,
one of the things that #BlackLivesMatter has accomplished or
started to accomplish is working away at the people who never
thought that kind of thing was true. Because there are still plenty
of people who don't believe, even now, that when I walk into
a store in La Cañada—a seventy-some-year-old woman, a retired naturalist, and an Olympian—people start to follow me
around.

I have a friend, Alex, who's white—she was one of my co-workers at Clear Creek—and one day I told her about it. "Why would they be following you around?" she asked. Not in a disbelieving way because she knows about racism and a lot of her friends are people of color. "You're a grown woman! Let's put it to the test."

"Okay," I said, "let's go."

So we go to the market, and I'm pushing my basket one way, and she's pushing her basket another, and it takes maybe five minutes before someone comes up to me and says, "Can I help you find something?"

My rule is always to say, "Sure! Here's my list." And I make sure to have three of four lists so that when the next person comes up to "help" me, I can say it again: "Sure! Here's my list."

On this particular occasion, Alex and I had set a time to meet at the checkout, and when that time came, I said to her, "Did you get everything accomplished?"

And Alex said, "Yeah, mostly. Did you?"

"Yes!" I told her. "These three lovely people helped me out." Because of course they were still standing there. "I didn't have to do anything but sit around."

After that, Alex could say she had seen it in action. But, you know, for a lot of people, if it doesn't happen to them, then it doesn't happen. It's not there. It can't be true. Even well-intentioned people can go in that direction. They think, *How could people do that? How could they still act that way? I just can't believe it.* And that can be difficult for the people who know, the people who easily see it. They can get impatient. But for me the question is: How do you bring those other people along? The ones who can't see or don't want to see—how do you bring them in? Because being inclusive means reaching out to all kinds of people, even people who have very different experiences. I always feel that the whole "They don't know our pain!" argument is not a strong argument. If you've felt pain, then you know pain. And everyone knows pain.

It's not going to be the same pain—absolutely not. If you lose a kid, and I'm a person who has never lost a kid, and I hear your story, I feel, but I will probably never feel the same pain or the same sorrow that the person who has lost a kid will feel. And I wouldn't want to take that from them. But we who are now speaking out for Black people will never know the pain of our forefathers or foremothers. Their pain was a different pain. I think back to my father and all the suffering and the labor that he had to do to get to where he was, which wasn't far. I see that, I understand that, and I say to my children just like he said to me: "I don't ever want you to have to work as hard as I've worked." But would I stand up for my father? Can I say that what happened to the people of his generation should never have happened? And would I want my children to stand up for me? Yes I can, and yes I would.

Not that I don't get impatient sometimes. It shouldn't take lives lost to bring those other people in, to have people who have never had to deal with it see that just because you're a policeman, it doesn't mean that you're not a racist. And just because you're in a position of authority, it doesn't mean you won't act on your racism. Racism *exists*. That's just a reality in our society. I think that people—all people, people who have had the experience and people who haven't—just have to be able to look down into themselves, deep down inside, and say, "Yes. I can see. That is racist." It is racist to beat or tase or shoot a young Black man who is lying on the ground or has his hands up or is walking or driving or just standing there breathing. It is racist to follow a Black woman around when she is doing her grocery shopping. But if you've been brought up all the time to think, *What I do is right; what you do is wrong*, it might take longer for you to see that. How do you correct that problem? I don't have all the answers. But people shouldn't have to be killed to correct it.

Sometimes I feel like we're just going back to long before I was born, when these things were happening but weren't getting any press. Now the tasing and shootings are getting lots of press, and some people are trying to act like it's a big surprise. But it's only a surprise for people who are looking for the first time. In any case, this is what's happening, and it is something that we need to look at, that the world needs to see, not just America. It bothers me that here we are in the twenty-first century and one of the only things that's changed is that there is more publicity.[36] Lives are still gone. People's lives are still being taken from them. And that has to change.

One aspect of the movement that reminds me of the old days, of my time in the Olympic Project for Human Rights, is the football players like Colin Kaepernick who are protesting during the national anthem. It takes all different kinds to make people aware of what is going on in the world today, and anybody who has a platform should use it. Of course, a lot of people are going to say, "How could they do that? How could they sit down or kneel or whatever? That's disrespecting the flag. It's an insult to veterans."

---

36 Sometimes the publicity seems to make precious little difference: Ron Bryant and J.W. Milam, the men who murdered Emmett Till, were put on trial and found not guilty two weeks after Till's funeral—during which time Till's mutilated body was displayed in an open casket because his mother, Mamie Bradley, wanted the world to see what racism had done to her son. It took over a month for George Zimmerman to be charged for the murder of Trayvon Martin and a year and a half before Zimmerman was found—incredibly—not guilty. See http:// www.history.com/this-day-in-history/the-death-of-emmett-till and http://www.cnn.com/2013/06/05/us/trayvon-martin-shooting-fast-facts/index.html.

To them I say: "Think about this: all the Black people who fought in wars and then came back home and had nothing and could do nothing—like the Tuskegee Airmen."

And if they come back with: "Well, those people still stood up for the flag," I say: "Yes, they did. But did the flag stand up for them? Does this country stand up for them?"

It didn't, and it doesn't. We all protest in our own way, and if the NFL players sitting through the anthem or taking a knee is going to bring awareness about what is going on in America, then I say let that be. Because of it, more people are talking about what's happening. Of course, some people are talking about it in a way that seems straight-up crazy to me, but even that can be good: it shows us all where they stand. We get moved from California where things are fuzzy to the South where everything is clear. There are some people out there who are such lovers of the flag that they can't bear to have anyone not worship it. But I say that no one is saying anything about not loving the flag. They're just not loving what is happening in America, and this is a platform for the world to see, or at least for more people to see and more people to start thinking. Think about why you dislike that kind of protest. Is it really because this country is so great? Come on. And I think, too, that if it was about another cause, if it was about farm subsidies, for example, I don't know if people would be so down on Colin Kaepernick taking a knee, or the multiple Women's National Basketball Assioncation (WNBA) teams—including the Minnesota Lynx, the New York Liberty, the Indiana Fever, and the Phoenix Mercury—that have been in the protest from the beginning.

When people ask me if I think I will get to see the changes I want to see, I have to admit that I don't. Not in my lifetime. But I have grandchildren, and I have hope for them. I feel like a whole lot is possible, a lot of change can happen. Is it ever going to be equal, with everybody sharing the same? I don't see that. But I also like to think positive. I like to think that it *could* change, and I am thinking that things *will* change, but they will change so slowly that I won't be around to really appreciate it. Still, you never know what will happen once someone lights a spark—like when Tommie Smith and John Carlos did their medal stand protest.

Sometimes it takes one person, sometimes it takes a group of people to be the spark. You don't know what will spark people, but whatever does—whatever brings people to more clear and conscious thinking and saying, "Hey, yes, this is happening, it's not right, how can we change it, what can we do?"—then that's a good thing. The people who are already in the know have to be tolerant and wait for and help those people who are still figuring things out—have to help those people to cross the finish line too. If every time they make two steps I make fifteen, it's not that they've failed; it's just that it's a slow process. And who knows? Maybe the next month, maybe the next day, a spark may hit them, and suddenly they'll be with you, they'll be where you are, on the front line, so to speak.

Once there's a spark, whether it's an individual spark or a group spark, conversations change—they change everywhere and for everyone. After the Olympics, probably in the eighties, when I was inducted into the Olympic Hall of Fame, I would get invited to a lot of banquet dinners. Half of the time, I just talked to the person right next to me, or sometimes someone from across the table would keep talking to me, and that's where my conversation would be. A lot of times, people would say things during the cocktail part of the party—the part before everybody sits down—that would make me think: *Hope I'm not sitting at that person's table.* But mainly, you knew what you were getting into. You knew you were going to be with corporate America. And you knew you were going to be with a lot of people who probably didn't know anything about you or what you had done, and that your views and their views might not be identical, and that you didn't want them identical anyway. You knew which things you should stay away from in your conversations. But once there's a spark, there's no way to stay away. *Someone* is going to bring it up.

That's what happened when Tommie Smith and John Carlos did what they did. A lot of people were unhappy about that. So I would go to those banquets, and before long someone would say, "What do you think about Smith and Carlos?"

And I would say, "What do you mean?"

"I mean, is that the place for it? The Olympics?"

"What they did made a statement. It started people looking and thinking and questioning a lot of things, and some of the people looking at it joined a movement. So yes. I think that was exactly the right place."

"But *you* didn't do it."

"No one else did it either. Tommie and Carlos did it, and it was so powerful, there was no room for anybody else. Did you know that I dedicated my medal to them?" And then I wouldn't have to say too much more.

Sometimes, somebody else at the table might say, "You did?!" in a positive way, and then you would get another conversation out of it—a conversation that everybody at the table would hear, whether they said anything or not, and whether they agreed or not.

Other times, when someone asked about that, and everybody heard me say, "I dedicated my medal to them, I believe in what they did," nobody else had anything more to say. Then I would know what kind of table I was sitting at. Things are clear when there's a spark. Whichever side they're on, people aren't left to just think their own thoughts.

That was one of the things that came up a lot at those tables, long after Tommie and Carlos did their thing. And every time it came up, it gave me an opportunity to speak out. Sometimes people weren't happy about it. I would come home and tell Duane, and he would say, "Maybe you need to think more carefully about what you're going to say."

"Well, they need to do the same." Because when someone says something that really offends me or someone else, I can't not react. I can't control it.

And when I said that to Duane, he would reply, "Well, you can take a deep breath, and you can excuse yourself, and you can walk away from the table. And then when you come back, dinner's over, and you don't even need to sit at that table again. 'Is it time to go already? I got lost,' you can say."

But that wouldn't work for me. I am a person who has trouble—actually, I don't think it's trouble. It's just that if it comes to my head to respond to something offensive someone has said, and I don't say it, I walk around with that burden. Some things have to be said.

If we can all say the things that need to be said, if we use our platforms when we have them, and if we can see a way not only to work with other people but to see other people *as* people, then hopefully my grandchildren will see change that *is* change—change that is enough. Hopefully there will be a different type of life for them, such that they don't have to worry about how other people see them because everyone will see everyone else as people. Hopefully, by the time they are thirty or forty, a lot will have changed, not just in one part of the country but all over.

I know that if things are going to change, it's going to be

a long fight and we are going to have to be on our guard for a long time. Because any time you win something, even the littlest thing, it's always the same: The powers-that-be want you to sit back down and be satisfied. They're like, "We gave it to you, right? You got to calm down now." And the minute we calm down, they try to take it back. So we have to try to focus on the big picture, and we have to be down for the long haul. Will it happen? I know I said I didn't think it was going to happen in my lifetime, but I plan to live to be a hundred, so we've got thirty years to get it right.

APPENDIX
The Tigerbelles

Coach Edward Stanley Temple
USA Olympic Women's Track Coach, 1960 and 1964
Pan-American Track Coach, 1959 and 1975

Olympic Gold Medals won by Tigerbelles
Mae Faggs, BS/MS[37]—1952 Helsinki, Finland (4x100-meter relay)

Barbara Jones, BS—1952 Helsinki, Finland (4x100-meter relay); 1960 Rome, Italy (4x100-meter relay)

Wilma Rudolph, BS—1960 Rome, Italy (100 meter, 200 meter, 4x100-meter relay)

Martha Hudson, BS—1960 Rome, Italy (4x100-meter relay)

Lucinda Williams, BS/MS—1960 Rome, Italy (4x100-meter relay)

Edith McGuire, BS—1964 Tokyo, Japan (200 meter)

Wyomia Tyus, BS—1964 Tokyo, Japan (100 meter); 1968 Mexico City, Mexico (100 meter, 4x100-meter relay)

Madeline Manning, BS/MDiv—1968 Mexico City, Mexico (800 meter)

Chandra Cheeseborough, BS—1984 Los Angeles, California (4x100-meter relay, 4x400-meter relay)

---

37 Please note that all degrees represent the best information that we could find at time of publication. If you or a Tigerbelle you know has earned another degree, let us know so that we may update the list in future printings.

Olympic Silver Medals won by Tigerbelles

Willye B. White, BA—1956 Melbourne, Australia (long jump); 1964 Tokyo, Japan (4x100-meter relay)

Edith McGuire, BS—1964 Tokyo, Japan (100 meter; 4x100-meter relay)

Wyomia Tyus, BS—1964 Tokyo, Japan (4x100-meter relay)

Madeline Manning, BS/MDiv—1972 Munich, Germay (4x400-meter relay)

Kathy McMillan, BS—1976 Montreal, Canada (long jump)

Chandra Cheeseborough, BS—1984 Los Angeles, California (400 meter)

Olympic Bronze Medals won by Tigerbelles

Audrey Patterson, BS—1948 London, England (200 meter)

Wilma Rudolph, BS—1956 Melbourne, Australia (4x100-meter relay)

Isabelle Daniels, BS—1956 Melbourne, Australia (4x100-meter relay)

Margaret Matthews, BS—1956 Melbourne, Australia (4x100-meter relay)

Mae Faggs, BS/MS—1956 Melbourne, Australia (4x100-meter relay)

Additional Tigerbelle Olympians (US)

Emma Reed, BS—1948 London, England (high jump)

Anna Louis Smith, BS/MS—1960 Rome, Italy (long jump)

Shirley Crowder, BS—1960 Rome, Italy (100-meter hurdles)

JoAnn Terry, BS/MS—1960 Rome, Italy (80-meter hurdles); 1964 Tokyo, Japan (long jump)

Vivian Brown, BS—1964 Tokyo, Japan (200 meter)

Estelle Baskerville, BS/MS—1964 Tokyo, Japan (long jump); 1968 Mexico City, Mexico (high jump)

Eleanor Montgomery, BS—1964 Tokyo, Japan (high jump); 1968 Mexico City, Mexico (high jump)

Martha Watson, BS—1964 Tokyo, Japan (long jump); 1968 Mexico City, Mexico (long jump); 1972 Munich, Germany (long jump); 1976 Montreal, Canada (long jump)

Iris Davis, BS/MS—1968 Mexico City, Mexico (100 meter); 1972 Munich, Germany (100 meter)

Mamie Rallins, BS—1968 Mexico City, Mexico (100-meter hurdles); 1972 Munich, Germany (100-meter hurdles)

Brenda Morehead, BS—1976 Montreal, Canada (100 meter)

Additional Tigerbelle Olympians (International)

Cynthia Thompson (Jamaica), BS/MD—1952 Helsinki, Finland, and 1956 Melbourne, Australia (100, 200 meter)

Lorraine Dunn (Panama), BS—1964 Tokyo, Japan (100-meter hurdles)

Marcella Daniels (Panama), BS—1964 Tokyo, Japan, and 1968 Mexico City, Mexico (100, 200 meter)

Debbie Jones (Bermuda), BS—1976 Montreal, Canada (100, 200 meter)

Helen Blake (Jamaica), BS—1976 Montreal, Canada (4x400-meter relay, 400 meter)

Una Morris (Jamaica), BS/MD—1964 Tokyo, Japan, 1968 Mexico City, Mexico, and 1972 Munich, Germany (4x400-meter relay, 200 meter)

Acknowledgments

Thank you, Elizabeth Terzakis—my cowriter—who from the first time we met said, "This is a story that must be told," and (because of you) now it has. I appreciate you so much. Your vision has helped give this story a platform beyond anything I ever could have imagined. You pushed me to remember so many things; you had me consider and reconsider the impact of experiences that I had seen as simply the way things were. Our long talks, and sharing of stories, along with reflections on race and reality then and now, helped me to grow and navigate the waters to make this book happen. Your open ear and supportive pen made it comfortable for me to open up, and as you know, that's no easy task. I appreciate all that you brought and gave on this journey. I started with a coauthor and ended with a friend.

Thank you, Johnny Temple and Akashic Books, for making it possible for my story to be told and shared with the general public. Your honest feedback and continuous support were instrumental.

Thank you, Dave Zirin, for bringing Elizabeth, Johnny, and me together. What a team. From the beginning, your knowledge of the Tigerbelles, your appreciation for the true legacy of these women and our coach, really moved me. Thank you for your time, your edits, and your support.

To the Tigerbelles who have come before me—with me—and after me: We are a sisterhood of strength, power, and determination. Thank you for being strong Black women, letting the world know that no matter where we came from, we could excel on the field, in the classroom, and around the globe. We worked hard to achieve our goals. And our story is worth being told.

To Edith: We have been on this journey together for over fifty years, and I couldn't have had a better friend to be with than you. You have been my wings when I couldn't fly. Like a sister I never had, you have always supported me and encouraged me to push outside my own comfort zone. Thank you and much love.

To Cora: Thank you for all the laughs you've given me and the fun we've shared. Most of all, thanks for your support and friendship, and for being the one who always understands. My sister, my friend. You are loved.

To my children—Simone and Tyus—my life: I love you! This book is for you and your families. So that you (they) will always know all things are possible. Thanks for making my life as a mom such a joy.

Finally, to my husband Duane Tillman: My love—who worked so hard on this book, making sure we had all the facts and history correct, staying on the Internet night and day to find every piece of documentation—you are my inspiration, through all my ups and downs. My deepest gratitude and love.